Lessons from the Asian Financial Crisis

Nearly ten years after the Asian Financial Crisis, financial turmoil has reappeared – this time it is ravaging the world's wealthiest countries and dragging the global economy along for the ride. It forces one to reflect on the last major financial crisis to afflict the global economy, and to consider whether there are any similarities, and whether there are any lessons from that crisis that we can apply to the current one.

In the crisis of 2008, easy money and lax standards on mortgage lending have created a bubble in the real estate markets of the US and Europe. This scenario is all too familiar to those knowledgeable about the Asian Financial Crisis – a real estate bubble enabled companies to inflate the worth of their assets and to borrow more. Banks were all too eager to lend to them. And in 2008, derivatives and excessive leveraging of Wall Street financial institutions have brought the global financial system to the brink of collapse. This too is similar to the situation in 1997, when the near collapse of Long Term Capital Management likewise threatened a global financial meltdown.

While the contributions to this volume were all written prior to the onset of the 2008 crisis, they nevertheless offer important insights into the nature of financial crises in the twenty-first century. Written by a distinguished group of individuals from government, the private sector, international organizations, and academia, the chapters provide an overview of developments in the main affected countries during the Asian Financial Crisis, as well as the lessons learned and corrective measures taken at the country, regional, and international levels. Importantly, attention is also paid to the areas where substantial improvements are needed. The current crisis heightens the relevance of these lessons.

Lessons from the Asian Financial Crisis will be invaluable to those studying international relations, international finance, international economics and East Asian studies.

Richard Carney is Assistant Professor in the S. Rajaratnam School of International Studies at Nanyang Technological University.

Routledge contemporary Asia series

Lessons from the Asian Financial Crisis

Edited by Richard Carney

LONDON AND NEW YORK

First published 2009
by Routledge
2 Park Square, Milton Park, Abingdon, Oxon, OX14 4RN

Simultaneously published in the USA and Canada
by Routledge
711 Third Avenue, New York, NY 10017

Routledge is an imprint of the Taylor & Francis Group, an informa business

First issued in paperback 2011

Typeset in Times by Wearset Ltd, Boldon, Tyne and Wear

British Library Cataloguing in Publication Data
A catalogue record for this book is available from the British Library

Library of Congress Cataloging in Publication Data
Lessons from the Asian financial crisis/edited by Richard Carney.
p. cm. – (Routledge contemporary Asia series; 9)
1. Financial crises–Asia. I. Carney, Richard.
HB3722.L47 2009
332′.042095–dc22   2008027280

ISBN10: 0-415-48190-2 (hbk)
ISBN10: 0-415-66710-0 (pbk)
ISBN10: 0-203-88477-9 (ebk)

ISBN13: 978-0-415-48190-8 (hbk)
ISBN13: 978-0-415-66710-4 (pbk)
ISBN13: 978-0-203-88477-5 (ebk)

Contents

Illustrations

Figures

Tables

Contributors

Manu Bhaskaran, Partner and Member of the Board, Centennial Group Inc.

Richard W. Carney, Assistant Professor of International Political Economy, S. Rajaratnam School of International Studies, Nanyang Technological University.

J. Soedradjad Djiwandono, Professor, S. Rajaratnam School of International Studies, Nanyang Technological University; Central Bank Governor of Indonesia during the crisis.

Peter Gourevitch, Professor of Political Science, School of International Relations and Pacific Studies, University of California San Diego.

Stephen Grenville, Adjunct Professor, The Crawford School of Economics and Government, The Australian National University; Visiting Fellow, Lowy Institute for International Policy; Deputy Governor, Federal Reserve Bank of Australia during the crisis.

Khor Hoe Ee, Assistant Managing Director (Economics), Monetary Authority of Singapore; Director of Research at the Monetary Authority of Singapore during the crisis.

Anwar Ibrahim, former Deputy Prime Minister and Finance Minister of Malaysia. He has held teaching positions at St Anthony's College, Oxford as a Visiting Fellow; Johns Hopkins School of Advanced International Studies, as a Distinguished Senior Visiting Fellow and Georgetown University's School of Foreign Service as a Visiting Professor.

Masahiro Kawai, Dean, Asian Development Bank Institute.

Hubert Neiss, Senior Advisor, Global Markets Asia, Deutsche Bank AG; Director for the Asia Pacific at the IMF during the crisis.

Pradumna B. Rana, Senior Fellow, Division of Economics, Nanyang Technological University; Former Senior Director, Office of Regional Economic Integration, Asian Development Bank.

John Ravenhill, Visiting Professor, S. Rajaratnam School of International Studies, Nanyang Technological University; Professor, Research School of Pacific and Asian Studies, Australian National University.

Jomo Kwame Sundaram, Assistant Secretary-General for Economic Development in the United Nations Department of Economic and Social Affairs.

Robert H. Wade, Professor of Political Economy and Development, London School of Economics.

Kit Wei Zheng, Senior Economist, Macroeconomic Surveillance Department, Monetary Authority of Singapore.

Preface

This volume was put together following a conference entitled, *The Asian Financial Crisis Ten Years Later: What Have We Learned?* at the Ritz-Carlton, Singapore on June 25–26, 2007. The timing was intended to coincide with the beginning of the Asian Financial Crisis on July 2, 1997, with the depreciation of the Thai baht. Though a tight timeline was followed in organizing the conference, an excellent team of people from the S. Rajaratnam School of International Studies (RSIS) ensured its success.

Ambassador Barry Desker, dean of RSIS, saw the opportunity to bring together a group of distinguished people to discuss this topic of great importance to the region, and ensured that the financial resources were available to make the conference a success.

Soedradjad Djiwandono, who became very busy giving talks at a variety of venues during this time, was instrumental in identifying people to invite. His guidance ensured that we had participants who would engage in lively, thought-provoking exchanges. While the papers were, for the most part, prepared in advance of the discussions, the key points that were batted around are succinctly summarized in Hubert Neiss's concluding chapter. In addition to the authors in this volume (except for Anwar Ibrahim), conference participants included Takatoshi Ito, Eisuke Sakakibara, and Atchana Waiquamdee, and Lim Chong Yah. Barkha Shah and Prakhar Sharma took notes and authored a conference report that summarizes some of the key themes that emerged during the lively discussions. It can be downloaded through RSIS's website: www.rsis.edu.sg.

Evelyn Yeoh, with characteristic efficiency, handled a large part of the organization of the conference; her vivacity and attention to detail were critical to its success. Yang Razali Kassim, Peter Ee, and Ben Ng were also instrumental in lining up and making appropriate arrangements for the speakers.

John Ravenhill and two anonymous referees made helpful comments on the introductory chapter. I would also like to thank Sonja van Leeuwen and Leanne Hinves at Routledge for their help in the timely publication of the book.

Richard Carney
Singapore, May 2008

1 Introduction

Richard W. Carney

For the five countries most heavily affected by the Asian financial crisis – Thailand, Korea, Indonesia, the Philippines, and Malaysia – the toll in both economic and human terms was enormous: in 1998, these countries saw their economies shrink by an average of 7.7 percent and many millions of people lost their jobs.[1] The magnitude of the crisis, and the contagion effects in Latin America and Russia, sounded alarm bells about the substantial risks and potential fragility of the international financial architecture. A voluminous literature has been written on the crisis as a result – what caused it, how it was handled by governments and international organizations, and the lessons learned or not learned. So in crafting an edited volume on this topic, there is legitimate concern with simply restating what has already been said. What makes this volume different is the unique combination of people directly involved with managing the crisis alongside leading academic specialists. By combining the perspectives of academics with practitioners, this volume complements other recent reflections on the crisis, including the recent series of scholar/practitioner papers in Oxford's Pathways through Financial Crises project (Woods, 2006) the special issues of *Asian Economic Policy Review* (Ito *et al.*, 2007) and *Asian Survey* (2007), as well as the scholarly collection in MacIntyre *et al.* (2008), to name just a few.

This chapter provides a brief overview of the economic and political circumstances discussed in detail by the contributing authors. It begins by presenting the prevailing thoughts on how financial crises generally occur before turning to an overview of the specific domestic conditions that led to the Asian crisis, followed by the international response that worsened its initial effects. But distilling the key causes and lessons of the crisis can lead to the glossing over of a 'multitude of questions' and risk oversimplification as Ravenhill admonishes in the opening of Chapter 2. For example, Jomo reminds us in Chapter 3 that Malaysia had a far heavier reliance on equities markets in comparison to the other affected countries, thus making it more susceptible to changes in portfolio flows as compared to bank lending. Djiwandono, Chapter 4, similarly sees Indonesia's problems as uniquely due to the series of inconsistent responses by the private sector, government, and international organizations, rather than resulting from the missteps of any single actor that would be found in other countries. His account also illuminates the personal stresses that accompanied decision makers' calculus in some of the countries in deciding how to react to the crisis; for example, three of his colleagues were jailed in connection with providing liquidity support to banks. Investigations and court hearings are still ongoing.

In the aftermath of the crisis, changes to macroeconomic policy and economic institutions were made to greater or lesser degrees among all the affected countries. While nations' macroeconomic policies have generally improved and are unlikely to contribute to a future exchange rate crisis, institutional reforms have been far more limited, as emphasized by several authors. Peter Gourevitch explains in Chapter 8 that this is largely attributable to the constellation of interests that wield political influence within these countries. The political–economic arrangements that enabled the crisis to occur were partly, if not mostly, due to particularistic interests that influenced government policies and the design of countries' institutions. Because they have largely retained their influence, the structure of the institutions has not changed substantially; actors' behaviors remain similar despite changes to the formal rules.

After reviewing the country-specific political circumstances, I then turn to an overview of changes in the region that have occurred since 1998. While the crisis galvanized political support for closer regional coordination, Kawai and Rana emphasize that the main impact on the regional architecture derives primarily from economic motivations. At the international level, Stephen Grenville (Chapter 10) and Hubert Neiss (Chapter 12) explain that some limited reforms have occurred. However, fundamental problems remain unresolved such as the lack of voting allotments within the IMF that reflect today's economic realities, an inadequate international lender of last resort, and the lack of institutionalization of private sector involvement to resolve crises. As Wade argues, these problems likely reflect a deeper underlying political reality that is contributing to the spread of standards and codes that conform to the preferences of Anglo-American financial interests, and which may be to the detriment of many developing nations. The last section reviews present risks to the stability of the international financial system. Kawai and Rana (Chapter 9), Neiss (Chapter 12), and Grenville (Chapter 10) consider whether nations are prepared for a disorderly wind-down of global payments imbalances, or for dealing with financial turmoil stemming from other sources of risk (e.g. an oil-induced shock). Attention is also paid to the gap between formal and behavioral compliance with international codes and standards, and other nonfinancial sources of potential crisis in the concluding section.

While the authors generally agree on the list of factors that contributed to the crisis, tensions clearly exist as to their relative weight, and with regard to the best way for countries to proceed in its wake. Two areas stand out:

1   the degree to which the crisis was due to common versus country-specific attributes; and
2   the suitability of advocating one style of regulatory reforms as 'best practice'.

These differences have important implications for how we interpret the key lessons of the crisis, and inform how preparations should be made for the next one. Thus, in contrast to the convention of opening with specific arguments about the causes and consequences of the crisis, I instead want to alert the reader to these concerns while poring over the chapters.

Causes of currency crises

As Krugman (1996) explains, if it is recognized that a country's costs of maintaining a fixed exchange rate relative to the costs of abandoning it are predictably increasing so that the country is likely to devalue at some future date, then speculators will try to get out of the currency ahead of the devaluation. But as a result, they worsen the government's tradeoff, leading to an earlier devaluation than would have otherwise occurred. Smart investors, realizing this, try to get out even earlier. The result is a crisis that ends the fixed exchange rate regime well before the fundamentals would appear to make devaluation necessary. The important point is that the crisis is ultimately provoked by the inconsistency of government policies, which makes the long-run survival of the fixed rate impossible. But that may not be how the government sees it since it may have been prepared to defend the exchange rate for a long time, yet it was forced to abandon it by a speculative attack. The financial markets simply bring home the news sooner than the country might have wanted to hear it.

However, many now recognize that a country's currency may be unfairly or arbitrarily attacked, as in the case of a self-fulfilling crisis. Countries with fixed exchange rates fall somewhere along a spectrum with regard to their capacity to defend it. At one end are those countries which are expected to defend their currency firmly and effectively, and so will probably not need to do so. At the other end are countries which appear very likely to abandon their peg eventually, and as a result will almost surely find their timetable accelerated by speculative pressure. Self-fulfilling crisis models say that there is an intermediate range between these two extremes where a crisis can happen, but need not. If self-fulfilling crises are a real possibility, what sets them off? The common answer is 'herding'. Because money managers are compensated based on comparison with other money managers, they may have strong incentives to act alike if they have imperfect information, or even if they have information suggesting that the market's judgment is wrong. As Keynes observed with regard to beauty contests, market participants are more concerned with predicting what everyone else will do, rather than predicting what the market will do based on an assessment of the fundamentals alone. Once one country's currency falls, the crisis often spreads, through 'contagion'. One simple explanation for this is that countries' economies are linked, and so if one country's economy suffers, another country with close trade or production links will also suffer. However, trade links are sometimes weak, yet contagion still occurs. One reason for this is the existence of some common but imperfectly observed characteristic among countries; for example, they may all share a common colonial heritage, or are located in geographical proximity yet lack substantial trade ties. This may partly explain Korea's vulnerability in the Asian financial crisis, as it lacked substantial trade links to Southeast Asian nations.[2] But if crises are at least partly, and initially, due to weaknesses at the domestic economic level, can we point to a common domestic cause among the affected countries without risking oversimplification?

Domestic and international causes

According to Jomo (Chapter 3), the domestic origins of the crisis are primarily due to the 'twin liberalizations' of national financial systems and the opening of countries' capital accounts in the 1980s. This led to four consequences that, in combination with high economic growth, intensified the demand for funds and developed the potential for the Asian crisis:

1   domestic financial institutions were given greater flexibility in offering interest rates to secure funds domestically and in bidding for foreign funds;
2   these institutions also became less reliant on lending to the government;
3   regulations, such as credit allocation rules and ceilings, were reduced; and
4   greater domestic competition among financial institutions led to an expansion of lending portfolios, often at the expense of prudence.

An abundant supply of capital from large financial institutions (banks, hedge funds, mutual funds, and pension funds), and the short-termism of fund managers' investment horizons contributed to the inherent risk in the supply of these funds, while the fixed exchange rates of Asian countries offered false assurances of limited currency risk. Overinvestment led to asset price bubbles (notably in real estate) and inflation. Declining export competitiveness, worsened by the increasing value of the US dollar relative to the yen, contributed to the deterioration of bank balance sheets and made it difficult for them to make loan repayments, which was exacerbated by the currency and lending mismatches. The double mismatch in financial intermediation was compounded by the smallness of the countries involved, which made them vulnerable to the decisions of one or two large overseas financial institutions. As Ravenhill explains, a 'rational panic' (Radelet and Sachs, 1998) ensued once investors became concerned that a country's foreign exchange reserves were insufficient to meet the foreign currency liabilities of its financial institutions, thus leading to an insolvency crisis driven by self-fulfilling expectations. Where foreign investors lacked good information about the countries, they were particularly susceptible to herd-like behavior.

However, countries varied in the types of vulnerabilities that they exhibited. While all the major affected countries were excessively dependent on short-term foreign borrowing, and their financial institutions had weak prudential supervision and were excessively exposed to the property sector, they differed along other dimensions that were seen as contributing to the crisis. These included the ratio of short-term debt to foreign reserves, the level of financial institutions' investment in equities, central bank management of foreign reserves, the slow-down of export growth, and the extent of exchange rate overvaluation. Indeed, some authors see the differences among these countries as more important to understanding the crisis than the similarities. As mentioned earlier, Jomo points to the more bank-based financial systems of Korea, Thailand, and Indonesia as contributing to their vulnerability to the sudden drop in the availability of short-term US dollar bank loans as international confidence fell, in comparison to Malaysia, where the vulnerability was mainly due to the volatility of inter-national portfolio flows into its stock market.

Djiwandono (Chapter 4) likewise sees Indonesia's crisis as not being driven purely by investors' herding behavior or by domestic institutional factors. After all, Bank Indonesia demonstrated that it could successfully defend the rupiah in response to an external shock, as occurred following Mexico's crisis in 1995, as well as from a shock with domestic origins, as occurred following the ransack-ing of Megawati's party headquarters in 1996. Further, Bank Indonesia was praised for its monetary and exchange rate policies by the IMF and others just prior to the onset of the crisis. Djiwandono instead emphasizes how inconsistent responses by the government, the private sector, and the IMF initially affected the financial sector, and soon brought the pre-existing institutional weaknesses in other areas of the economy into the open, thereby exposing the whole system to destructive attacks. The erosion of market confidence fueled contagion in the national economy and generated widespread social and political turmoil, culmi-nating in the toppling of Soeharto's regime. Although it exhibited vulnerabilities like the other affected countries and initially implemented policies that were considered prudent, Indonesia suffered the most and has taken the longest time to recover. Both economic growth and investment levels are below the pre-crisis levels, and well below those of the other affected countries. Strong accusations have been leveled at the government's mismanagement of the crisis, and its failure to restore growth and investor confidence since. In response to these critics, Djiwandono offers an illuminating explanation of how the lack of a coordinated response undermined the capacity to successfully weather the crisis as Indonesia had accomplished before.

Insofar as countries exhibited unique vulnerabilities, the IMF's cookie-cutter approach aggravated the situation, especially if viewed from the perspective of a self-fulfilling crisis in which countries' (macro)economic fundamentals are actually sound. Many have criticized the IMF's recommendations; for example, although countries had sound fiscal balances before the crisis, the IMF asked the affected countries to cut government spending in order to restore confidence in their currencies despite the negative implications for economic recovery. Except for Indonesia, which could not raise the financing required, the crisis-affected countries eventually ignored this advice and undertook Keynesian-style refla-tionary, countercyclical measures starting in the second half of 1998 which, in combination with export-led growth, was critical to their recovery.

As Director of the IMF for the Asia-Pacific during the crisis, Hubert Neiss (Chapter 12) provides rare insight into the thinking that went into the fund's decisions, and the difficult circumstances under which it had to make them – frequently within very tight timeframes and with incomplete information. He acknowledges that with the benefit of hindsight, it is easier to recognize policy missteps, such as recommendations for fiscal tightening, interest rate increases, overly intrusive structural reforms unrelated to the crisis, delayed corporate restructuring, the hesitation of guaranteeing all bank deposits (rather than only those of individual depositors), and inadequate social protection. He argues, however, that while the IMF may be at fault for certain policy mistakes, the international community and other international institutions must also share in the blame as the content of the rescue programs and the amounts to be disbursed depended upon their support. And although important lessons have been learned, and the IMF would react differently the next time around, fundamental problems remain. The international financial architecture is in particular need of reform, including the expansion of lender of last resort capability, the institutionalization of private sector involvement, and the adjustment of voting rights to reflect today's economic realities. Since the next crisis is unlikely to be a replica of the last one, leaving these fundamental problems unattended may allow the next crisis to be deeper and to spread more quickly to other countries as capital flows increase in magnitude, speed, and reach.

National economic consequences

Since the crisis, most of the affected countries have made substantial improvements in their macroeconomic policies. Khor Hoe Ee and Wei Zheng (Chapter 6) argue that countries now exhibit greater credibility with regard to inflation targeting, and exchange rate flexibility has reduced countries' vulnerability to a capital flow-induced crisis.[3] Economic recovery has likewise occurred quickly; GDP levels are higher in 2007 than before the crisis, growth rates are around 4–6 percent (which is 2–3 percentage points lower than the 1990s, possibly suggesting that pre-crisis rates were unsustainably high or, as Grenville argues (Chapter 10), that current investment rates are too low), and since 2005 the value of capital flows into these countries has exceeded the pre-crisis peaks. Additionally, the crisis-hit countries have reduced their external debt positions from a peak of over 70 percent of GDP in 1998 to around 30 percent currently. The bolstering of countries' external positions has been accompanied by a massive build-up of foreign reserves as self-insurance against the risk of a sudden stop in capital flows.

Institutional reforms have also been introduced. For example, banking system reforms have been implemented in several of the crisis-affected countries; they are now better capitalized, lending rules and regulatory oversight have improved, and bankruptcy laws and procedures have been strengthened. But in addition to this, financing via capital markets is increasing as a result of authorities' active encouragement of the development of bond markets, which many are hoping will continue as reforms to accounting, corporate governance, and disclosure standards occur.

However, Manu Bhaskaran (Chapter 7) emphasizes that while these reforms look good on paper, they have in fact remained quite limited, and considerable improvements are needed. Although the corporate sector across most countries has seen increased privatization since the crisis – and the reduction of the state's influence – progress has been slow. This is largely attributable to underlying political interests which remain entrenched and influential, thereby preventing necessary corporate governance reforms that would enhance transparency, protect minority investors (and foreign investors), and remove any vestiges of crony capitalism. Of all the affected countries, Indonesia has the furthest to go. With regard to its banking institutions, Grenville (Chapter 10) explains that the most pressing problem is the lack of prudential regulation, including the implementation of strict lending criteria to ensure loans are repaid (i.e. no connected lending and no special relationships between state banks and state enterprises), as well as a strong legal system and well-functioning bankruptcy procedures. The continuing underdevelopment of the country's capital markets denies alternative financing sources to many domestic firms, reflecting the continuance of close business–government ties.

Most of the affected countries have successfully recovered and surpassed their positions prior to the crisis. Regional integration and cooperation has likewise improved, particularly in the areas of trade, production networks, and finance. But, 'if we go beyond this veneer, reality bites hard', Anwar Ibrahim (Chapter 5) avers. Most Southeast Asian countries still have not developed a durable base of manufacturing capacity nor a services industry to effectively compete in the global marketplace. And income inequality is rising.

Although Malaysia's equity markets are well developed and seem to have emerged from the crisis in good shape, to Anwar Ibrahim the country is in need of reforms that go beyond preparing for the next crisis. The main concern for Malaysia, which applies generally to the development paths of other East Asian countries, is the lack of equitable or 'humane' development. Prior to the crisis, many observers saw East Asia as pursuing a growth with equity model. But since 1998, income inequality has markedly increased. Ibrahim (Chapter 5) and Wade (Chapter 11) see this as a natural consequence of following the kinds of market reforms typically advocated by the IMF and World Bank, which generate further income inequality and undercut the state's capacity to offer a social safety net. Ibrahim asserts that Malaysia and other countries in the region are in need of adopting Keynesian style reforms – governments need to shield their domestic economies from the excesses that so often accompany global capital flows.

Domestic politics: impediments to reform

A good deal of the resistance to implementing reforms that would improve prudential regulation of the banking system, reduce the extent of government-influenced lending, and expand capital markets, is the consequence of regulatory capture. In particular, large corporations who benefit from a cozy relationship with the government are seen as blocking these initiatives. John Ravenhill (Chapter 2) discusses examples of how this kind of political arrangement fostered corruption and economic mismanagement prior to the crisis in Thailand, Indonesia, and Korea. Anwar Ibrahim likewise criticizes the huge government lending programs that persist in Malaysia. The continuance of these business–government relationships has prevented many reforms from being fully or meaningfully implemented. As Gourevitch (Chapter 8) notes, what has resulted is 'mock compliance' – change in the formal rules, but not change in actual practice (Walter, 2008). For the formal rules to take effect, political support needs to exist. This does not necessarily mean that convergence on an Anglo-Saxon type of financial model is the necessary outcome; financial systems in continental Europe work well, yet are different. The outcome often depends on the way in which various interests form political power-sharing coalitions. For example, in the United States, farmers (whose power is magnified by over-representation in the Senate) struck bargains with business owners over financial regulation in the early twentieth century that led to a fragmented banking system and dispersed corporate ownership. In post-World War II Germany, anti-Communist American occupiers struck a bargain with German labor that solidified the country's postwar capitalist economy which has been organized around large universal banks and concentrated corporate ownership (Carney, forthcoming). As a result, German firms have depended on a different kind of corporate model and a different set of institutional arrangements from their American counterparts, yet these arrangements have enabled them to successfully compete in the global marketplace. The key lesson is that a variety of financial outcomes are possible, and work; imposing a cookie-cutter model onto a country without consideration for the political circumstances that have generated its institutional arrangements will likely lead to mock compliance and lure investors into a false sense of complacency about the safety of their investments.

Regional economic changes

Before the crisis, formal regional institutions were limited to the Association of Southeast Asian Nations (ASEAN) and two pan-Pacific institutions, the ASEAN regional forum and Asia Pacific Economic Cooperation (APEC). The crisis shocked countries in the region into a recognition of their common vulnerability to global financial forces, which were sure to increase with the expansion of trade, production networks, and financial development. As a result, a variety of initiatives at regional cooperation were implemented, especially in the financial arena, as Kawai and Rana (Chapter 9) discuss in detail. For example, the ASEAN Plus Three (APT) has helped to establish regulatory standards that are more sensitive to countries' specific political economic arrangements than international rules, yet which promote improvements that are likely to be viewed as legitimate by the international community. Central bank governors have also developed regional fora for policy dialogues on monetary policy, banking, and exchange rate management. And through the Chiang Mai Initiative, progress has occurred in creating a regional reserve pooling framework in which a swap agreement exists among Southeast Asian nations. While it has been strengthened over time, a heavy reliance on IMF support remains since only 20 percent of the initial amount requested would come from the swap agreement without IMF support; the remaining 80 percent depends on support from the IMF before funds are released. But the substantial amount of reserves accumulated by individual countries lessens the perceived need to bolster this regional framework.[4]

Additionally, initiatives aimed at developing and deepening regional bond markets were introduced as a way to reduce the double-mismatch problem that led to the 1997 crisis by attracting funds from the region (largely countries' foreign exchange reserves) via bond sales. These funds are then used as an alternative to financial intermediaries outside of the region for long-term investments. While there is a greater emphasis after the crisis on developing regional economic cooperation, political support is lacking. Thus, a 'parallel' as opposed to a 'European' approach to regional financial cooperation seems more likely to succeed in the long-run, and would facilitate intraregional trade and lessen currency risk (Eichengreen, 2006).

Enhancing the possibilities for regional financial cooperation is the expansion of, and changing geographic distribution of, trade relations since the crisis. Before 1998, Japan and, to a lesser degree, the United States were the key national economies driving regional growth. However, China has become a pivotal economic hub due to a massive inflow of foreign investment in manufacturing. China's rapid growth has occurred in tandem with the repositioning of regional production networks that increasingly place it at the center. Yet at the same time, Asian trade relations are increasing even more with the global economy than they are with other countries within the region. But the increasing reliance on exports from a single sector – electronics – increases the region's trade vulnerability. While preferential trading agreements have proliferated, which some claim can help to limit vulnerability to trade dimensions of future economic crises, they may be significant more for their political–strategic value (Ravenhill, 2008).

Thus, regional cooperation has expanded since the crisis, especially in the financial arena. Yet the depth of this cooperation is limited by countries' increased self-reliance, as demonstrated by the accumulation of foreign reserves. While increased trade relations offer the possibility of expanding regional cooperation, few meaningful region-wide trade agreements have been struck, and the growing reliance on electronics exports raises concerns about trade vulnerability in the future. Because regional cooperation has increased primarily as a result of economic and business-related motivations, rather than being a politically driven process, the breadth and depth remains limited.

International financial system

On the international dimension, the IMF has improved its surveillance of countries vulnerable to crisis, and the IMF and World Bank are taking a more nuanced approach to managing them. However, there are areas where reforms are needed. If another financial crisis occurs, despite more flexible exchange rates, Stephen Grenville (Chapter 10) poses the question: how well does the IMF support the range of options available? He observes that short-term capital controls are not clearly endorsed by the IMF, although some evidence indicates that they can be useful in certain circumstances. Additionally, the IMF lacks a firm commitment to acting as a lender of last resort in all cases where equal need is demonstrated without the backing of a powerful sponsor (e.g. the US or EU). Consequently, the amount of capital needed to stave off a liquidity crunch may be insufficient and not available quickly enough in today's fast-moving capital markets. Thus, a reallocation of voting powers to reflect toady's economic realities is needed. Kawai and Rana (Chapter 9), and Neiss (Chapter 12), likewise point to the inadequate institutionalization of private involvement in helping to resolve a crisis.

On top of this, Kawai and Rana see the need for the effective implementation of standards and codes which have been promoted by the IMF and World Bank, and which fall under the broad categories of policy transparency, financial sector regulation and supervision, and market integrity. Data dissemination standards that involve consistent and reliable data updates are seen as a necessary component of strengthening the international financial landscape, and helping countries gain access to global capital markets.

However, Wade (Chapter 11) warns that the adoption of these uniform standards across countries may have undesirable consequences for developing nations. Since the standards that are recommended derive from the Anglo-American market economy model, they tend to grant financial institutions working in these systems an advantage when competing for business internationally. Implementing US–UK rules reduces the space for the state to lead the development process, as it did before the crisis, or as it has in many, now industrialized, nations (e.g. Japan, Korea, and France). By observing the income distribution effects within the US and UK, Wade raises legitimate concerns about the potential consequences for the world economy as a result of implementing these standards globally. As mentioned earlier, income inequality has increased among East Asian countries since the crisis. The worry is heightened by the exclusion of developing countries from the fora in which these standards are decided (e.g. the Bank for International Settlements and the Financial Stability Forum). Despite the incentives to adhere to these rules (e.g. lower cost financing), developing countries have displayed mixed results, either in formally or behaviorally complying with them. And where they have formally implemented these rules, there has tended to be a lack of behavioral compliance. This then raises the question of when do we observe de facto (behavioral), as opposed to *de jure* (formal), compliance and leads us back to an examination of domestic interests and the political environment in which policy is made. If the groups with the political power to enforce these rules domestically do not benefit from behavioral compliance, then real movement toward an Anglo-American financial model will be lacking. Before behavioral compliance occurs, there is a need to build good institutions (legal, property rights, information provision, and monitoring). Thus, sequencing reforms to these underlying institutions is necessary first, and will take time.

Future risks

Since 1998, East Asian countries have kept interest rates low and stable to encourage export-led growth and to build up reserves to insure against a repeat of the crisis. A low exchange rate is also important for maintaining competitiveness with China. But keeping the exchange rate artificially low delays the inevitable appreciation; if the nominal rate doesn't appreciate at some point, the real rate will via increasing inflation. Indeed, some countries have witnessed run-ups in the prices of their stock markets and real estate, as Hoe Ee and Wei Zheng (Chapter 6) observe; Kawai and Rana (Chapter 9) explain that this is a particular concern in the case of China. Seeing that appreciation is inevitable, speculation ensues which makes the costs of adjustment greater. The problem for these other countries is maintaining competitiveness relative to China if their currency appreciates.

Higher equities and real estate prices create greater risks for the banking sector in these countries, which have been ramping up their business activities in the securities arena. With the exception of Hong Kong and Singapore, many countries' banking systems already suffer from a continuing lack of transparency and full disclosure, uncertainty about the continuing level of non-performing loans, as well as the effectiveness of supervision, regulation, and risk management.

Further, the persistence of global payments imbalances is not sustainable in the long-run, and heightens the existing risks. There are several adjustment possibilities that could be made to accommodate an orderly wind-down, including stronger domestic demand in East Asia, a savings increase in the US, an orderly depreciation of the real effective exchange rate of the US dollar, and an appreciation of East Asian currencies to reduce the US current account deficit and the East Asian surplus. The risk is that these adjustments will not be orderly, and that further increases in the imbalances could trigger abrupt exchange rate swings, or perhaps more likely, rapid adjustments in domestic economies and financial markets. The risks to the banking and corporate sectors are exacerbated by the gap between formal and behavioral compliance since substantial problems may exist beneath a sanguine surface. If an economic downturn exposes this gap, foreign investors may run for the exits – again.

But other, potentially graver, risks may arise from nonfinancial arenas, which then lead to economic and financial troubles. For example, natural disasters, which many see as increasing as a result of global warming, could incite social turmoil as the gap between poor and wealthy increases. The recent rise in food prices could likewise exacerbate growing tensions arising from increasing inequality. An unexpected increase in the cost of certain commodities – notably oil – may also cause strains, particularly as more countries compete for scarce resources to fuel their development. Pollution, and other related consequences of rapid development, may also foster social tensions both within and between countries. Moreover, the recent mortgage crisis illustrates that shocks to the global financial system can come from unexpected places, even from the supposedly 'safe' capital markets of the United States. This time, most Asian countries have not been affected simply because their financial institutions are not yet sophisticated enough to participate. But as their institutions mature, Asian nations are unlikely to be immune the next time around. Since information is often incomplete at the onset of a crisis, from whatever source the next crisis emerges, and whatever form it takes, it would be wise to remember Neiss's counsel: 'in the event of a new crisis, be quite flexible in the policy response and be prepared to change policies as events unfold and the situation becomes clearer.'

Notes

1 Economic growth is measured with purchasing power parity.
2 Of course, Korea's fragile financial system contributed to its vulnerability.
3 Note, however, that this is in contrast to the views of Benjamin Cohen (2008), among others.
4 Amyx (2008) offers a detailed account of political initiatives for regional financial cooperation, including the establishment of a regional monetary fund via the Chiang Mai Initiative, regional bond markets, and the increasing interest in establishing an Asian currency unit.

References

Amyx, J. (2008) 'Regional Financial Cooperation in East Asia since the Asian Financial Crisis', in A. MacIntyre, T.J. Pempel, and J. Ravenhill *East Asia in the Wake of the Financial Crisis*, Ithaca, NY: Cornell University Press.
Asian Survey (2007) 47(6).
Carney, R. (forthcoming) *Contested Capitalism: Political Origins of Financial Institutions*, Book Manuscript.
Cohen, B. (2008) 'After the Fall: East Asian Exchange Rates since the Crisis', in A. MacIntyre, T.J. Pempel, and J. Ravenhill *East Asia in the Wake of the Financial Crisis*, Ithaca, NY: Cornell University Press.
Eichengreen, B. (2006) 'The Parallel-Currency Approach to Asian Monetary Integration', *American Economic Review* 96(2), pp. 432–436.
Ito, T., Kojima, A., McKenzie, C., and Urata, S. (eds.) (2007) 'Ten Years After the Asian Crisis: What Have We Learned or Not Learned?' *Asian Economic Policy Review* 2(1), pp. 1–168.
Krugman, P. (1996) 'Are Currency Crises Self-Fulfilling?', *NBER Macroeconomics Annual*.
MacIntyre, A., Pempel, T.J., and Ravenhill, J. (2008) *East Asia in the Wake of the Financial Crisis*, Ithaca, NY: Cornell University Press.
Radelet, S. and Sachs, J. (1998) 'The Onset of the East Asian Financial Crisis', *NBER Working Paper No. W6680*.
Ravenhill, J. (2008) 'Trading Out of Crisis', in A. MacIntyre, T.J. Pempel, and J. Ravenhill *East Asia in the Wake of the Financial Crisis*, Ithaca, NY: Cornell University Press.
Walter, A. (2008) *Governing Finance: East Asia's Adoption of International Standards*, Ithaca, NY: Cornell University Press.
Woods, N. (ed.) (2006) 'Understanding Pathways Through Financial Crises and the Impact of the IMF', *Global Governance* 12(4).

Part I
Overview

2 From miracle to misadventure

The political economy of the 1997–98 crises

John Ravenhill

At one level of generality, an explanation for the misadventure that befell many East Asian economies in 1997–98 is straightforward. The devastating (if, save for Indonesia, short-term) reversal of economic growth was the product of mutually reinforcing currency and banking crises. These quickly spilled over into the real economy when the collapse of financial institutions led to the non-renewal of loans and/or companies were unable to service their debts under a higher interest rate regime. The proximate cause of the crisis was a massive reversal in capital flows – with net international bank and bond finance for the five most severely affected economies (Indonesia, Korea, Malaysia, the Philippines, and Thailand) moving from an inflow of $54 billion in the 12 months from the fourth quarter of 1996 to the third quarter of 1997, to an outflow of $68 billion in the fourth quarter of 1997 and the first quarter of 1998 (Grenville 2000: Table 2.3, p. 42). The turn-around in bank lending between 1996 and 1997 was equivalent to 9.5 percent of the combined GDP of the five crisis economies (Radelet and Sachs 1998: 6)

Moving beyond this level of generality is like peeling the layers of skin from an onion – or perhaps, given the interrelated character of many of the factors contributing to the crisis, akin to attempting to understand the atomic composition of a DNA molecule. For the straightforward explanation of the crisis presented above hides a multitude of questions. Why did economies whose fundamentals were widely regarded as sound (and therefore would not be identified as vulnerable under conventional modelling of financial crises)[1] collapse in 1997? Why were financial systems so fragile? Why did countries with among the highest rates of domestic savings in the world come to depend so heavily on foreign lending? Why was so large a portion of foreign capital inflows short term in nature and denominated in foreign currency? Why did the process of liberalization that had occurred in financial sectors in East Asian economies over the previous decade produce such flawed outcomes? Would controls over short-term capital inflows have reduced the vulnerability to crisis? Were the close relations between the state and business that many commentators – including even the World Bank in its "miracle" study (World Bank 1993) – had identified as a positive factor in East Asia's rapid economic growth, a hindrance in an era of financial liberalization? What was the relationship between weaknesses in the financial sector and problems in the real economy? How significant a problem was contagion in the rapid spread of crisis across the region? Was East Asia's high debt model (Wade and Veneroso 1998) of industrial financing obsolete given rapidly changing domestic and international economic and political contexts? How can demand for investment funds in rapidly growing economies best be met? Was the crisis exacerbated by inappropriate responses? If so, to what extent was this the fault of the IMF? What is an appropriate exchange rate regime for small rapidly-growing East Asian economies heavily dependent on extra-regional markets?

To be able to take action against the occurrence of similar crises in the future, we need to know both what went wrong and why "things fell apart." To answer these questions requires an explanation grounded in political economy as well as economic theory. This chapter, following the division of labour drawn up by the conference organizers, examines the background and context of the crises, leaving to others the provision of a more detailed account of the experience of individual economies and of the lessons that can be drawn from the unhappy experience of 1997–98.[2]

Given the complexities and interrelationships involved, the story of the unfolding of the crisis can be told in various ways. A good starting point is the excessive investment that occurred in the crisis economies from the late 1980s – excessive in the sense that the inflow of funds could not be absorbed productively or managed in a manner that did not cause macroeconomic imbalances. The significance of this investment boom was threefold:

- it created the underlying vulnerability of East Asian economies to a sudden reversal of flows of foreign lending by generating a gap between (already high levels) of domestic savings on the one hand, and desired investment on the other, a gap that was filled by foreign borrowing;
- it stoked an asset price bubble that contributed to an acceleration of domestic inflation, which in turn caused a loss of competitiveness for the exports of the crisis economies; and
- it contributed – through a concentration of investment in property and equities – to a further deterioration of the balance sheets of banks and other financial institutions in the crisis economies.

The savings–investment gap

Figure 2.1 presents data on the average ratio of investment to GDP for the five crisis economies in the years from 1985 to 1996. In the second half of the 1980s, this ratio was already over 25 percent for all the economies except for the Philippines. In the period from 1990–96, the mean figure jumped substantially for all economies, most spectacularly for Malaysia and Thailand, where the ratio climbed to close to 45 percent.

By the late 1980s, for all the crisis economies except for Indonesia, levels of domestic savings were insufficient to fully finance the investment boom (Figure 2.2). For Korea and Malaysia (except in 1995), the gap between domestic savings and gross fixed capital formation was relatively small as a

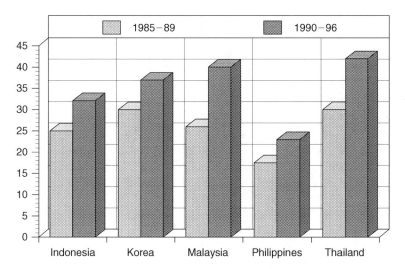

Figure 2.1 Mean investment/GDP ratio (%) (source: calculated from data in World Bank, *World Development Indicators* online database).

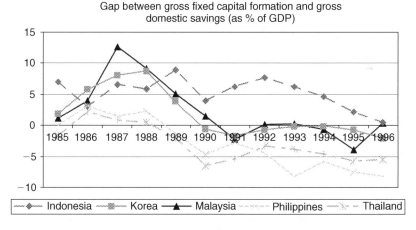

Figure 2.2 The savings–investment gap (source: World Bank, *World Development Indicators* online database).

percentage of GDP; for the Philippines and Thailand it was much more substantial, averaging over 5 percent for the years from 1990 to 1996.

The investment boom was financed by massive capital inflows. These increased from an annual average of 1.4 percent of GDP over the years 1986–90 to 6.7 percent in the years 1990–96. The pace of inflows increased markedly between 1994 and 1996. In the latter year, they were equivalent to about 15 percent of GDP for Thailand and the Philippines, 8 percent for Malaysia, and 5 percent for Indonesia and Korea (World Bank 1998: Figure 1.3). In all of the crisis economies save for Malaysia, the vast majority of capital inflows originated in overseas borrowing by financial intermediaries and by the corporate sector.

From the perspective of both borrowers and lenders, this activity appeared rational. The relative stability of exchange rates in the region (and their seemingly implicit guarantee by governments) reduced the apparent risk for both parties to a transaction. For borrowers from within the region, foreign loans offered the opportunity to access money at rates lower than those prevailing domestically for lenders and borrowers alike (and therefore, a chance for financial institutions to profit from intermediation). For financial institutions in high-income economies, faced with relatively low interest rates at home, especially for those from Japan, supplying loans to the rapidly growing economies of East Asia also appeared an attractive proposition – providing them with the opportunity to earn relatively high returns with apparently little risk. A necessary condition for the outbreak of financial crisis was the vast increase in funds in industrialized economies in search of profitable outlets.

Inflation and the exchange rate

In most countries, inflation trended upwards in the 1990s with the emergence of asset bubbles. The economies were committed to fixed or heavily managed exchange rates with little flexibility. Success in managing inflation and the exchange rate, however, varied substantially across the crisis economies. Indonesia experienced one of the crisis group's higher rates of inflation but its currency depreciated consistently through the late 1980s and early 1990s so that on the eve of the crisis the nominal exchange rate against the US dollar was only half that prevailing in 1985 (Figure 2.3). The Philippines also experienced a substantial nominal depreciation against the US dollar (but this was concentrated in the second half of the 1980s, the peso trading in a fairly narrow range between 1991 and the crisis).

While Malaysia experienced relatively low rates of inflation, the nominal exchange rate against the dollar in the year before the crisis was less than 2 percent below that in 1985. The two most problematic cases, however, were Korea and Thailand, both of which had annual rates of inflation in the first half of the 1990s that averaged over 5 percent, yet their currencies actually appreciated (Thailand) or traded within a very narrow range (Korea after 1992) against the US dollar.[3] With the dollar itself appreciating against the yen, and China effectively devaluing the yuan in 1994 through consolidating its official and market exchange rates, it is scarcely surprising that some Korean and Thai goods lost competitiveness in international markets. The impact on the balance of trade was exacerbated in some instances by sharp declines in export prices.[4]

The overall impact of inflation and real exchange rate appreciation on the real economy, as measured by annual rates of export growth, was mixed, however (Figure 2.4). Export growth in the Philippines was on a markedly upward trend in the mid-1990s. Korea's record was patchy, but 1996 seemed to be an exception to an otherwise positive trajectory. Only in the other three Southeast Asian crisis economies – Indonesia, Malaysia, and Thailand – did there appear to be a downward direction in export growth in the mid-1990s compared with the beginning of the decade. In themselves, these fluctuations were certainly of no greater magnitude than those experienced by the region in the past (and only in Thailand did exports actually *decline* – in the year immediately preceding the crisis – rather than the growth rate slowing), and something that most analysts might reasonably expect to be accommodated through appropriate policy adjustments. The downturn in export performance in the mid-1990s was sufficient, however, when combined with evidence of growing problems in the financial systems, to trigger concerns about the overall health of the economies, which led directly to the onset of speculative attacks against the currencies.

Financial sector problems

The effects of the investment boom on the financial sector were particularly problematic. One dimension was the misallocation of funds toward largely speculative investments. On the eve of the crisis, it was estimated that the share of bank lending that was directed towards the property sector ranged from 15–20 percent in the Philippines, 15 to 25 percent in Korea, 25–30 percent in Indonesia, to 30 to 40 percent in Malaysia and Thailand (Goldstein 1998: Table 4b, p. 8). In addition, in some countries, notably Korea, banks themselves had substantial investments in stocks.[5] There, the new lending in the 1990s financed the building of massive excess capacity in sectors such as steel and automobiles (Noble and Ravenhill 2000). Risky lending further weakened banks' balance sheets, with non-performing loans estimated as constituting at least 15 percent of total loans in the five economies.[6] Small wonder, then, that by the mid-1990s some financial advisors were warning clients of the vulnerability of the region's financial institutions.[7] Once the speculative bubble burst, financial institutions quickly found themselves in trouble – and it was the accumulation of non-performing loans by non-bank financial intermediaries in Thailand that triggered the initial waves of speculation against the baht.

The problems of the financial sector were compounded by what has become known as the "double mismatch" in financial intermediation. The first was a currency mismatch between financial institutions' borrowing through unhedged foreign-currency-denominated loans and their lending of these funds in domestic currencies.[8] The second was a maturity mismatch between the short-term foreign currency borrowing of the financial institutions and their medium-term domestic lending.[9] The double mismatch generated several vulnerabilities. The dependence on short-term loans made the system of investment financing vulnerable to a massive reduction in the availability of funds in a short time period – a reversal of capital flows that could occur for reasons that had little to do with the situation in the borrowing country.[10] In this context it is important to remind oneself of the relatively small size of the financial systems in the crisis economies: decisions by one

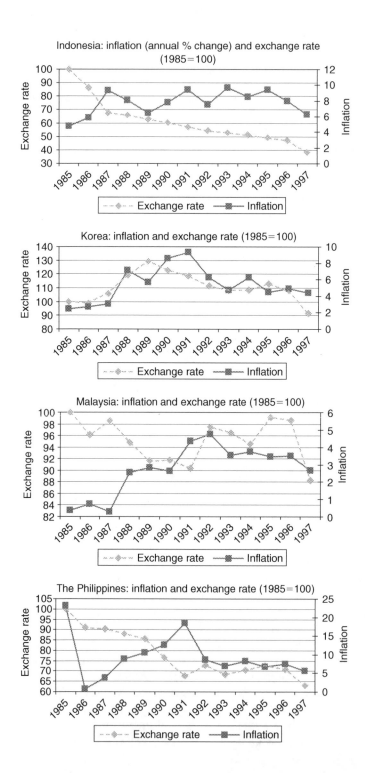

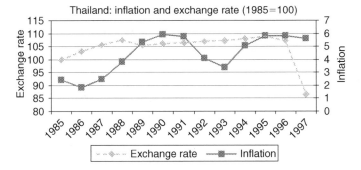

Figure 2.3 Inflation (annual percentage change) [right axis] and nominal exchange rates (market exchange rates – local currency to the US dollar, period average, 1985 = 100) [left axis] (source: exchange rate data from World Bank, *World Development Indicators*).

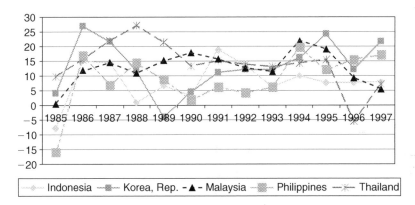

Figure 2.4 Annual average growth of exports (%) (source: World Bank, *World Development Indicators*).

or two large overseas financial institutions to withdraw from lending could have a disproportionate impact on the local economy.

And, any depreciation of the exchange rate would generate a gap between the financial institutions' international obligations and the value of their loan portfolios. Devaluation simply increased the local currency value of financial institutions' liabilities. Heavy dependence on unhedged foreign loans also rendered the whole financial system vulnerable to "rational panic" (Radelet and Sachs 1998) if investors became concerned that a country's foreign exchange reserves were insufficient to meet the foreign currency liabilities of its financial institutions. The situation was ripe for an insolvency crisis driven by self-fulfilling expectations. And, as Grenville (2000: 44) notes, foreign lenders were particularly susceptible to herd-like behavior in a context where they had little knowledge of, and understanding of, the local economy.

The trigger for the crisis, then, was the realization by foreign lenders of how dire was the relationship between short-term debt and available foreign exchange reserves in Thailand, Indonesia, and Korea (Figure 2.5), and the risk that this posed to their recovering their loans. By 1995, in all three countries, short-term debts exceeded available foreign exchange – and the ratio rose to as high as 300 percent in Korea. The situation in Korea was exacerbated by the central bank's lending reserves to commercial banks – and everywhere by doubts over the accuracy of the asset sheets presented by the central banks.[11]

Once the crisis began, its various elements – in the currency market, the financial sector, and the real economy – became self-sustaining and mutually reinforcing. An attack on the currency took the form of non-renewal of lending, which caused problems for banks and the corporate sector; currency depreciation increased the local currency liabilities of domestic financial institutions; attempts to stem capital outflows and currency depreciation by raising interest rates caused further corporate defaults; these defaults in turn further exacerbated the problem of non-performing loans, generating more concern among foreign investors about the health of the financial sector.

A summary of the sources of vulnerability of the crisis economies is provided in Table 2.1. While considerable commonalities are evident across all five economies, it is important to note that, just as the East Asian "model" was far from uniform,[12] so too were there some cross-country differences in vulnerability, a reflection of variance in policy choice by incumbent governments.

The political economy of vulnerability

One commonality across the divergent views in what was often a heated debate in academic circles on the East Asian Crisis in the late 1990s was to blame a

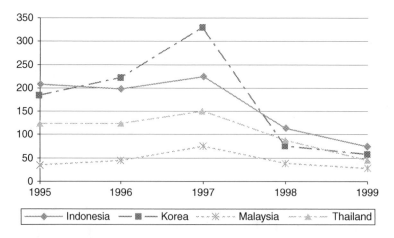

Figure 2.5 Ratio of short-term external debt to foreign reserves (%) (source: data from Goldstein and Turner 2004: Table 2.1, p. 12).

Table 2.1 Sources of vulnerability in the crisis economies

	Indonesia	Korea	Malaysia	Philippines	Thailand
Excessive dependence on short-term foreign borrowing	Y	Y	Y	Y	Y
Ratio of short-term debt to foreign reserves	Y	Y	N	N	Y
Exchange rate inflexibility	?	Y	Y	?	Y
Significant exchange rate overvaluation	N	?	N	N	Y
Slowdown of export growth	Y	?	Y	N	Y
Significant financial institution exposure to the property sector	Y	Y	Y	Y	Y
Significant financial institution investment in equities	N	Y	Y	N	N
Central bank mismanagement of foreign reserves	N	Y	N	N	Y
Weak prudential supervision	Y	Y	Y	Y	Y

flawed process of financial liberalization for the countries' vulnerability. Identifying the origins of the liberalization push – whether it came from domestic forces strengthened by democratization, from rent-seeking interests, or from the US Treasury and international financial institutions – and especially the prescriptions on how to overcome the flaws (a reversal of liberalization, improved prudential regulation, or more comprehensive liberalization?) were among the more contentious issues.

The dependence on short-term foreign borrowing reflected not only the arguably "excessive" levels of investment discussed above but also the absence of other sources of investment finance. In some countries offshore borrowing (especially for short-term loans) by financial institutions had been liberalized before inward foreign direct investment (FDI) – a sequence that could alternatively be seen as reflecting longstanding statist preferences and/or those of powerful domestic corporate actors. In the first half of the 1990s, Korea remained substantially closed to inward FDI, these flows averaging only $0.8 billion each year in the period 1990–94 (Urata 2001: Table 11.2, p. 414). The four ASEAN economies had become far more welcoming of FDI, in part in response to the perceived challenge from China's liberalization and growth, but only in Malaysia did FDI inflows in the early 1990s exceed borrowing by financial institutions and corporate actors.

Other potential sources of investment financing were similarly limited. Of the five countries, only in Malaysia did the domestic stock market provide a significant proportion of corporate finance. And bond markets were almost non-existent. With governments typically running fiscal surpluses or maintaining a balanced budget, there was little call for the issue of government bonds. Together with the ongoing reservations about foreign investor participation in such markets, this lack of government demand for financing effectively precluded the emergence of a vibrant domestic bond market.[13]

A move away from dependence on bank financing inevitably would have taken time – and this was a luxury that governments may not have been able to afford given the pressures that they were under to liberalize their financial sectors. These pressures were frequently both internal and external in origin. Much of the attention at the time of the crisis focused on demands from the US, other Western governments, and the international financial institutions – the significance of which varied from country to country, Korea being particularly vulnerable after it announced its application to join the OECD. Domestic sources, however, were also important. Some sections of the government and the academic world had been persuaded by the logic of liberalization and served as a transmission belt for the ideas that became known as the "Washington consensus." Other actors, notably in the financial and corporate as well as the political worlds supported liberalization because they believed that it would bring institutional and/or individual gain. Democratization in some countries increased the effectiveness of the clamor for reducing the state's role in the economy in general, and in the financial sector in particular.[14]

As Haggard (2000: 8) notes, the weakness of prudential regulation in the crisis economies might reflect either sins of commission or omission (or, indeed, one might add, a combination of the two). Sins of omission arise where the state simply lacks the administrative capacity and knowledge to implement effective regimes of liberalization and prudential regulation. Sins of commission, in contrast, are the product of the capture of these regimes by self-seeking actors.

The experience of disasters in the regulation of the financial and corporate sectors in the industrialized world over the past quarter of a century has demonstrated how difficult it is to "get the settings right." The informational demands are enormous – especially for agencies that have little experience with the challenges of liberalization in a globalizing economy, and which may be significantly understaffed.[15] Moreover, in countries where domestic economic activity is dominated by relatively few, powerful economic actors, liberalization may pose a particular challenge – taking the state out of the market may simply open the way for oligopolies to seize opportunities to dominate new market sectors (as was very much the concern in Korea).

Governments, moreover, have to overcome a variety of collective action problems – situations where what is rational for an individual actor, e.g. offshore borrowing by a financial institution in foreign currencies, may, when multiplied across numerous independent actors, be detrimental for the health of the economy as a whole. The Financial Stability Forum (2000: 14) reminds us succinctly of the difficulties governments face: "A country is not, of course, a single legal entity under one management, and it cannot control its balance sheet in the same way as a company."

A number of commentators have suggested that at least part of the failure of the Thai government to respond appropriately to the massive inflows of foreign capital in the 1990s can be attributed to a lack of full appreciation of the constraints on the independence of monetary policy imposed by capital account liberalization. Thailand's difficulties arose from what Benjamin Cohen (1993) has termed the "unholy Trinity" – the problem that governments cannot simultaneously pursue a fixed exchange rate, an open capital account, and an autonomous monetary policy.[16] From 1990 onwards, Thailand liberalized its capital account, in part because the government hoped to establish Bangkok as a regional financial center. To attempt to maintain export competitiveness in its largest market, the Thai government adopted an exchange rate regime that effectively pegged the baht to the US dollar. Nonetheless, it persisted in attempting to use a conventional monetary policy approach, namely, increasing interest rates, to dampen the effects of capital inflows. But with an open capital account, an increase in interest rates can have a perverse effect: rather than dampening activity, they can lead to an increase in capital inflows – precisely what appeared to happen in Thailand in the early 1990s.[17] Moreover, by widening the differential between domestic and international interest rates, a policy of monetary tightening further encouraged offshore borrowing by domestic financial institutions.

With the effectiveness of monetary policy constrained by the open capital account and by a pegged exchange rate, more of a burden falls on fiscal policy in attempting to contain the adverse effect of a boom sustained by large capital inflows. Despite their good record in maintaining fiscal balances or surpluses, it seems that East Asian governments generally, and Thailand in particular, did not appreciate that an even tighter fiscal policy would be necessary to cope with a boom in the context of monetary policy ineffectiveness (Corbett and Vines 1999: 75). Fiscal policy in the years running up to the crisis was widely regarded as being pro-cyclical, that is, expansionary, in a period when the economy was already over-heating (Alba *et al.* 1999: 33).

One way of escaping from the shackles of the "unholy Trinity" would have been to allow exchange rates to float. A policy of maintaining a "soft peg," which in effect was followed by all of the crisis economies, rendered them particularly vulnerable to speculative attack. Moreover, an apparently implicit government guarantee of exchange rate stability was a significant source of "moral hazard," encouraging financial institutions to engage in unhedged offshore borrowing.[18] Yet this exchange rate regime offered advantages to governments: it reduced uncertainty for international traders, an important consideration for economies so heavily dependent on exports. And, while one can argue that governments were foolish in putting all their eggs in one basket by pegging their currencies to the US dollar, they may be considered to have been unlucky when the dollar appreciated against the yen in the years immediately preceding the crisis.

More fundamentally, however, the decision to continue with a soft peg arguably reflected both excessive caution – an unwillingness to move beyond the familiar to the uncertainties of a more flexible exchange rate regime – and a failure to absorb the lessons of crises in Europe (the Exchange Rate Mechanism crisis of 1992–93) and Mexico (the peso crisis of 1994). Both of these crises illustrated how costly it could be, in a context of ever larger volumes of mobile capital controlled by private sector actors, to attempt to defend an exchange rate peg in the face of determined speculative attack.

Regulatory capture

If some of the problems in the process of partial liberalization of the financial regimes in the crisis economies can be attributed to sins of omission – reflecting lack of full understanding of the new context of globalized financial markets, problems of incomplete information or, in some instances, unfortunate timing or sheer bad luck – others reflected sins of commission, a consequence of regulatory capture.

A classic case in point is the creation in Thailand in 1993 of the Bangkok International Banking Facilities (BIBF), termed by the *Bangkok Post* "a pompous name for a good idea that went wildly wrong."[19] These arrangements were intended to establish Thailand as a major regional financial center, with the hope that it would be able to capture some of Hong Kong's banking business after the island was returned to the mainland in 1997. The BIBF was originally intended to engage solely in offshore transactions whereby banks borrowed overseas funds and lent them overseas with the funds not entering the local economy, so-called "out–out" trade. Foreign banks were attracted to the Facilities with a promise that they would subsequently be permitted to enter the local banking market. Domestic banks were also offered BIBF status. In the process of negotiating the working rules of the Facilities, however, the government caved in to demands that it permit the BIBF to be used to source offshore funds for onward lending into the domestic economy – a decision that facilitated the emergence of currency mismatches. Immediately before the crisis, estimates were that fully two-thirds of BIBF financing was devoted to the "out–in" trade, that is, to offshore funds being lent to the domestic economy (Delhaise 1998: 84).

In the 1990s the region's central banks struggled against a tide of increasing political interference. In Thailand, a commission of enquiry set up to investigate the causes of the crisis found that the Bank of Thailand had become increasingly politicized, with the consequence that it was less and less willing to make the interventions necessary for it to fulfill its supervisory role (Haggard 2000: 35). The Bank of Thailand's ineffective response to the problems at the Bangkok Bank of Commerce (BBC), which did much to tarnish the central bank's reputation and ultimately led to the resignation of its governor, reflected political interference by politicians from the ruling party who had been beneficiaries of BBC loans (Haggard and MacIntyre 2000: 63).

Similarly, in Indonesia, Cole and Slade (1998: 65) note that although central bank examiners were "very capable," they were unable to play an appropriate supervisory role when banks were politically connected. Banks enjoying a "Soeharto Connection" were effectively untouchable. Liberalization of the financial sector, through widespread reforms in 1988, led to a proliferation of banks and of non-bank financial institutions, many of which had powerful political connections. In the words of Natasha Hamilton-Hart (2000: 110), "rapid growth in the deregu-lated private banking sector sustained rather than eroded a patronage-based political economy." And political interference in the financial system was, of course, a major factor in the early ineffectiveness of the IMF program in Indonesia.

In Korea, a flawed process of liberalization reflected the difficulties of financial sector liberalization in a system where existing financial institutions were very weak because of the burden of large quantities of non-performing loans, where responsibility for bank supervision was divided between rival agencies, and where political interference by powerful corporate actors keen to gain a foothold in the financial sector was rife. The weakness of domestic financial institutions on the eve of liberalization, a legacy of decades of directed lending to projects favored by the state, caused supervisory authorities to dilute, ignore or circumvent the new prudential rules that had been established.[20] As Cho (2002: 5) records:

> the introduction of global standards overnight in an economy where the accounting and supervisory practices were very backward, pushed the long accumulated (but veiled) non-performing assets to the surface at a pace which the political economy of the country could not readily accommodate. A consequence was granting forbearance, benignly neglecting the applica-tion of the already introduced rules, or relying on the old intervention syn-drome to roll over credit to troubled firms to disguise bad loans. All these measures undermined the credibility of the reform program and made the future restructuring more difficult.

Moreover, banks were able to take advantage of disparities between deregulation of various types of accounts and their assignment to different agencies for pru-dential supervision. The Office of Banking Supervision, part of the Bank of Korea, was responsible for supervising regular accounts in banks, whereas the Ministry of Finance and Economy (MoFE) had oversight of banks' trust accounts and most non-bank financial institutions. Cho (2002: 43) notes that the two agen-cies failed to share information and to coordinate their supervisory activities. The MoFE had fewer than ten officers to supervise the non-bank financial institutions (Ji 1998: 3), and failed to establish even a minimal regulatory framework such as capital adequacy ratios for these institutions (Shin and Hahm 1998: 28).

In Korea, the government had long sought to limit chaebol dominance of the financial system by barring them from bank ownership. From the 1980s, however, the chaebol had circumvented these controls through their ownership of most of the non-bank financial institutions (NBFIs). These institutions were not as closely regulated as the banks on matters such as interest rates and asset management, one reason why they expanded much more quickly than conventional banks in the 1980s. With the adoption of a deregulation drive by the Kim Young-Sam administration as part of its commitment to globalization when it took office in February 1993, the way was open for pressure – both foreign and domestic – to remove entry barriers to the financial sector. The chaebol seized the opportunity to increase their dominance of non-bank financial institutions. As Cho (2002: 54) notes, their cementing of control over the NBFIs "strengthened the internal capital market of the chaebols, and further weakened the role of financial institutions in corporate governance." The NBFIs, meanwhile, lobbied to extend their reach. A particularly attractive route was through obtaining a merchant banking licence – 24 of which were issued between 1994 and 1996. Haggard (2000: 37) records how the licensing process was riddled with corruption. The merchant banks were amongst the earliest casualties of the financial crisis.

In a situation of financial distress, Korean banks, confident in their belief that the government had at least implicitly extended a guarantee to them, had every incentive to "gamble for redemption" – in this instance through high-risk international investment. Korean financial institutions purchased 40 percent of the first Eurobond issue by the Russian Federation, an entire Deutschmark issue by the Colombian government, and more that 20 percent of total bonds issues by Mexico and Brazil. They also began to speculate heavily in derivatives, including substantial volumes of domestic Indonesian debt. Most of these instruments proved to be illiquid once the financial panic began in Southeast Asia (International Monetary Fund 1998: 55).

Korea's attempt to move from administrative *fiat* to market mechanisms as a means of managing the financial regime proved fatally flawed. In a newly democratic context, bolstered by international pressure to liberalize the economy, the chaebol were able to capture the deregulation process. As Cho (2002: 53) concludes: "*Chaebols*, through their influence over the public media and strong political lobbying, frustrated all government attempts to introduce new rules that ran against their interests."

The problems in Korea's financial system and its highly indebted corporate sector fed off one another. Many of Korea's financial institutions were in difficulties even before a number of the larger chaebol went bankrupt in early 1997. In Woo-Cumings's (2001: 363) words: the crisis of 1997–98 "was a disaster waiting to happen."

Conclusion

Ten years after the crisis, it is evident that the abrupt reversal of opinion that occurred in some quarters regarding East Asia's rapid economic growth was unwarranted. With the partial exception of Indonesia, East Asian economies quickly ascended the reverse leg of a marked "V-shaped" curve. Economies have returned to rates of economic growth that are rapid in comparison with those of most developing economies, albeit lower rates than those prevailing in the pre-crisis period. The financial crisis appears as a relatively small, albeit painful, detour in an otherwise phenomenally successful record.

It was not really a single crisis but a combination of crises that undid East Asia in 1997–98. In the financial sector, the region suffered mutually reinforcing currency and liquidity crises; these in turn exacerbated insolvency problems in the real sector and were further reinforced by them. Dependence on short-term unhedged loans to finance the excessive investment that occurred in the region in the first half of the 1990s rendered economies vulnerable to a withdrawal of funds. The massive reversal of international lending that precipitated the crisis was a rational response by investors who were driven by not unreasonable fears that they would be unable to recoup their assets.

Economics provides part of the explanation for why the crisis countries were so vulnerable: they were victims of the "unholy Trinity," with governments failing to fully comprehend (or at least failing to act effectively in response to) the implications for domestic policy instruments of attempting to pursue "soft pegging" while opening the capital account. By appearing to provide a guarantee both of the exchange rate and of financial institutions, governments encouraged the reckless behavior in the financial sector that rendered economies vulnerable to attack.

A more complete understanding of vulnerability – an explanation of why governments pursued policies that seemed to guarantee perverse outcomes requires the use of political economy approaches. The flawed process of financial sector liberalization can be explained in part by the difficulties that governments faced in responding to dramatically new challenges in a rapidly changing international financial environment. Arguably far more important, however, was the capture of the process of financial liberalization by particularistic interests. In all five countries, deregulation proved a new fertile ground for rent-seeking interests. Addressing the political economy sources of the 1997–98 crisis would prove to be just as challenging as attempting to rectify the economic factors underlying the dramatic interruption of growth.

Notes

1 The principal reference is Krugman (1979), where a major determinant of a crisis is a change in the domestic money supply resulting from budgetary deficits.
2 I also will not look at recovery from the crisis or address the debate of whether or not an end to East Asia's rapid growth was inevitable because there was, in reality, no "miracle" (Young 1993; Krugman 1994). I do, however, find persuasive arguments about the limitations of growth accounting estimates of total factor productivity pointed out, for instance, by Ito (2001) and Stiglitz (2001).
3 Warr (1998: 53) estimates that by the onset of the crisis the baht had appreciated in real terms by close to 40 percent over the previous decade.
4 Most notably for semiconductors. For the Korean experience see Noble and Ravenhill (2000).
5 An IMF staff study noted that:

> While on the whole the Fund and the authorities were aware of the magnitude of these inflows, and some concern was expressed, this concern was tempered by the perception that the inflows were attributable mainly to favorable investment

prospects associated with a stable macroeconomic environment and high growth. In hindsight, however, it appears that the inflows were to a considerable extent financing asset price inflation and an accumulation of poor-quality loans in the portfolios of banks and other financial intermediaries.

(Lane *et al.* 1999: 10)

6 During 1996, stock prices fell by more than 20 percent in Korea and by almost one-third in Thailand. Property prices in Thailand also declined before the crisis began (Lane *et al.* 1999: 15).
7 On private sector warnings about the health of financial institutions in the crisis countries see Delhaise (1998) and Hale (2007).
8 On the eve of the crisis, 45 percent of Korea's and 50 percent of Thailand's domestic bank lending to the private sector was funded by borrowing from international banks (Goldstein and Turner 2004: Table 2.2, p. 13).
9 The Financial Stability Forum (2000: 10) estimated that the share of short-term debt to banks in the total external debt of East Asian and Pacific countries rose from 20 percent to 30 percent from the end of 1990 to the end of 1996.
10 Some observers, e.g. Wade (1998), suggest that problems in the Japanese financial system contributed to decisions by Japanese banks not to renew short-term lending to the region in the second half of 1997.
11 On the Korean situation see Cho (2002); on the dubious accounting practices of banks in the region see Delhaise (1998).
12 See, for instance, Mackie (1988) and Jomo (2001).
13 In Korea, bonds and equities each accounted for less than 15 percent of corporate sector finance in the first half of the 1990s (Cho 2002: Table 16, p. 41).
14 For the Korean case, see Cho (2002: 2).
15 On the difficulties that governments face in collecting data to provide effective monitoring of the financial system see Financial Stability Forum (2000).
16 Otherwise known as the Mundell–Fleming model. See Mundell (1963) and Fleming (1962).
17 For further discussion of Thailand see Warr (1998).
18 On implicit government guarantees of exchange rate stability generating a "moral hazard" see Dooley (1999); McKinnon and Pill (1997); and Krugman (1998).
19 Quoted in International Monetary Fund (2002).
20 Korean banks' return on assets averaged 0.56 percent from 1990 to 1993; by 1996 the ratio had slumped to 0.26 percent (OECD 1999: Table 14). The World Bank (1998: Figure 3.3, p. 37) estimated that Korean banks in the first half of the 1990s had the highest percentage of non-performing loans, highest cost:income ratios and lowest returns on equity and on assets of the various Asian banking systems it surveyed.

References

Alba, P., Bhattacharya, A., Claessens, S., Ghosh, S., and Hernandez, L. (1999) "The Role of Macroeconomic and Financial Sector Linkages in East Asia's Financial Crisis," in P.-R. Agénor, M. Miller, D. Vines, and A. Weber (eds.) *The Asian Financial Crisis: Causes, Contagion and Consequences*, Cambridge: Cambridge University Press.

Cho, Y.J. (2002) "Financial Repression, Liberalization, Crisis and Restructuring: Lessons of Korea's Financial Sector Policies," Research Paper 47, Asian Development Bank Institute, Tokyo.

Cohen, B. (1993) "Triad and the Unholy Trinity: Problems of International Monetary Cooperation," in R. Higgott, R. Leaver, and J. Ravenhill (eds.) *Pacific Economic Relations in the 1990s: Cooperation or Conflict?* Boulder: Lynne Rienner.

Cole, D.C. and Slade, B.F. (1998) "Why Has Indonesia's Financial Crisis Been So Bad?" *Bulletin of Indonesian Economic Studies* 34, no. 2: 61–6.

Corbett, J. and Vines, D. (1999) "The Asian Crisis: Lessons from the Collapse of Financial Systems, Exchange Rates and Macroeconomic Policy," in P.-R. Agénor, M. Miller, D. Vines, and A. Weber (eds.) *The Asian Financial Crisis: Causes, Contagion and Consequences*, Cambridge: Cambridge University Press.

Delhaise, P.F. (1998) *Asia in Crisis: The Implosion of the Banking and Finance Systems*, Singapore: John Wiley & Sons.

Dooley, M.F. (1999) "Are Capital Inflows to Developing Countries a Vote for or against Economic Policy Reforms?" in P.-R. Agénor, M. Miller, D. Vines, and A. Weber (eds.) *The Asian Financial Crisis: Causes, Contagion and Consequences*, Cambridge: Cambridge University Press.

Financial Stability Forum (2000) "Report of the Working Group on Capital Flows," Financial Stability Forum, Singapore.

Fleming, J.M. (1962) "Domestic Financial Policies under Fixed and Floating Exchange Rates," *IMF Staff Papers* 9: 369–79.

Goldstein, M. (1998) *The Asian Financial Crisis: Causes, Cures, and Systemic Implications*, Washington, DC: Institute for International Economics.

Goldstein, M. and Turner, P. (2004) *Controlling Currency Mismatches in Emerging Economies*, Washington, DC: Institute for International Economics.

Grenville, S. (2000) "Capital Flows and Crises," in G. Noble and J. Ravenhill (eds.) *The Asian Financial Crises and the Global Financial Architecture*, Cambridge: Cambridge University Press.

Haggard, S. (2000) *The Political Economy of the Asian Financial Crisis*, Washington, DC: Institute for International Economics.

Haggard, S. and MacIntyre, A. (2000) "The Political Economy of the Asian Financial Crisis: Korea and Thailand Compared," in G. Noble and J. Ravenhill (eds.) *The Asian Financial Crises and the Global Financial Architecture*, Cambridge: Cambridge University Press.

Hale, D. (2007) "The East Asian Financial Crisis," in *A Decade Later: Asia's New Responsibilities in the International Monetary System*, Seoul: Reinventing Bretton Woods Committee.

Hamilton-Hart, N. (2000) "Indonesia: Reforming the Institutions of Financial Governance?" in G. Noble and J. Ravenhill (eds.) *The Asian Financial Crises and the Global Financial Architecture*, Cambridge: Cambridge University Press.

International Monetary Fund (1998) *International Capital Markets: Developments, Prospects, and Key Policy Issues*, Washington, DC: International Monetary Fund.

—— (2002) *The IMF's Role in Asia: Part of the Problem or Part of the Solution?* Remarks by Thomas C. Dawson, Director, External Relations Department, International Monetary Fund. Prepared Text for Remarks at the Institute of Policy Studies and Singapore Management University Forum, Singapore, July 10, 2002, IMF [cited June 14, 2007]. Online, available at: www.imf.org/external/np/speeches/2002/071002.htm.

Ito, T. (2001) "Growth, Crisis, and the Future of Economic Recovery in East Asia," in J.E. Stiglitz and S. Yusuf (eds.) *Rethinking the East Asia Miracle*, New York: Oxford University Press.

Ji, D. (1998) "Prudential Supervision of Korean Financial Institutions," Paper for a conference on Financial Reform and Macroeconomic Policy and Management in Korea Australian National University, Canberra.

Jomo, K.S. (2001) "Growth after the Asian Crisis: What Remains of the East Asian

Model?" G-24 Discussion Paper series 10, United Nations Conference on Trade and Development, New York and Geneva.

Krugman, P. (1979) "A Model of Balance-of-Payments Crises," *Journal of Money, Credit and Banking* 11, no. 3: 311–25.

—— (1994) "The Myth of Asia's Miracle," *Foreign Affairs* 73, no. 6: 62–78.

—— (1998) *What Happened to Asia?* MIT. Online, available at: http://web.mit.edu/krugman/www/DISINTER.html.

Lane, T., Ghosh, A.R., Hamann, J., Phillips, S., Schulze-Ghattas, M., and Tsikata, T. (1999) "IMF-Supported Programs in Indonesia, Korea, and Thailand: A Preliminary Assessment," Occasional Paper 178, International Monetary Fund, Washington, DC.

Mackie, J.A.C. (1988) "Economic Growth in the ASEAN Region: The Political Underpinnings," in H. Hughes (ed.) *Achieving Industrialization in East Asia*, Cambridge: Cambridge University Press.

McKinnon, R.I. and Pill, H. (1997) "Credible Economic Liberalizations and Overborrowing," *American Economic Review* 87, no. 2: 189–93.

Mundell, R.A. (1963) "Capital Mobility and Stabilization Policy under Fixed and Flexible Exchange Rates," *Canadian Journal of Economics and Political Science* 29: 475–85.

Noble, G. and Ravenhill, J. (2000) "The Good, the Bad and the Ugly? Korea, Taiwan and the Asian Financial Crisis," in G. Noble and J. Ravenhill (eds.) *The Asian Financial Crises and the Global Financial Architecture*, Cambridge: Cambridge University Press.

OECD (1999) *OECD Economic Surveys: Korea*, Paris: OECD.

Radelet, S. and Sachs, J. (1998) "The Onset of the East Asian Financial Crisis," mimeo, Harvard Institute for International Development, Cambridge, MA.

Shin, I. and Hahm, J.-H. (1998) "The Korean Crisis – Causes and Resolution," paper for the East-West Center/KDI Conference on the Korean Crisis East-West Center, Hawaii.

Stiglitz, J.E. (2001) "From Miracle to Crisis to Recovery: Lessons from Four Decades of East Asian Experience," in J.E. Stiglitz and S. Yusuf (eds.) *Rethinking the East Asia Miracle*, New York: Oxford University Press.

Urata, S. (2001) "Emergence of an FDI-Trade Nexus and Economic Growth in East Asia," in J.E. Stiglitz and S. Yusuf (eds.) *Rethinking the East Asia Miracle*, New York: Oxford University Press.

Wade, R. (1998) "The Asian Debt-and-Development Crisis of 1997–?: Causes and Consequences," *World Development* 26, no. 8: 1535–53.

Wade, R. and Veneroso, F. (1998) "The Asian Crisis: The High Debt Model Versus the Wall Street-Treasury-IMF Complex," *New Left Review*, no. 228: 3–23.

Warr, Peter G. (1998) "Thailand," in R.H. McLeod and R. Garnaut (eds.) *East Asia in Crisis: From Being a Miracle to Needing One?*, London: Routledge.

Woo-Cumings, M. (2001) "Miracle as Prologue: The State and the Reform of the Corporate Sector in Korea," in J.E. Stiglitz and S. Yusuf (eds.) *Rethinking the East Asia Miracle*, New York: Oxford University Press.

World Bank (1993) *The East Asian Miracle: Economic Growth and Public Policy*, New York: Oxford University Press.

—— (1998) *East Asia: The Road to Recovery*, Washington, DC: The World Bank.

Young, A. (1993) "Lessons from the East Asian NICs: A Contrarian View," Working Paper 4482, National Bureau of Economic Research, Cambridge, MA.

3   Causes of the 1997–1998 East Asian crises and obstacles to implementing lessons

Jomo Kwame Sundaram

The East Asian crises of 1997–1998 gave rise to two major responses from mainstream or orthodox economists. The first was an attempt to explain the unexpected events from mid-1997 in terms of several aspects of the orthodoxy, especially theories of currency crisis. Proponents of this explanation made much of current account or fiscal deficits, real as well as imagined. When this line of reasoning clearly proved to be wrong, inadequate, or unpersuasive, the second line of defence was to turn the preceding celebration of the East Asian miracle on its head by suggesting that key elements of East Asian exceptionalism, for example, government intervention and social capital, were responsible for the crises. Those promoting this explanation emphasized cronyism (government favouritism for particular business interests) and poor corporate governance – both genuine problems, but irrelevant in this context – with some grudging acknowledgement of the poor or wrong sequencing of financial liberalization, rather than the implications of liberalization itself with its open capital accounts.

Two consequences of this failure to deal with the full implications of the East Asian debacle require revisiting the crises to try to ensure that their most important lessons are not lost. Subsequent currency and financial crises elsewhere suggest that many important lessons have not been appreciated or translated into appropriate policy. First, erroneous lessons drawn by orthodox economists, financial analysts, and the media have obscured the important policy-relevant analysis that has emerged. Second, the policies and policymakers responsible for creating the conditions that culminated in the crises need to be identified. Perhaps more importantly, the wrong lessons have diverted attention away from the intellectual and ideological bases of the erroneous thinking, analyses, and policies responsible for the crises. Suggesting that such ideas are associated with the so-called Washington consensus' advocacy of economic liberalization at both the national and global levels would not be an exaggeration. Needless to say, drawing the right lessons would likely undermine the intellectual, analytical, and policy authority of the interests and institutions upholding this consensus.

This chapter considers various views of the origins of the crisis and its development and spread throughout the region (referred to as contagion). This is then set against the larger drama of the transformation of the East Asian miracle into a debacle. All this is placed in the larger context of policy advocacy for financial liberalization, especially since the late 1980s. It focuses on the consequences of financial liberalization in the region. It also argues that the crises were of a new type and were somewhat different from earlier currency and financial crises. In particular, it emphasizes the implications of easily reversible capital flows. While much of the literature emphasizes the problems associated with foreign bank borrowing, this chapter also draws attention to the dangers of portfolio capital flows. It looks at the role of the International Monetary Fund (IMF) in exacerbating the crises. The chapter then suggests six urgent areas for international financial system reform from a development perspective that go beyond crisis avoidance and management. It concludes with a consideration of why there has not been more progress in making needed reforms since the Asian crises.

Even though considerable work was critical of East Asia's record and potential, none actually anticipated the East Asian debacle of 1997–1998 (Krugman 1994). While certain aspects of the crises were common to all four of the most adversely affected East Asian economies – Indonesia, the Republic of Korea, Malaysia, and Thailand – others were unique to a particular country or common only to the more open economies of Southeast Asia, namely, Indonesia, Malaysia, and Thailand. Of course, some of the weaknesses identified in the literature did imply that the region was economically vulnerable. The dominance of manufacturing activities, especially the most technologically sophisticated and dynamic ones, by foreign transnationals subordinated domestic industrial capital in the region, allowing finance capital, both domestic and foreign, to become more influential (Jomo 1998, 2004).

None of the critical writing seriously addressed the crucial implications of the greater role and fluidity of foreign capital in Southeast Asia, particularly with regard to international financial liberalization, which had become more pronounced in the 1990s. Indeed, financial capital developed a complex symbiotic relationship with politically influential rentiers, dubbed cronies in the aftermath of 1997–1998. Although threatened by the full implications of international financial liberalization, Southeast Asian financial interests were quick to identify and secure new possibilities for capturing rents from arbitrage, as well as other opportunities offered by gradual international financial integration. In these and other ways (Gomez and Jomo 1999; Khan and Jomo 2000), transnational dominance of Southeast Asian industrialization facilitated the ascendance and consolidation of financial interests and politically influential rentiers. This increasingly powerful alliance was primarily responsible for promoting financial liberalization in the region, both externally and internally.

However, insofar as the interests of domestic financial capital did not entirely coincide with those of international finance capital, the processes of international financial liberalization were partial and uneven. The varying policy influence of domestic financial interests in different parts of the region also played a part. History too was relevant. For example, the banking crisis in Malaysia in the late 1980s led to the introduction of a prudential regulatory framework unlike those anywhere else in the region, yet caution was thrown to the wind as early external liberalization measures succeeded in securing capital inflows. Both Malaysia and

Thailand wanted such flows to finance current account deficits caused primarily by service account deficits (mainly for imported financial services and investment income payments abroad) and growing imports for consumption; speculative activity in regional stock markets; and output of non-tradables, mainly in the real estate sector.

There is little evidence that such capital inflows contributed significantly to accelerating the pace of economic growth, especially of the tradable sectors. Instead, they probably contributed greatly to the asset price bubbles, whose inevitable deflation was accelerated by the advent of the crises, with their devastating economic, social, and political consequences. After months of international speculative attacks on the Thai baht, the Bank of Thailand let its currency float from 2 July 1997, allowing it to drop suddenly. By mid-July 1997, the currencies of Indonesia, Malaysia, and the Philippines had also fallen precipitously after being floated, with their stock market price indexes following suit. In the following months, currencies and stock markets throughout the region came under pressure as easily reversible short-term capital inflows took flight in herd-like fashion. In November 1997, despite Korea's somewhat different economic structure, the won too had collapsed following the withdrawal of official support. Most other economies in East Asia were also under considerable pressure, either directly (for example, the attack on the Hong Kong dollar) or indirectly (for instance, due to the desire to maintain a competitive cost advantage against the devalued currencies of Southeast Asian exporters).

Contrary to the impression conveyed mainly by the business media, as well as by the IMF, consensus on how to understand and characterize the crises is still lacking. One manifestation of this has been the debates between the IMF and its various critics about the appropriateness of its negotiated programmes in Indonesia, Korea, and Thailand. While policy debates have understandably captured the most attention, especially among the public at large, the East Asian crises have also challenged previously accepted international economic theories. However, contrary to the popular impression promoted by the Western-dominated financial media of crony capitalism as the main culprit, most serious analysts now agree that the crises essentially began as currency crises of a new type, different from those previously identified with either fiscal profligacy or macroeconomic indiscipline. A growing number of observers also seem to agree that the crises started off as currency crises and quickly became more generalized financial crises, before affecting the real economy. Reduced liquidity in the financial system, the consequences of inappropriate official policy and ill-informed, herd-like market responses contributed to this chain of events.

From miracle to debacle

Rapid economic growth and structural change, mainly associated with export-led industrialization in the region, can generally be traced back to the mid-1980s. Then devaluation of the currencies of Indonesia, Malaysia, and Thailand, as well as selective deregulation of onerous rules, helped to create attractive conditions for the relocation of production facilities in these countries and elsewhere in Southeast Asia and in China. This was especially attractive for Japan and the first-tier or first-generation newly industrializing economies, that is, Hong Kong (China), Korea, Singapore, and Taiwan (China), most of which experienced currency appreciation, tight labour markets, and higher production costs.

This sustained export-oriented industrialization well into the 1990s and was accompanied by the growth of other manufacturing, services, and construction activities. High growth was sustained for about a decade, during much of which fiscal surpluses were maintained, monetary expansion was not excessive, and inflation was generally under control. Table 3.1 shows various summary macroeconomic indicators for the 1990s, paying greater attention to the period since 1996. Prior to 1997, savings and investment rates were high and rising in all three Southeast Asian economies. Foreign savings supplemented high domestic savings in all four East Asian crisis economies, especially in Malaysia and Thailand. Unemployment was low, while fiscal balances generally remained positive until 1997–1998. This is not to suggest, however, that fundamentals in East Asia were not experiencing any problems (Rasiah 2001). As Table 3.1 shows, the incremental capital–output ratio rose in all three Southeast Asian economies during the 1990s before 1997, suggesting declining returns to new investments before the crises linked to asset price inflation, especially the property and share market booms.

Export-led growth had been followed by a construction and property boom, fuelled by financial systems favouring such "short-termist" investments – which involved loans with collateral, that is, the kind that bankers like – over more productive, but also seemingly more risky, investments in manufacturing and agriculture. The exaggerated expansion of investment in such non-tradables exacerbated the economies' current account deficits. Although widespread in East Asia, the property–finance nexus was particularly strong in Thailand, which made it especially vulnerable to the inevitable bursting of the bubble (Jomo 1998, 2004; Pasuk and Baker 2000). Financial liberalization from the 1980s had major ramifications in the region, as foreign savings supplemented the already high domestic savings rates to further accelerate the rate of capital accumulation, albeit in increasingly unproductive activities, because of the foreign domination of most internationally competitive industries. The rapid growth of the previous decade gave rise to several related macroeconomic concerns that had emerged by the mid-1990s.

First, the savings–investment gap had historically been financed by heavy reliance on foreign direct investment (FDI), as well as by public sector foreign borrowing, with the latter declining rapidly from the mid-1980s. Both FDI and foreign debt, in turn, caused investment income outflows abroad.[1] In the 1990s, the current account deficit was increasingly being financed by short-term capital inflows, as in 1993 and 1995–1996, with disastrous consequences later when such flows reversed.[2]

Many subsequent confidence restoration measures have sought to induce such short-term inflows once again, but they cannot be relied upon to address the underlying problem in the medium to long term. Although always in the minority,

Table 3.1 East Asian four: macroeconomic indicators, 1990–1999

| Country | Savings/GDP (%) | | | | |
	1990–1995	1996	1997	1998	1999
Indonesia	31.0	26.2	26.4	26.1	23.7
South Korea	35.6	33.7	33.3	33.8	33.5
Malaysia	36.6	37.1	37.3	39.6	38.0
Thailand	34.4	33.0	32.5	34.9	31.0
	(Savings–investment)/GDP (%)				
	1990–1995	1996	1997	1998	1999
Indonesia	−0.3	−3.4	−2.3	4.0	4.4
South Korea	−1.2	−3.1	−1.8	4.1	5.5
Malaysia	−0.9	−5.4	−5.8	12.8	15.7
Thailand	−5.6	−8.1	−0.9	12.8	10.0
	Investment/GDP (%)				
	1990–1995	1996	1997	1998	1999
Indonesia	31.3	29.6	28.7	22.1	19.3
South Korea	36.8	36.8	35.1	29.8	28.0
Malaysia	37.5	42.5	43.1	26.8	22.3
Thailand	41.0	41.1	33.3	22.2	21.0
	Incremental capital–output ratios				
	1987–1989	1990–1992	1993–1995	1997	1998
Indonesia	4.0	3.9	4.4	1.7	0.4
South Korea	3.5	5.1	5.1	4.2	−15.1
Malaysia	3.6	4.4	5.0	3.9	28.2
Thailand	2.9	4.6	5.2	12.9	−11.5
	Fiscal balance/GDP (%)				
	1990–1995	1996	1997	1998	1999
Indonesia	0.2	1.4	1.3	−2.6	−3.4
South Korea	0.2	0.5	−1.4	−4.2	−2.9
Malaysia	−0.4	0.7	2.4	−1.8	−3.2
Thailand	3.2	2.4	−0.9	−3.4	−3.0
	Unemployment rate (%)				
	1990	1996	1997	1998	1999
Indonesia	n/a	4.1	4.6	5.5	6.3
South Korea	2.4	3.0	2.6	6.8	6.3
Malaysia	6.0	2.5	2.4	3.2	3.0
Thailand	4.9	1.1	0.9	3.5	4.1

Sources: ADB (1999); Radelet and Sachs (1998: Table 11); Bank of Thailand, Bank Indonesia, Bank of Korea, and Bank Negara Malaysia data.

foreign portfolio investments increasingly influenced stock markets in the region in the 1990s. With incomplete information exacerbated by limited transparency, the presence of foreign portfolio investment, the biased nature of fund managers' incentives and remuneration, and the short-termism of fund managers' investment horizons, foreign financial institutions were much more prone to herd behaviour than they might otherwise have been, and thus contributed decisively to regional contagion. Second, private sector debt exploded in the 1990s, especially from abroad, not least because of the efforts of debt-pushers keen to secure higher returns from the fast-growing region.[3] Commercial banks' foreign liabilities also increased quickly, as the ratio of loans to gross national product rose rapidly during the period.

Overinvestment of investible funds, especially from abroad, in non-tradables only made things worse, especially in relation to the current account. Only a small proportion of commercial banks and other lending agencies were involved with manufacturing and other productive activities. This share is likely to have been even smaller with foreign borrowing, most of which was collateralized with such assets as real estate and stock.[4] Thus, much of the inflow of foreign savings actually contributed to asset price inflation, mainly involving real estate and share prices. Insofar as such investments did not increase the production of tradables, they actually exacerbated the current account deficit rather than allevi-ated it as they were thought to be doing.

This, in turn, worsened the problem of currency mismatch, with borrowing in US dollars invested in activities that did not generate foreign exchange. As a high proportion of this foreign borrowing was short term in nature and deployed to finance medium- to long-term projects, a term mismatch problem also arose. According to the Bank for International Settlements (BIS) (*Asian Wall Street Journal*, 6 January 1998), well over half of the foreign borrowing by commer-cial banks was short-term in nature: 56 per cent in Malaysia, 59 per cent in Indonesia, 66 per cent in Thailand, and 68 per cent in Korea. More generally, the foreign exchange risks of investment generally rose, increasing the vulnerability of these economies to the maintenance of currency pegs to the US dollar.[5]

The pegs encouraged a great deal of un-hedged borrowing by an influential constituency with a strong stake in defending the pegs regardless of their adverse consequences for the economy. Because of the foreign domination of export-oriented industries in Southeast Asia, unlike in Northeast Asia, no politically influential industrial community that was oriented toward national exports was available to lobby for floating or depreciating the Southeast Asian currencies, despite the obvious adverse consequences of the pegs for inter-national cost competitiveness.

Instead, after pegging their currencies to the US dollar from the early 1990s, and especially from the mid-1990s, most Southeast Asian central banks resisted downward adjustments to their exchange rates, which would have reduced, if not averted, some of the more disruptive consequences of the 1997–1998 currency collapses.[6] Yet, economists now generally agree that the 1997–1998 East Asian crises saw tremendous "overshooting" in exchange rate adjustments well in excess of expected corrections. The economic literature before the crises tended to characterize the affected Southeast Asian economies in terms of the following key fundamentals: viability of domestic financial systems;[7] responsiveness of domestic output and exports to nominal devaluations;[8] sustainability of current account deficits;[9] prevalence of high savings rates and robust public finances.

Financial liberalization and the East Asian crises

Montes (1998) attributed the Southeast Asian currency crises to the "twin liberalizations" of domestic financial systems and opening of the capital account. Financial liberalization induced new behaviour in financial systems, notably:

- Domestic financial institutions had greater flexibility in offering interest rates to secure funds domestically and in bidding for foreign funds.
- Domestic financial institutions became less reliant on lending to the government.
- Regulations, such as credit allocation rules and ceilings, were reduced.
- Greater domestic competition meant that ascendance depended on expanding lending portfolios, often at the expense of prudence.

Kaminsky and Reinhart's (1996) study of 71 balance-of-payments crises and 25 banking crises during 1970–1995 finds that only three banking crises were associated with the 25 balance-of-payments crises during 1970–1979. However, during 1980–1995, 22 banking crises coincided with 46 balance-of-payments crises, which the authors attribute to the financial liberalization of the 1980s, with a private lending boom culminating in a banking crisis and then a currency crisis. In their review of 57 countries during 1970–1996, Carleton *et al.* (2000) find that inflationary macroeconomic policies and small foreign reserves stocks reliably predicted currency collapses. They argue that financial contagion is a better explanation than weak domestic fundamentals, as the probability of Indonesia, Malaysia, Korea, and Thailand experiencing currency collapse in 1997 was about 20 per cent, but all four currencies (and economies) collapsed – rather than just one, as expected.

One of the most cited crisis explanations (Montes 1998) suggests that they stemmed from the banking sector because of imprudent expansion and diversification of domestic financial markets, fuelled by short-term private borrowing. While this may have been true of Thailand, it was certainly less true for Indonesia, Malaysia, the Philippines, and Korea (in order of decreasing relevance). Instead, the significance of contagion cannot be exaggerated, as "the differences raise questions about how sensitive the currency knockdowns (and the associated divestment from these economies) are to economic fundamentals" (Montes 1998: 3).

Even though East Asia's financial systems were quite varied and were hardly clones of the Japanese main bank system (as often incorrectly alleged), they had nevertheless become prone to similar asset price bubbles, albeit for somewhat different reasons. Arguably, the more bank-based systems of Indonesia, Korea, and Thailand had a stronger nexus of this kind compared with, say, Malaysia's much more market-oriented financial system. Rapid growth, based on export-oriented industrialization from the late 1980s, gave rise to accelerated financial expansion, which contributed to asset price bubbles, including property booms, both in more market-oriented or Anglo-American Malaysia, as well as in the other more bank-oriented economies badly hit by the crises.[10]

Little was achieved by insisting that the crises should not have happened because East Asia's economic fundamentals were fine, even if that were true. In some instances, such official denials exacerbated the problem, because the authorities did not seem to be responding to ostensible problems in ways deemed appropriate by market opinion-makers. Unfortunately, as East Asia has painfully learnt, financial markets are driven by sentiments as much as by funda-mentals. Hence, even though much more serious current account deficits in 1995, for instance, did not result in crises, this does not mean that an economy can maintain such deficits indefinitely without being vulnerable to speculative attack or loss of confidence. Governments cannot, for example, liberalize the capital account and then complain when short-term portfolio investors suddenly withdraw following their whims and fancies. Capital controls can make rapidly withdrawing capital from an economy difficult, costly, or both. Many govern-ments treat FDI quite differently from portfolio investments.

Some authorities try to distinguish between speculative investments by hedge funds that are clearly short-termist from, say, pension funds with more medium-term orientations. In the early and mid-1990s, some Southeast Asian economies had become excessively reliant on short-term capital inflows to finance their current account deficits. This problem was exacerbated by excessive imports to manufacture more items that could not be exported, such as buildings, infra-structure, and heavily protected import substitutes. Ostensibly prudent financial institutions often preferred to lend for real property and stock purchases, and thereby secure assets with rising values as collateral, rather than to provide credit for more productive uses. While foreign banks were more than happy to lend US dollars at higher interest rates than were available in their home economies, East Asian businesses were keen to borrow at lower interest rates than were available domestically.

The sustained dollar pegs of the Southeast Asian currencies may have induced some moral hazard by discouraging borrowers from hedging their loans, but little systematic evidence of the extent of this problem is available. In any case, the existence of well-developed swap markets allowed Southeast Asian companies to tap into foreign capital markets, at low cost, by swapping away the currency risk. Hence, many such loans remained un-hedged as Southeast Asian currencies had been pegged to the US dollar since the 1970s, despite the official fictions of exchange rates moving with the baskets of the currencies of coun-tries' major foreign trading partners. The growth in foreign banking in the region in the 1990s led to lending competition reminiscent of the loans to devel-oping country governments in the late 1970s (which led to the debt crises of the 1980s). However, the new belief in international policymaking circles before the crises was that such accumulation of private sector debt did not matter as long as public sector debt was reined in.

Meanwhile, portfolio investors moved into newly emerging stock markets in East Asia with encouragement from the International Finance Corporation, an arm of the World Bank. In Malaysia, for example, net inflows soared in 1992–3, only to withdraw even more suddenly from late 1993, leaving most retail stockholders in the lurch. The government introduced some capital control measures, only to abrogate them later in 1994. Unfortunately, policymakers did not learn the lessons from that experience, as the new, unsustainable stock market build-up from 1995 sent stock prices soaring once again despite declining price–earnings ratios.

Clearly, investor panic was the principal cause of the Asian financial crises (McKibbin 1998; Montes 1998). The tightening of macroeconomic policies in response to the panic served to exacerbate, rather than to check, the crises. Economic disasters are not necessarily punishment for economic sins, and while cronyism is wrong, it was not the cause of the East Asian crises, and as the crises demonstrated, even sound macroeconomic fundamentals cannot guarantee immunity from contagion and crisis. With the currency collapses, the assets acquired by portfolio and other investors in the region depreciated correspondingly in value from their perspectives, precipitating an even greater sell-off and panic, causing herd behaviour and contagion to spread across national borders to the rest of the region. Meanwhile, liberalizing the capital account essentially guaranteed residents and non-residents ease of exit and placed fewer limitations on nationals holding foreign assets, thereby inadvertently facilitating capital flight. Thus, financial liberalization allowed lucrative opportunities for taking advantage of falling currencies, accelerating and exacerbating the volatility of regional currency and share markets. All this, together with injudicious official responses, transformed the inevitable correction of overvalued currencies in the region into a collapse of the currencies and the stock markets aggravated by herd behaviour and contagion.

Crises of a new type

Many economists were obliged to reconsider their earlier assessments of the causes of the Asian crises, most notably Krugman. In the immediate aftermath of its outbreak, some saw the crises as vindication of Krugman's earlier popularization of a critique of the East Asian miracle as primarily due to massive factor inputs subject to diminishing returns (Krugman 1994). In March 1998, Krugman dissented from the view – associated with Radelet and Sachs (1998) – of the East Asian crises as being due to a "good old-fashioned financial panic … a panic need not be a punishment for your sins … an economy can be 'fundamentally sound' … and yet be subjected to a devastating run started by nothing more than a self-fulfilling rumor." Instead, Krugman (1998c) argued that:

> The preconditions for that panic were created by bad policies in the years running up to the crisis. The crisis, in short, was a punishment for Asian

crimes, even if the punishment was disproportionate to the crime ... The specific spirit that pushed Asia to the brink was the problem of moral hazard in lending, mainly domestic lending.

Krugman associated the crises with crony capitalism. Attributing the crises to cronyism turned on its head one of the main arguments about how intimate business–government relations in East Asian economies had helped to create the conditions for the regional miracle. However, by October 1998, Krugman (1998a) had completely changed his view:

> When the Asian crisis struck ... countries were told to raise interest rates, not cut them, in order to persuade some foreign investors to keep their money in place and thereby limit the exchange-rate plunge ... In effect, countries were told to forget about macroeconomic policy; instead of trying to prevent or even alleviate the looming slumps in their economies, they were told to follow policies that would actually deepen those slumps ... But, because crises can be self-fulfilling, sound economic policy is not sufficient to gain market confidence; one must cater to the perceptions, the prejudices, and the whims of the market. Or, rather, one must cater to what one hopes will be the perceptions of the market ... The perceived need to play the confidence game supersedes the normal concerns of economic policy.

Later, Krugman (1999) added:

> The scope of global "contagion"–the rapid spread of the crisis to countries with no real economic links to the original victim – convinced me that IMF critics such as Jeffrey Sachs were right in insisting that this was less a matter of economic fundamentals than it was a case of self-fulfilling prophecy, of market panic that, by causing a collapse of the real economy, ends up validating itself.

Clearly, no one fully anticipated the crises in East Asia, mainly because they were crises of a new type. Some observers argued that the crises had important parallels with the Mexican tequila crisis of 1995, while others emphasized the differences (Kregel 1998). There were, of course, sceptics who regarded the claims of an East Asian economic miracle as somewhat exaggerated in the first place (for example, Krugman 1994). However, these were different criticisms of the East Asian miracle and certainly did not anticipate, let alone predict, the East Asian debacle of 1997–1998. The East Asian crises differed from conventional currency crisis scenarios in at least several important ways (Krugman 1998a), namely:[11]

- the absence of the usual sources of currency stress, whether fiscal deficits or macroeconomic indiscipline;[12]
- the governments' lack of any incentive to abandon their pegged exchange rates, for instance, to reduce unemployment;

- the pronounced boom and bust cycles in asset prices (real estate and stock markets) preceded the currency crises, especially in Thailand, where the crises began;
- the fact that financial intermediaries were key players in all the economies involved;
- the severity of the crises in the absence of strong, adverse shocks;
- the rapid spread of the initial crisis from Thailand even to economies with few links or similarities to the first victims.

Thus, the traditional indexes of vulnerability did not signal crises, because the source of the problem was not to be found in government fiscal balances, or even in national income accounts. The liabilities of the mainly private financial intermediaries were not part of the governments' liabilities until after the crises, after foreign lenders and the international financial institutions "persuaded" them to nationalize much of the private foreign debt. Other issues also need to be taken into account for an adequate analysis of the East Asian crises, namely:

- The crises had severe adverse effects on growth by disrupting the productive contribution of financial intermediation.
- The crises involved not only excessive investment, but also unwise investment.
- The huge real currency depreciations caused large output declines and seemed to do little to promote exports.

Other kinds of market failure also need to be taken into account. Furman and Stiglitz (1998) emphasize that economic downturns caused by financial crises are far more severe and have longer-lasting effects than those caused by inventory cycles. High leveraging by companies and high lending for asset price (stock or property market) booms enhance financial fragility and increased insolvencies disrupt the credit mechanism. Large unanticipated interest rate increases may not only precipitate financial crises, but are also likely to cause economic downturns as the value of bank assets and highly indebted firms collapse. Such adverse effects are likely to persist well after the interest rate has returned to more normal levels. In addition to asset price bubbles, excessive investments, and other problems caused by moral hazard, resulting from implicit government guarantees for weakly regulated financial intermediaries as well as the exchange rate peg, a more comprehensive analysis must also consider the following phenomena:

- The implications of the growth in currency trading and speculation for the post-Bretton Woods international monetary system.
- The reasons why the Southeast Asian monetary authorities defended their quasi pegs against the strengthening US dollar, despite the obvious adverse consequences for export competitiveness, and hence, for growth.
- The consequences of financial liberalization, including the creation of conditions that contributed to the magnitude of the crises.

- The role of herd behaviour in exacerbating the crises.
- The factors accounting for the contagion effects.

Reversible capital inflows

Analysts have increasingly acknowledged the role of easily reversible capital flows into the East Asian region as the principal cause of the 1997–1998 crises. They now generally accept that the national financial systems in the region did not adapt well to international financial liberalization (Jomo 1998, 2004). The bank-based financial systems of most of the East Asian economies affected by the crises were especially vulnerable to the sudden drop in the availability of short-term loans as international confidence in the region dropped suddenly during 1997. Available foreign exchange reserves were exposed as inadequate to meet financial obligations abroad, requiring governments to seek temporary credit facilities to meet such obligations that had been incurred mainly by their private sectors. Data from the BIS show that the banks were responsible for much of this short-term debt, though some of it did consist of trade credit and other short-term debt deemed essential for ensuring liquidity in an economy.

However, the rapid growth of short-term bank debt during stock market and property boom periods suggests that much short-term debt is due to factors other than trade credit expansion. In Malaysia, the temporary capital controls the central bank introduced in early 1994 momentarily dampened the growth of such debt, but by 1996 and early 1997, a new short-term borrowing frenzy was evident that involved not only the banks, but also other large, private companies with enough political influence to circumvent the central bank's guidelines. As Table 3.2 shows, in Indonesia, Malaysia, and Thailand, the non-bank private sector was the major recipient of international bank loans, accounting for more than half of total foreign borrowing by the end of June 1997, that is, well above the developing country average of slightly under half. In contrast, 65 per cent of borrowing in Korea was by banks, with only 31 per cent by the non-bank private sector. Government borrowing was low, and was lowest in Korea and Malaysia, although the data do not permit differentiating between state-owned public companies and partially private, but corporatized previously fully state-owned enterprises.

Jomo (2001b: appendix tables 2a–2d; Wong *et al.* 2005) shows the remarkable growth of mainly private foreign debt in the early and mid-1990s, especially in the three most externally indebted economies of Indonesia, Korea, and Thailand. While FDI grew in all four economies in the 1990s, it grew least in Korea. Profit remittances on FDI were lowest from Korea and Thailand and highest from Malaysia, reflecting its historically greater role, although FDI in Indonesia was actually higher in 1995–1996. Portfolio equity flows into all four economies grew strongly in the mid-1990s. External debt as a share of export earnings rose from 112 per cent in 1995 to 120 per cent in 1996 in Thailand and from 57 to 74 per cent over the same period in Korea, but declined in Indonesia and grew more modestly in Malaysia. By 1996, foreign exchange reserves as a share of external debt were 15 per cent in Indonesia, 30 per cent in Korea, 43 per

Table 3.2 Lending by banks reporting to BIS by sector, East Asian four and developing
countries, end June 1997 (US$ bn)

Sector	Indonesia	S. Korea	Malaysia	Thailand	Developing countries
Total borrowing, of which:	58.6	103.4	28.9	79.4	743.8
Bank	12.4	67.3	10.5	26.1	275.3
	(21.1)	(65.1)	(36.3)	(32.9)	(37.0)
Private non-bank	39.7	31.7	16.5	41.3	352.9
	(67.7)	(30.6)	(57.1)	(52.0)	(47.4)
Government	6.5	4.4	1.9	12.0	115.6
	(11.1)	(4.3)	(6.6)	(15.1)	(15.5)

Source: BIS data.

Note
Figures in parentheses are percentages.

Table 3.3 Exposure of banks reporting to BIS and non-BIS
borrowers, end-June 1997 (US$ bn)

Banks' national location	Amount
Total	1,054.9
Germany	178.2
Japan	172.7
United States	131.0
France	100.2
United Kingdom	77.8
Percentage of private non-bank borrowers	45

Source: BIS data.

cent in Thailand, and 70 per cent in Malaysia. By 1997, this ratio had dropped
further to 15 per cent in Korea, 29 per cent in Thailand, and 46 per cent in
Malaysia, reflecting the reserves lost in futile currency defence efforts.

Despite recessions in 1998, reserves picked up in all four economies, mainly
because of the effects of currency devaluations on exports and imports. The
short-term debt share of total external debt in 1996 stood at 58 per cent in Korea,
41 per cent in Thailand, 28 per cent in Malaysia, and 25 per cent in Indonesia.
Table 3.3 shows that French, German, Japanese, UK, and US banks that
reported to the BIS accounted for much of the lending to developing countries,
with the share of UK and US banks being far less significant than lending to
other emerging markets. This pattern was quite different from that of lending
before the 1980s debt crises, and suggests that Anglo-American banks were
generally far more reluctant to lend in the 1990s following their experiences in
the 1980s. Little evidence suggests that such banks were more averse to lending

either to governments or to developing economies. Indeed, the pattern of lending in the late 1970s and early 1980s suggests the contrary.

From the beginning of the 1990s, Malaysia sustained a current account deficit. Overinvestment of investible funds in non-tradables only made things worse. Insofar as such investments did not contribute to export earnings, for example, in power generation and telecommunications, they aggravated the problem of currency mismatch, with foreign borrowing invested in activities that did not generate foreign exchange. An additional problem of term mismatch also arose, as a high proportion of the foreign borrowing was short-term in nature (Table 3.4), but was deployed to finance medium- to long-term projects.

Foreign capital inflows into East Asia augmented the high domestic savings rate to boost the domestic investment rate and East Asian investments abroad in the 1990s. Thus, even though some evidence suggests that foreign capital inflows may have had an indirect adverse effect on the domestic savings rate, they generally supplemented, rather than substituted for, domestic savings (Wong with Jomo 2005). Being conclusive on this point is difficult, because the nature of foreign capital inflows has changed significantly over time. Hence, even if earlier foreign capital inflows may have adversely affected domestic savings, one possibility is that the changed composition of foreign capital inflows just before the crises no longer adversely affected domestic savings.

International financial liberalization undoubtedly succeeded in temporarily generating massive net capital inflows into East Asia, unlike many other developing and transition economies, some of which experienced net outflows. However, it also exacerbated systemic instability and reduced the scope for the government interventions responsible for the region's economic miracle. Increased foreign capital inflows reduced foreign exchange constraints, allowing the financing of additional imports, but thereby also inadvertently encouraging current account deficits. Finally, foreign capital inflows adversely affected factor payment outflows, export and import propensities, terms of trade, and capital flight, and thus, the balance of payments.

These consequences suggest that governments should be cautious when determining the extent to which they should encourage foreign capital inflows.

Table 3.4 Maturity distribution of lending by banks reporting to the BIS to the East Asian four, 1996–1997 (US$ million.)

Country	All loans			Under 1 year			1–2 years		
	June 1996	*Dec. 1996*	*June 1997*	*June 1996*	*Dec. 1996*	*June 1997*	*June 1996*	*Dec. 1996*	*June 1997*
Indonesia	49,306	55,523	58,726	29,587	34,248	34,661	3,473	3,589	3,541
S. Korea	88,027	99,953	103,432	62,332	67,506	70,182	3,438	4,107	4,139
Malaysia	20,100	22,234	28,820	9,991	11,178	16,268	834	721	615
Thailand	69,409	70,147	69,382	47,834	45,702	45,567	4,083	4,829	4,592

Source: BIS data.

Furthermore, the Southeast Asian trio's heavy dependence on FDI in relation to gross domestic capital formation, especially for manufacturing investments, probably also limited the development of domestic entrepreneurship, as well as many other indigenous economic capabilities, by the increased reliance on foreign capabilities usually associated with some types of FDI (Jomo *et al.* 1997).

As noted earlier, starting in the mid-1990s, three major indicators began to cause concern. The current account of the balance of payments and the savings–investment gap were recording large imbalances in the Southeast Asian economies, especially Malaysia and Thailand. However, as Table 3.5 shows, the short-term foreign debt and current account deficits as proportions of inter-national reserves were better in Malaysia than in Indonesia, Korea, and Thailand, thereby averting the need for IMF emergency credit. Domestic credit expansion had also soared in all four countries by the mid-1990s. Prior to the crises, since the mid-1980s, East Asia had moved steadily toward financial liberalization, including bank liberalization, promotion of the region's newly emerging stock markets, and greater capital account convertibility. Thus, East Asia succeeded in attracting a great deal of capital inflows.

Whereas the other three crisis-affected East Asian economies succeeded in attracting considerable, mainly short-term, US dollar bank loans into their more bank-based financed systems, Malaysia's vulnerability was mainly due to the volatility of international portfolio capital flows into its stock market. As a con-sequence, the nature of Malaysia's external liabilities at the beginning of the crisis was quite different from that of the other crisis-stricken East Asian economies. A greater proportion of Malaysia's external liabilities consisted of equity rather than debt. Compared with Malaysia's exposure in the mid-1980s, many of the liabilities, including the debt, were private rather than public. In addition, much of Malaysia's debt in the late 1990s was long-term rather than short-term in nature, again in contrast to the other crisis-affected economies.

Monetary policy and banking supervision had generally been much more prudent in Malaysia than in the other victims of the crises; for example, Malaysian

Table 3.5 Debt service and short-term debt, East Asian four, selected years

Country	Debt service as a percentage of exports			Short-term debt (US$ billions)[a]				Current account deficit plus short-term debt as a percentage of international reserves			
	1980	1992	1995	1992	1994	1995	1996	1992	1994	1995	1996
Indonesia	13.9	32.1	30.9	18.2	14.0	16.2	17.9	191	139	169	138
S. Korea	14.5	6.9	5.8	11.9	31.6	46.6	66.6	133	125	131	127
Malaysia	6.3	6.6	7.8	3.6	7.6	7.5	8.5	29	46	60	55
Thailand	18.9	14.1	10.2	14.7	29.2	41.1	44.0	101	127	152	153

Sources: UNCTAD (1997: Table 14); World Bank (1994: Tables 20, 23; 1997: Table 17).

Note
a Year-end figures.

banks had not been allowed to borrow heavily from abroad to lend on the domestic market. Such practices involved currency and term mismatches, which increased the vulnerability of countries' financial systems to foreign bankers' confidence and exerted pressure on the exchange rate pegs. These differences have lent support to the claim that Malaysia was an innocent bystander that fell victim to regional contagion by being in the wrong part of the world at the wrong time.

Such a view takes a benign view of portfolio investment inflows and does not recognize that such inflows are even more easily reversible and volatile than bank loan inflows (Jomo 2001a). Contrary to the innocent bystander hypothesis, Malaysia's experience actually suggests greater vulnerability because of its greater reliance on the capital market. As a consequence, the Malaysian economy became hostage to international portfolio investors' confidence. Hence, when government leaders engaged in rhetoric and policy initiatives that upset such investors' confidence, Malaysia paid a heavy price when portfolio divestment accelerated.

International financial liberalization

An explosion of international financial flows followed the substitution of the Bretton Woods system of fixed exchange rates with the prevailing system of flexible exchange rates. Analysts have ascribed strong speculative motives to most of the international capital flows not associated with FDI. Much recent FDI, especially into East Asia in the wake of the crises, has been for mergers and acquisitions rather than to add new economic capacity through greenfield investments. The demise of fixed exchange rate regimes also encouraged capital account liberalization. Recent financial developments have resulted in a proliferation of financial instruments, enabling investors to diversify their holdings of financial assets.

These trends gathered steam with international financial liberalization in the wake of the international debt crises of the 1980s and picked up further momentum in the 1990s. By 1995, the volume of foreign exchange spot transactions had grown to well over a trillion US dollars per day, or more than 67 times the total value of the international trade in goods by 1995, or more than 40 times the value of all international trade (including services). Estimates put the daily foreign exchange market in 1997 at US$1,250 billion. In a world economy where foreign exchange spot transactions are now worth more than 70 times the total value of international commodity trade transactions, the financial sector has become increasingly divorced from the real economy.

Viewed from a historical perspective, such currency trading is hardly natural, inevitable, or even desirable. For most of human history, it has not been "integral to global trade in goods and services," as then US Treasury Secretary Robert Rubin (1998) claimed. Indeed, critics have offered various alternatives to the current system. With the recent proliferation of new financial instruments and markets, the financial sector has an even greater capacity to inflict damage on the real economy. Ever since Keynes (1936) advocated "throwing sand" into the financial system to halt the potentially disastrous consequences of unfettered liberalization, Keynesians and others have been wary of the financial liberalization advocated by ideological neo-liberals and their often naïve allies. Furthermore, many of the promised benefits of international financial liberalization have not been realized (Eatwell 1997), namely:

- Liberalization was expected to move financial resources from capital-rich to capital-poor countries.[13] Instead, such net flows of finance – and of real resources – over time have been modest and have tended to go to the capital-rich economies.[14] Of course, most net flows to the capital-poor states were mainly to the most attractive emerging markets, especially in East Asia before 1998. The rush to convertibility and capital control deregulation in most transition economies has resulted in many of them becoming significant net capital exporters, for example, the Russian Federation.[15] Such flows arguably contributed to asset price bubbles and, eventually, to financial panic, and thus, to currency and stock market collapses.
- Liberalization was expected to enhance options and returns for savers and to lower the cost of funds to borrowers; however, savers have benefited most from higher real interest rates. It has been claimed that the lower cost of funds in the late 1970s was attributable to the exceptional circumstances caused by financial repression, enhanced liquidity brought about by the availability of petroleum revenues, and high inflation.
- New financial derivatives, which were expected to improve risk management and have undoubtedly reduced some of the older sources of volatility and instability, also generated new systemic risks especially vulnerable to sudden changes in sentiment.
- Improved macroeconomic performance resulting in greater investment and growth that was expected from better allocative efficiency has not been realized. Instead, overall macroeconomic performance has been worse than during the post-war "golden age" before financial liberalization.
- Financial liberalization has introduced a persistent deflationary bias in economic policy as governments try to gain credibility in financial markets to avert destabilizing capital outflows, instead of exerting the healthy discipline on governments that was expected to improve macroeconomic stability.

More generally, financial liberalization has further constrained the role of the state, and governments face reduced options in both monetary and fiscal policies. In addition to such macroeconomic policy limitations, the room for discretionary state interventions has been much reduced, for example, in the form of selective industrial promotion, which was so crucial to late industrialization. Thus, financial liberalization has greatly weakened governments' capacity in relation to development. Given the desirability of preserving the limited, but still significant, scope for monetary independence, liberalization should not be allowed to frustrate the sound development of a country's financial system and its effective deployment for development purposes. The scope for monetary independence depends partly on the soundness of macroeconomic management, as well as on political will.

Financial markets seem to function in such a way as to impose their own expectations on the real economy, thereby defining their own fundamentals and logic, and in turn become self-fulfilling prophecies. In other words, financial markets do not simply process information in order to allocate resources efficiently. The threat of instability in the now massive capital market forces both governments and private investors to pursue risk-averse strategies, resulting in low growth and employment creation. A deflationary bias in government policy and the private sector emerges in response to the costly risks of violating the rules of the game. This is exacerbated by the high costs of debt caused by high real interest rates that result from efforts to maintain financial stability in a potentially volatile world.

Thus, long-term price stability supersedes a high and stable level of employment as the macroeconomic policy priority. A successfully liberalized financial system that gives high priority to flexibility or the possibility of easy exit necessarily tends to become fragile, as reflected in:

- liquidity crises that reduce real output;
- private sector risk aversion that encourages short-termism;
- public sector risk aversion that results in a deflationary policy bias;
- persistent pressure for ever greater flexibility that increases the ease of exit.

The benefits of reduced financial controls to emerging markets must be weighed against the increased instability resulting from enhanced ease and speed of exit.

While increased (real) FDI flows generally require countries to agree to unrestricted repatriation of profits, this is quite different from the instant exit conditions financial markets demand. Considerable evidence indicates that in the longer term, economic development has been associated with developmental states effectively promoting selected new economic activities by the use of industrial or selective investment policy. The post-war golden age – which saw high levels of output and employment and short-run efficiency – was based on the premise of active macroeconomic management under the Bretton Woods system. Post-war European reconstruction was achieved with tight capital controls. Similarly, Japan, Korea, and Taiwan (Province of China) all began their industrialization and achieved rapid capital accumulation with the aid of capital controls.

The adverse consequences for economic development of financial disintermediation and of grossly undervalued currencies also deserve attention, particularly as the crises threatened the future of growth and structural change in the region, not only directly, but also as a consequence of policy responses. The typically deflationary policies the international financial community and others favour may well throw out the baby of economic development with the bathwater of financial crisis. Some dangers associated with financial liberalization have now become evident, but most have not been sufficiently recognized, let alone debated and addressed. Most initiatives in this regard cannot be undertaken unilaterally without great cost, as market reactions to Malaysian Prime Minister Mahathir's critical remarks in the second half of 1997 showed (see Jomo 2001b).

The few options available for unilateral initiatives need to be carefully considered and only implemented if deemed desirable. Selectively invoking instances of bad or incompetent policymaking or implementation does not justify leaving matters to liberalized markets that render systematic policymaking impossible. Instead, the experience of financial crisis emphasizes the importance of creating an environment and developing the capability such that good and competent policy is effective. Many policies need to be actively pursued through multilateral initiatives, for which governments need the support of neighbouring countries and others. Given the power of the dominant ideology that infuses the prevailing international system, asserting control over the financial system is virtually impossible without a fundamental change in priorities and thinking by the governments of the major economic powers. The currencies of a small number of countries – Germany, Japan, the United Kingdom, and the United States – were involved in more than three-quarters of currency transactions in 1995; thus, such countries have the capacity to monitor and control trans-border capital flows by acting in concert, especially with further concentration since the emergence of the Euro zone.

The role of the IMF

Critical consideration of the causes and consequences of the East Asian crises requires paying close and careful attention to the nature and implications of IMF rescue programmes and conditionalities, as well as policies favoured by international, as distinct from domestic, financial communities. IMF prescriptions and conventional policymaking wisdom urged bank closures, government spending cuts, and higher interest rates in the wake of the crises. Such contractionary measures transformed what had started as currency crises, and then became full-blown financial crises, into crises of the real economy. Thus, Indonesia, Korea, and Malaysia, which had previously enjoyed massive capital inflows in the form of short-term bank loans or portfolio investments, went into recession during 1998, following Thailand, which went into recession in 1997.

Not only did the IMF underestimate the severity of the collapse in all the East Asian economies, it also underestimated the speed and strength of recovery (IMF 1997, 1998; Lane *et al.* 1999). This suggests that the IMF not only did not understand the causes of the crises, but was also incapable of designing optimal policies in response to it. Critics still doubt whether the IMF recognized the novel elements of the crises and their implications, especially at the outset. The IMF's apparent failure to anticipate the crises in its generally glowing reports on the region prior to the crises and its role in exacerbating the downturns in Indonesia, Korea, and Thailand certainly did not inspire much confidence. In addition, even though the Philippines had long been involved in IMF programmes and supervision, it was not spared the contagion.[16]

International scepticism about the IMF's role in and prescriptions for the East Asian crises is considerable. Most economists now agree that the early IMF programmes for Indonesia, Korea, and Thailand were ill-conceived, although they do not seem able to agree on why the IMF made such mistakes. Perhaps partly out of force of habit from dealing with situations in Africa, Eastern Europe, Latin America, and elsewhere where fiscal deficits had been part of the problem, the IMF insisted on the same prescription of deflationary policies in its early policy responses to the East Asian crises.

Thus, many of its programmes were effectively contractionary, though this was sometimes disguised by poorly conceived measures to provide social safety nets for the poor. Hence, what started off as currency and financial crises led – partly because of policy responses recommended or imposed by the IMF – to economic recessions in much of the region in 1998. The accounts vary with the different countries involved (Jomo 1998, 2004; *Cambridge Journal of Economics* November 1998; see Jomo 2001a: Chapter 1; Wong *et al.* 2005 for accounts of the Malaysian experience).

The early IMF policy prescription to raise domestic interest rates not only failed to stem capital flight, but instead exacerbated the impact of the crises, causing financial pain through currency depreciation, stock market collapses, and rising interest rates. Even if higher interest rates had succeeded in preventing capital flight, it can only be halted temporarily, and even then at great and permanent costs to productive investments in the real economy. When inflows are eventually reversed in the precipitous manner East Asia experienced from the second half of 1997, a large amount of collateral damage is inevitable.

Furman and Stiglitz (1998) provide a critical review of the literature and argue against raising interest rates to protect the exchange rate. In particular, where leveraging is high, as in East Asia, high interest rates will take a huge toll by weakening aggregate demand and increasing the likelihood and frequency of insolvencies. Unexpected interest rate hikes tend to weaken financial institutions, lower investment, and thereby reduce output. Furman and Stiglitz (1998) offer the following three main reasons why keeping interest rates low while letting the exchange rate depreciate may be a preferable option in light of the trade-off involved:

- To avoid crisis, policymakers should be more concerned about interest rate increases than about exchange rate declines (Demirguc-Kunt and Detragiache 1998; Furman and Stiglitz 1998).
- Any government intervention to stabilize the exchange rate is likely to encourage economic agents to take positions they would otherwise not take, later compelling the government to support the exchange rate to avoid the now larger adverse effects. This point is based on a moral hazard argument.
- When a government defends its currency, it is often making a one-way bet, where the expected loss is speculators' expected gain. In contrast, if the government does not wager any reserves, the gains of some speculators are simply the losses of others. Thus invoking an equity argument, they ask why borrowers, workers, firms, and others adversely affected by higher interest rates should be compelled to pay for speculators' profits.

Despite their sound fiscal balances before the crises, the IMF also asked the East Asian economies to cut government spending to restore confidence in their currencies, despite the ominous implications for economic recovery. Even though all the affected East Asian economies had been running fiscal surpluses in the years preceding the crises (except Indonesia, which had a small deficit in 1996), the IMF expected the governments to slash public expenditure. With the possible exception of Indonesia, which could not raise the financing required, the other crises-affected economies eventually ignored this advice and began to undertake Keynesian-style reflationary, countercyclical measures starting in the second half of 1998, which have been primarily responsible for their economic recovery. Incredibly, the IMF did not seem to be cognizant of the subjective elements that had contributed to the crises and seemed to approach the situation as if it was solely due to weaknesses in the countries' macroeconomic or financial systems.

Examining the changing risk premiums on Eurobonds issued by East Asia, Woo (2000) finds evidence of "irrational exuberance," implying that the potential for investor panic also existed. Moreover, even though the risk premiums on Thai Eurobonds increased by ten basis points following the July 1997 devaluation, they jumped by four times as much with the acceptance of the IMF programme for Thailand in August 1997. This suggests that the latter's deflationary macroeconomic policies and abrupt closure of financial institutions had undermined, rather than restored, investor confidence. Insolvent financial institutions should have been restructured so as to avoid the possibility of triggering bank runs and consequent social instability.

By insisting on closing down banks and other financial institutions in Indonesia, Korea, and Thailand, the IMF undermined much of the remaining confidence, inducing further panic in the process. Nasution (2000) points out that the IMF's way of taking insolvent banks out of Indonesia's financial system in late 1997 exacerbated the country's economic crisis. He argues that the Indonesian government should have temporarily taken over the insolvent banks rather than closing them down suddenly to sustain credit to solvent borrowers and to retain depositors' confidence.

Also, even though the IMF insisted on greater transparency by the crises-affected governments and those under their jurisdiction, it continued to operate under considerable secrecy. Such double standards on the part of the IMF, reflected by the priority it gave to protecting the interests of foreign banks and governments, also compromised its ostensible role as an impartial agent working in the interests of affected economies.

The burden of IMF programmes invariably fell on countries' domestic financial sectors and, eventually, on the public at large, which has borne most of the costs of adjustment and reform. The social costs of the public policy responses have been considerable, usually involving bailouts of much of the financial sector and of the corporate sector more generally.

Unhappiness in East Asia about how differently the IMF responded to the East Asian crises compared with the earlier Mexican one is widespread. People generally believe that the IMF was far more generous in helping Mexico because of the interest of the United States in ensuring that the tequila crisis was not seen as an adverse consequence of Mexico joining the North American Free

Trade Agreement. In contrast, East Asians saw the IMF as far less generous and more demanding with all three countries, which had long seen themselves as allies of the United States and of the West in general.

The IMF has invariably given priority to liabilities and other commitments to foreign banks, even though both foreign and domestic banks may have been equally irresponsible or imprudent in their lending practices. As the BIS noted: "In spite of growing strains in Southeast Asia, overall bank lending to Asian developing countries showed no evidence of abating in the first half of 1997" (Raghavan 1998). From mid-1996 to mid-1997, Korea received US$15 billion in new loans while Indonesia received US$9 billion from the banks. Short-term lending continued to dominate, with 70 per cent due within one year, while the share of lending to private non-bank borrowers rose to 45 per cent by the end of June 1997.

The banks were also actively acquiring non-traditional assets in the region, for instance, in higher-yielding local money markets and other debt securities. Most of this lending was by Japanese and European banks. Thus, Japanese and Western banks have emerged from the crises relatively unscathed and stronger than the domestic financial sectors of the crises-affected economies, which have taken the brunt of the cost of adjustment. Some merchant banks and other financial institutions were also able to make lucrative commissions from marketing sovereign debt, as the short-term private borrowing that precipitated the crises is converted into longer-term, government-guaranteed bonds under the terms of IMF programmes.

Priorities for international financial system reform

The experiences of the 1997–1998 East Asian crises give rise to six major lessons for international financial reform. First, existing mechanisms and institutions for *preventing financial crises* are grossly inadequate. As recent experiences suggest, current trends in financial liberalization are likely to increase rather than decrease the likelihood, frequency, and severity of currency and financial crises. Too little was done by the national authorities and their foreign advisers to discourage short-term capital flows and too much emphasis has been placed on the expected protection provided by international adherence to codes and standards (Rodrik 1999).[17]

Financial liberalization has also reduced the macroeconomic instruments available to governments for crisis aversion, and has instead left governments with little choice but to react pro-cyclically, which tends to exacerbate economic downturns. Governments need to be assured of autonomy in their national macroeconomic policy to enable them to intervene countercyclically to avoid crises, which have had much more devastating consequences in developing countries than elsewhere. Recognition of the exaggerated effects of currency movements at the international level should also lead to greater surveillance and coordination among the three major international currency issuers: Japan, the United States, and Europe.

Second, existing mechanisms and institutions for financial *crisis management* are also grossly inadequate. The greater likelihood, frequency, and severity of currency and financial crises in middle-income developing countries in recent times – with devastating consequences for the real economy and for innocent bystanders "in the neighbourhood," as in the East Asian crises – makes speedy crisis resolution imperative. There is an urgent need to increase emergency financing during crises and to establish adequate new procedures for timely and orderly debt standstills and work-outs.[18] International financial institutions, including regional institutions, should be able to provide adequate countercyclical financing, for instance, for social safety nets during crises (Ocampo 2000).[19] Instead of current arrangements, which tend to benefit foreign creditors, new procedures and mechanisms are needed to ensure that they too share responsibility for the consequences of their lending practices.

Third, the agenda for international financial reform needs to go beyond the recent preoccupation with crisis prevention and resolution to address the declining availability and provision of *development finance*, especially to small and poor countries (Ocampo 2000) that have limited and expensive access to capital markets. The IMF, in particular, is facing growing pressure to return to its supposedly core function of providing emergency credit and core competencies of crisis prevention and mitigation.[20] Furthermore, the World Bank and other multilateral development banks have either abandoned or sharply reduced industrial financing, further limiting the likelihood that developing countries will be able to secure funding to develop new manufacturing capacities and capabilities. The United Nations Conference on Financing for Development, held in Mexico in March 2002, clearly did not address this challenge adequately despite the promise of the Monterrey consensus after the modest proposals of the Zedillo group report commissioned by the UN's Secretary-General.

Fourth, inertia and vested interests stand in the way of urgently needed international institutional reforms. The *international financial institutions* need to reform their *governance* to ensure greater and more equitable participation and decision-making – and hence, ownership – by developing countries at all levels and in various tasks that the new international financial system must begin to address more adequately. There is also a need to reduce the concentration of power in and the power of some apex institutions, such as the IMF, by delegating authority to other agencies, for example, the proposed World Financial Organization or World Financial Authority, as well as by encouraging decentralization, devolution, complementarity, and competition with other international financial institutions, including regional ones.[21] The Group of Seven must engage in more serious consultations with developing countries in relation to international economic issues to avoid insensitive and potentially disastrous oversights and further loss of policy legitimacy (Rodrik 1999).

Fifth, the reforms should restore and ensure *national economic authority and autonomy*, which have been greatly undermined by international liberalization and regulation, and which have proved essential for more effective, especially expansionary and countercyclical macroeconomic management and initiatives pertaining to equitable development such as ensuring the availability of development finance as well as more inclusive access to financial facilities. Policy conditionalities accompanying IMF financing must be minimized, if not eliminated altogether.[22] One size clearly does not fit all, and imposed policies have not contributed much to either economic recovery or growth (Weisbrot *et al.* 2000), let alone sustainable development. Such ownership will ensure greater legitimacy for public policies and must include regulation of the capital account and choice of exchange rate regime.[23] Because international financial reforms in the foreseeable future are unlikely to adequately provide the global public goods and other international financial services most developing countries need, it is imperative that reforms of the international system assure national policy independence so that governments are better able to address regulatory and interventionist functions beyond a global and regional purview.

Finally, appreciation is growing of the desirability of *regional monetary cooperation* in the face of growing capital mobility and the increasing frequency of currency and related financial crises, often with devastating consequences for the real economy. Some observers argue, for instance, that growing European monetary integration in recent decades arose out of governments' recognition of their declining sovereignty in the face of growing capital mobility, especially as their capital accounts were liberalized (Baines 2002). Instead of trying to assert greater national control with probably limited efficacy, cooperation among governments in a region is more likely to be effective in the face of the larger magnitude and velocity of capital flows. However, no single formula or trajectory for fostering such cooperation is available, and it probably cannot be promoted successfully independently of economic cooperation on other fronts.

The existence of such regional arrangements also offers an intermediate alternative between national and global levels of action and intervention and reduces the possibly monopolistic powers of global authorities. To be successful and effective, such regional arrangements must be flexible, but credible, and must be capable of both effective countercyclical initiatives for crisis prevention and management. In East Asia, the Japanese proposal for an Asian monetary facility soon after the outbreak of the Asian crises could have made a major difference in checking and managing the crises, but Western opposition blocked the proposal. With the growing reluctance in the West – especially the United States – to allow the IMF to serve as a lender of last resort (as in the last Argentine crisis), it should at least be more tolerant of regional cooperative arrangements as alternatives.

Conclusion

The conventional wisdom was to blame the crisis on bad economic policies by the governments concerned. Citing the first and second generation currency crisis theories, the initial emphasis was on poor macroeconomic policies, especially fiscal policies. Ignoring the fact that most East Asian economies had been maintaining budgetary surpluses for some years at least, the IMF and others, including the influential international business media, recommended spending cuts and other pro-cyclical policies (e.g. monetary policies raising interest rates) which served to exacerbate the downturns. Such policies were adopted in much of the region in the second half of 1997 or in early 1998, precipitating sharp economic collapses.

By the second quarter of 1998, however, it was increasingly widely recognized that these policy recommendations and conditionalities had actually worsened, rather than ameliorated, the deteriorating economic situation, transforming currency and financial crises into crises of the real economy. In early 1998, however, as the macroeconomic explanations lost credibility, a new line of criticism focused on the political economy of the region, condemning cronyism in corporate governance as the source of the regional financial crises. US Federal Reserve Bank chair Alan Greenspan, US Treasury Deputy Secretary Lawrence Summers and IMF Managing Director Michel Camdessus formed a chorus criticizing Asian corporate governance in quick sequence over a month from late January.

The failure of fiscal as well as corporate governance explanations of the Asian crises was not only evident to heterodox economists in the region and beyond, but was also recognized by relatively orthodox economists familiar with the actual situation in the affected economies. The World Bank's senior vice-president and chief economist Joseph Stiglitz as well as other prominent economists such as Jeffrey Sachs and Paul Krugman provided important international support for adopting countercyclical policies.

The heterodox view emphasized the transformation of the region's economies and financial systems from the late 1980s. As a consequence, the economies had become much more vulnerable and fragile. The rapid economic growth of the region and the liberalized financial institutions served to attract massive inflows of capital. Much of these inflows came from Japanese and continental European banks as UK and US banks continued to recover from the 1980s debt crises, and generally exercised greater prudence in lending internationally. BIS regulations encouraged short-term lending, which was generally rolled over in good times, but which could be quickly reversed when conditions became less favourable, as happened when the crisis began.

Significant inflows were also attracted by the stock market and other asset price bubbles in the region. Such flows were even more easily reversible. The herd behaviour especially characteristic of capital markets, particularly in situations of constrained information, served to exacerbate pro-cyclical market behaviour, worsening panic during downturns. Such fickle market behaviour also exacerbated contagion effects, worsening regional neighbourhood effects.

A year after the crisis began in July 1997, US President Clinton acknowledged the need for a new international financial architecture in a speech in mid-1998, triggering significant discussion for a brief time. The apparent spread of the crisis to Brazil and Russia around the same time gave further momentum to the new discourse. The collapse of Long-Term Capital Management (LTCM) following the Russian crisis led the US Federal Reserve to coordinate a private sector bailout of the hedge fund in a successful attempt to contain the problem. This legitimized government interventions in East Asia to ensure functioning financial systems and the availability of liquidity to finance economic recovery. The US Fed also lowered interest rates, encouraging capital to flow to East Asia once again. The Malaysian government's establishment of bailout institutions and mechanisms in mid-1998 and its imposition of capital controls on outflows at the beginning of September 1998 may also have warned the West of the possibility of other countries going their own way.

Ironically, the successful and rapid V-shaped economic recoveries in the region from the last quarter of 1998 may well have weakened the pressure to address flaws in the international financial system. Talk of a new international financial architecture began to fade as the rapid recovery in the region was seen as proof of the resilience of the international financial system. Of course, there continues to be some interest in crisis avoidance, crisis management, development finance, governance of the Bretton Woods institutions, reasserting national economic sovereignty and regional financial cooperation.

The Japanese government's offer of $100 billion to the Asian region to manage the crisis during the third quarter of 1997 was blocked by Western governments and the IMF. Later, a more modest amount was made available under the Miyazawa Plan for more modest facilities, institutions, and instruments. From around 2000, following a regional meeting of finance ministers in Chiang Mai, Thailand, a series of bilateral credit lines emerged but with the condition of requiring an IMF programme. In May 2007, the finance ministers of Japan, China, and the Republic of Korea agreed to multilateralize the arrangements and to increase the amount of the credit facility; however, it is still not clear at the time of writing whether the IMF programme requirement will remain. There have also been other regional initiatives, including the Asian bond market, which have made varying degrees of progress. An important new initiative is the idea of an Asian Investment Bank mobilizing private funds for long-term investments, e.g. in infrastructure. However, progress on these various initiatives has generally been slow and contingent on cooperation between Japan and China.

Hence, it is clear that various different and sometimes contradictory lessons have been drawn from the Asian crisis experiences. The ideological implications and political differences involved have generally complicated the possibility of drawing shared lessons from the crises. The seeming calm and increased growth in most developing countries in the period since 2001 have also served to undermine the possibility of far-reaching reforms following the experience. Perhaps most importantly, the vested interests supporting existing international financial governance arrangements continue to impede the possibility of greater progress. Such interests are supported by conventional (market) wisdom, reinforced by the business media and its pervasive influence on the political economy of international monetary and financial governance.

Notes

1 Of course, the availability of cheap foreign funds, for example, because of a low real interest rate, can help to temporarily close both domestic savings–investments and foreign exchange gaps, especially if well invested or deployed.

2 Financial analysts had become fixated with the current account deficit, especially since the Mexican meltdown of early 1995. In earlier times, some economies

sustained similar deficits for much longer without comparable consequences. In the immediate aftermath of the Mexican crisis, several Southeast Asian economies already had comparable current account deficits, despite, or rather because of, rapid economic growth.

3 In some countries, government-owned, non-financial, public enterprises were very much part of the growth of supposedly private sector debt.

4 There is also no evidence that the stock market boom of the mid-1990s raised funds for productive investment more effectively. Indeed, the converse was true, with financial dis-intermediation from commercial banks to the stock market.

5 Even though the US economy was strengthening, the Southeast Asian economies were growing even faster.

6 In the mid-1990s, as the US dollar strengthened along with the US economy, both Germany and Japan allowed their currencies to depreciate against the US dollar, with relatively little disruption, in an effort to regain international competitiveness.

7 Sentiments can influence fundamentals and the health of financial systems either favourably or unfavourably (Montes 1998). In particular, the collapse of the Southeast Asian currencies because of sentiments adversely affected the viability of investments made at different exchange rates, which in turn exacerbated the domestic banking crises.

8 Montes (1998) argues that the more rural-based Southeast Asian economies were better able to carry out real devaluations from nominal changes in currency value, because their export sectors were not too tied down by supply-side inflexibilities to respond to real devaluations. After asserting that stock markets served to share risks among asset owners rather than to raise financing, he notes that, except for financial system weaknesses, Southeast Asian real sectors were relatively immune from the 1997–1998 asset market frenzy.

9 Equity and portfolio investments had overtaken direct investment, loans, and trade credit in providing external financing by the 1990s. Montes (1998: 34) cites Reisen's warning that offers of foreign financing should be resisted if they would "cause unsustainable currency appreciation, excessive risk-taking in the banking system, and a sharp drop in private savings." Hence, in a sentiment-driven market, currencies become too strong with the prospect of strong external financing and too weak when capital withdraws or threatens to.

10 Woo (2000) argues that occasional excessive price movements in financial markets should not be too readily attributed to the rational anticipation of changes in government policies that were not eventually realized, the main argument usually invoked to reject claims of speculative bubbles.

11 Krugman's (1998c) attempt at theoretical catching-up is particularly worthy of consideration in light of his own previous attempts to understand related international economic phenomena as well as East Asian economic growth. As the crises were still unfolding, such an attempt was hardly definitive, especially without the benefit of hindsight. Yet, as policy was very much being made on the hoof, his attempt to highlight certain relationships were illuminating. Hence, Krugman (1998c) argues that:

> It is necessary to adopt an approach quite different from that of traditional currency crisis theory. Of course Asian economies did experience currency crises, and the usual channels of speculation were operative here as always. However, the currency crises were only part of a broader financial crisis, which had very little to do with currencies or even monetary issues per se. Nor did the crisis have much to do with traditional fiscal issues. Instead, to make sense of what went wrong, we need to focus on two issues normally neglected in currency crisis analysis. These are the role of financial intermediaries (and of the moral hazard associated with such intermediaries when they are poorly regulated), and the prices of real assets such as capital and land.

12 None of the fundamentals usually emphasized seemed to have been important in the affected economies: all the governments had fiscal surpluses and none were involved in excessive monetary expansion, while inflation rates were generally low.

13 Recent findings suggest that national savings tend to equal national investment, indicating that flows of capital to the best possible use are far from universal and much smaller than simple theories predict. Lack of information or other risks and uncertainties tend to reduce cross-border capital flows.

14 Eatwell (1997) suggests a negative correlation between dependence on foreign savings and economic performance. This is true if foreign savings are not broken down into their components. The numbers are strongly biased by the inclusion of short-term money market flows, which may include efforts by governments to prop up their currencies with high interest rates, which temporarily suck in money from overseas. Brazil, Mexico, and especially Venezuela typified this a few years ago. If only long-term direct (or equity) investment was considered, many poorly performing Latin American economies would not be considered to be heavily dependent on foreign savings any more. Southeast Asian countries, especially Malaysia and Singapore, would then rank high in both foreign savings (measured "appropriately") and economic performance.

15 Of course, capital flight is not an inevitable consequence of financial liberalization, but may reflect locals' fears and hedging behaviour.

16 Arguably, the Philippines currency did not take quite as hard a hit as those of the other crises-affected economies, in part because its banking and accounting standards were relatively better, but also because its short-term capital inflows before the crises were relatively low.

17 Pistor (2000) demonstrates that international legal standards are unlikely to have the desired outcomes because of the significance of historical original conditions and varied path dependence.

18 Consensus is growing on the need to set up standstill and other procedures for international debt work-outs akin to US bankruptcy provisions for corporations and municipal authorities, although IMF Deputy Managing Director Anne Krueger's (2002) proposals have not been well received by those governments most likely to be affected by them because of their adverse selection consequences for such governments.

19 Social safety nets should not be seen as a substitute for social policy, which should be adequate to ensure a decent standard of living within a government's means in addition to enhancing human resources for development.

20 Then US Treasury Secretary and former World Bank Vice-President and Chief Economist Lawrence Summers is a prominent proponent of this view. See, for example, Summers (1999).

21 As Ocampo (2000) puts it:

> The required financial architecture should in some cases have the nature of a network of institutions that provide the services required in a complementary fashion (in the areas of emergency financing, surveillance of macroeconomic policies, prudential regulation and supervision of domestic financial systems, etc.), and in others (particularly in development finance) should exhibit the characteristics of a system of competitive organizations.

22 They have been shown to be ill-informed, erroneous, and irrelevant to the problems at hand, and as noted, also exacerbated the East Asian crises.

23 Then IMF Senior Deputy Managing Director Stanley Fischer (2001) admitted that

> willingly or otherwise, a growing number of countries have come to accept [the belief that intermediate regimes between hard pegs and free floating are unsustainable] ... Proponents of the bipolar view – myself included – have perhaps exaggerated their argument for dramatic effect.

References

ADB (Asian Development Bank) (1999) *Asian Development Outlook*, Hong Kong: Oxford University Press.

Baines, A. (2002) "Capital Mobility and European Financial and Monetary Integration: A Structural Analysis," *Review of International Studies* 28: 337–357.

Carleton, P. D., Rosario, B. P., and Woo, W. T. (2000) "The Unorthodox Origins of the Asian Financial Crisis: Evidence from Logit Estimations," *ASEAN Economic Bulletin* Special Issue, April.

Demirguc-Kunt, A. and Detragiache, E. (1998) "The Determinants of Banking Crises in Developing and Developed Countries," *IMF Staff Papers* 45(1): 81–109.

Eatwell, J. (1997) *International Financial Liberalization: The Impact on World Development*, Discussion Paper series, New York: United Nations Development Programme, Office of Development Studies.

Fischer, S. (2001) "Exchange Rate Regimes: Is the Bipolar View Correct?" *Finance and Development* 38(2): 18–21.

Furman, J. and Stiglitz, J. E. (1998) "Economic Crises: Evidence and Insights from East Asia," in *Brookings Papers on Economic Activity* no. 2. Washington, DC: Brookings Institution.

Gomez, E. T. and Jomo, K. S. (1999) *Malaysia's Political Economy: Politics, Patronage, and Profits*, Cambridge: Cambridge University Press.

IMF (1997) *World Economic Outlook: Interim Assessment*, Washington, DC: International Monetary Fund.

IMF (1998) *World Economic Outlook and International Financial Markets: Interim Assessment*, Washington, DC: International Monetary Fund.

Jomo, K. S. (ed.) (1998) *Tigers in Trouble: Financial Governance, Liberalisation and Crises in East Asia*, London: Zed Books.

Jomo, K. S. (2001a) "Growth After the Asian Crisis: What Remains of the East Asian Model?" Group of 24 Discussion Paper no. 10. Geneva and Cambridge, MA: United Nations Conference on Trade and Development and Harvard University, Kennedy School of Government.

Jomo, K. S. (ed.) (2001b) *Malaysian Eclipse: Economic Crisis and Recovery*, London: Zed Books.

Jomo, K. S. (ed.) (2004) *After The Storm: Crisis, Recovery and Sustaining Development in East Asia*, Singapore: Singapore University Press.

Jomo, K. S., Chung, C. Y., Folk, B. C., ul-Haque, I., Phongpaichit, P., Simatupang, B., and Tateishi, M. (1997) *Southeast Asia's Misunderstood Miracle: Industrial Policy and Economic Development in Thailand, Malaysia, and Indonesia*, Boulder: Westview.

Kaminsky, G. and Reinhart, C. M. (1996) "The Twin Crises: The Causes of Banking and Balance-of-Payments Problems," Working Paper no. 17, Center for International Economics, University of Maryland, Baltimore.

Keynes, J. M. (1936) *The General Theory of Employment, Interest, and Money*, New York: Harcourt Brace.

Khan, M. and Jomo, K. S. (eds) (2000) *Rents, Rent-Seeking, and Economic Development: Theory and Evidence in Asia*, Cambridge: Cambridge University Press.

Kregel, J. (1998) "East Asia Is Not Mexico: The Differences between Balance of Payments Crises and Debt Deflation," in K. S. Jomo (ed.) *Tigers in Trouble: Financial Governance, Liberalisation, and Crises in East Asia*, London: Zed Books.

Krueger, A. (2002) Speech on a sovereign debt restructuring mechanism, International Monetary Fund, Washington, DC.

Krugman, P. (1994) "The Myth of the Asian Miracle," *Foreign Affairs*, November/December.

Krugman, P. (1998a) "The Confidence Game: How Washington Worsened Asia's Crash," *The New Republic*, 5 October.

Krugman, P. (1998b) "What Happened to Asia?" Paper prepared for a conference in Japan, January. Online, available at: www.mit.edu/krugman/www/DISINTER/html.

Krugman, P. (1998c) "Will Asia Bounce Back?" Speech for Credit Suisse First Boston, Hong Kong. Online, available at: http://web.mit.edu/krugman/www.

Krugman, P. (1999) *The Return of Depression Economics*, London: Allen Lane.

Lane, T., Ghrosh, A., Hamann, J., Phillips, S., Schulze-Ghattas, M., and Tsikata, T. (1999) *IMF-Supported Programs in Indonesia, Korea, and Thailand: A Preliminary Assessment*, Washington, DC: International Monetary Fund.

McKibbin, W. (1998) "Modelling the Crisis in Asia," *ASEAN Economic Bulletin*, December.

Montes, M. F. (1998) *The Currency Crisis in Southeast Asia*, Singapore: Institute of Southeast Asian Studies.

Nasution, A. (2000) "The Meltdown of the Indonesian Economy: Causes, Responses, and Lessons," *ASEAN Economic Bulletin* Special Issue, April.

Ocampo, J. A. (2000) "A Broad Agenda for International Financial Reform," in *Financial Globalization and the Emerging Economies*, Santiago: United Nations Economic Commission for Latin America and the Caribbean.

Pasuk, P. and Baker, C. (2000) *Thailand's Crisis*, Chiang Mai, Thailand: Silkworm Books.

Pistor, K. (2000) "The Standardization of Law and Its Effect on Developing Economies," Group of 24 Discussion Paper series no. 4, Geneva and Cambridge, MA: United Nations Conference on Trade and Development and Harvard University, Center for International Development.

Radelet, S. and Sachs, J. (1998) "The East Asian Financial Crisis: Diagnosis, Remedies, Prospects," *Brookings Papers on Economic Activity* 1: 190.

Raghavan, C. (1998) "BIS Banks Kept Shovelling Funds to Asia Despite Warnings," *Third World Economics*, January: 16–31.

Rasiah, R. (2001) "Pre-Crisis Economic Weaknesses and Vulnerabilities," in K. S. Jomo (ed.) *Malaysian Eclipse: Economic Crisis and Recovery*, London: Zed Books.

Rodrik, D. (1999) "Governing the Global Economy: Does One Architectural Style Fit All?" Paper prepared for the Brookings Institution Trade Policy Forum Conference on Governing in a Global Economy, 14–16 April, Washington, DC.

Rubin, R. (1998) "Strengthening the Architecture of the International Financial System," Public statement delivered at the Brookings Institution, 14 April, Washington, DC.

Summers, L. (1999) Speech at the London Business School, 14 December, *Financial Times*, 15 December. Online, available at: www.lbs.ac.uk/news-events/scripts/summers.

UNCTAD (1997) *Trade and Development Report, 1997*, Geneva: United Nations Conference on Trade and Development.

Weisbrot, M., Naiman, R., and Kim, J. (2000) *The Emperor Has No Growth: Declining Economic Growth Rates in the Era of Globalization*, Washington, DC: Center for Economic Policy Research.

Wong, H. K. and Jomo, K. S. (2005) "Before the Storm: The Impact of Foreign Capital Inflows on the Malaysian Economy, 1966–1996," *Journal of Asia-Pacific Economy* 10(1), February: 56–69.

Wong, S. C., Jomo K. S., and Fay, C. K. (2005) *Malaysian "Bail-Outs"? Capital Controls, Restructuring & Recovery in Malaysia*, Singapore: Singapore University Press.

Woo, W. T. (2000) "Coping with Accelerated Capital Flows from the Globalization of Financial Markets," *ASEAN Economic Bulletin* Special Issue, April.

World Bank (1994) *World Development Report, 1994: Infrastructure for Development*, New York: Oxford University Press.

World Bank (1997) *World Development Report, 1997: The State in a Changing World*, New York: Oxford University Press.

Part II

Lessons learned and not learned

4 Indonesian financial crisis ten years after

An insider's view

J. Soedradjad Djiwandono

There have been many books, articles and reports, as well as conferences and seminars discussing what happened a decade ago in the economies of Asia: the causes and effects, descriptions and analyses, as well as lessons learned or not learned together with attempts to theorize about what is generally labeled as the Asian financial crisis. Curiously, there is actually no consensus which could be accepted as a single specific explanation on what caused the crisis and why it became a contagion that dramatically affected practically all aspects of human lives in so many Asian economies.

However, one could also claim that it has been generally accepted that the Asian crisis was triggered by a rapid depreciation of the Thai baht on July 2, 1997, and that weak financial institutions together with unsustainable foreign exposure of the corporate sector were very prominent. This may explain why, aside from the obvious reason of its tenth anniversary, there is tremendous interest in revisiting the crisis in different forums – especially in looking at what governments, the private sector and regional as well as multilateral institutions (and their stakeholders) have learned or not learned in order for the affected countries to avoid a repeat in the future and to cope with it better if a new crisis arises.

But discussing complex matters like the financial and economic crisis a decade ago is not an easy thing. For Indonesia, the challenge is even bigger because the crisis has been very complex indeed and in a way it is unique, as I will discuss below. In addition, I would conjecture that, as a nation, Indonesia has great difficulty in facing up to and being at peace with its own past. Writing about the Indonesian crisis is therefore difficult.

However, it is precisely because of these reasons that, after ten years, it is still relevant to talk about the Asian financial crisis. Even reminiscing about how it happened and speculating about what actually caused the contagion as well as the policy responses and reactions of the stakeholders are important lessons to learn in order to avoid similar mistakes in the future. But this is a discussion about the already much discussed events of the past, so I will highlight only the areas that, in my view, need straightening out or correction. This is what this chapter is about – an Indonesian insider's view of the Asian crisis. It will start with a descriptive analysis of what happened by looking at the similarities and differences among the affected countries, and by examining what seem to have been the causes of the crisis for Indonesia in particular. The description will also include the initial policy responses by the government, both within the context of regional cooperation and with the support of multilateral institutions – especially the International Monetary Fund (IMF) through its standby arrangements. The chapter concludes on the positive note that Indonesia is unlikely to face a similar crisis in the near future, and that Indonesia has, to some extent, learned lessons from the crisis.

Home grown but not home alone

It is instructive to look at the similarities of how the crisis developed in different economies in Asia, as well as comparing them with other cases outside Asia, both before and after the 1997 crisis. However, it is also as important, and I would even suggest that it is actually more important, to recognize their differences, as with the policy responses of the stakeholders in each crisis country, the effects of the crisis in different countries, and the lessons learned or not learned by them.

Let me mention some of the findings that others have made regarding these issues – in particular those that have either added to or corrected earlier studies, some of which have become standard interpretation. One important thing I learned from these studies is that the differences of one crisis from another seem to be more prominent than the similarities. In a way, the crisis seems to be more country-specific even though one could find certain patterns in some of the characteristics of the crisis.

In terms of its sequence, the Asian crisis started with a drastic Thai baht depreciation on July 2, 1997 – almost immediately after its flotation. But it was immediately followed by a process of contagion, spreading to other currencies in the region. There is a characteristic, which was only recently demonstrated with the publication of an article on the Asian crisis by Professor Ito (Ito, 2007), that in terms of the speed of the currency depreciation, the Asian contagion proceeded with a much slower pace than what happened with the peso in the Mexican crisis of December 1994. Second, Ito showed that the leading country in terms of currency depreciation – what he called the epicenter of the crisis – had moved from the Thai baht (July to September, 1997) and then to the Indonesian rupiah and Korean won (September 1997 to January 1998). From January 1998 the rupiah was the epicenter. After the Asian contagion, the crisis then erupted in Russia (1998), Brazil (1998–1999), Turkey (2000–2001) and Argentina (2000–2001).

Despite the consensus on the contagion of the Asian crisis across most economies in Asia, the currency depreciation turned out to be different between countries suffering from the crisis. Ito (2007) showed that there were four groups of countries in terms of the intensity of the depreciation. The Thai baht suffered the most, followed by Malaysia, Indonesia and the Philippines, followed later by Singapore and Taiwan, which suffered only mild depreciations. Meanwhile, the China renminbi and the Hong Kong dollar did not suffer depreciations, the former due to capital controls while the latter was due to the working of a hard peg system; i.e. the Hong Kong dollar was pegged to the US dollar with the effective support of a currency board.

After the crisis, most Asian currencies have strengthened, but only to levels less than their pre-crisis ones. The appreciation of currencies has not been similar for all currencies. Ten years after the crisis, the Korean won and the Singapore dollar recovered 90 to 95 percent of their respective rates. The Thai baht and the Malaysian ringgit recovered 70 percent of the pre-crisis levels, the Philippines peso 50 percent, while the Indonesian rupiah has recovered only 25 percent.

All Asian economies have also exhibited recoveries in their economic growth rates; however, their GDP growth rates (4–6 percent) are lower than the pre-crisis levels (7–9 percent) and their investment rates have also been lower than the pre-crisis levels.

The immediate issue associated with the above has been the question of undervalued currencies: which ones, by how much, and what to do about them. There has also been the issue of whether the pre- or post-crisis growth rates (and investment rates) are the normal pattern, and the related debate on whether savings gluts and investment deficits, or excessive spending and lack of savings, offers the correct explanation for the existence of global imbalances (Bernanke, 2005; Rajan, 2006; Wolf, 2007).

With a view to the numerous discussions and theories about the causes and development of the crisis, it has been my contention that the Indonesian crisis was initially triggered by external financial contagion, i.e. the rapid depreciation of the Thai baht in early July 1997, almost immediately after its floatation. But when the external contagion hit Indonesia's financial system, it ushered in a different type of domestic contagion, starting with a foreign exchange market crisis which was then followed by a banking crisis, which in turn caused a general economic crisis and ultimately led to a socio-political crisis, culminating in the fall of the 32-year reign of Soeharto in May 1998.

In the case of Indonesia, the crisis was due to two important factors – a contagious shock, which then hit an institutionally weak national economy. First, Indonesia's crisis was triggered by a financial shock in the form of contagious external currency depreciation. In other words, the Thai baht's rapid depreciation was contagious and it served as the triggering factor to the ensuing crisis. It is my contention that the trigger must be contagious. However, it does not have to be a financial shock like the rapid depreciation of the baht. It is also my contention that the trigger could come from other factors, such as economic, financial or socio-political shocks. If the shock is not contagious, a crisis may not develop. In January 1995 Indonesia experienced a currency shock originating from the Mexican crisis, which caused the currency (rupiah) to depreciate quickly. But it was easily stabilized by way of Bank Indonesia's intervention – close to USD 600 million, supported by the tightening of monetary policy and the widening of the intervention bands in a managed floating framework. This is a financial shock which does not develop into contagion, and no crisis develops.

Second, the contagion hit the Indonesian economy, whose institutions were structurally weak, i.e. the banking sector, the corporate sector, and the socio-political institutions and their governance. In this environment the trigger from the financial sector in effect brings the weaknesses out into the open and the whole system gets exposed to destructive attacks. Indonesia also suffered another currency shock in July 1996, which originated from social unrest after Megawati's Party headquarters were ransacked. The rupiah took a beating, but Bank Indonesia successfully stabilized the currency before it developed into a contagion. Of course, the intervention cost Bank Indonesia another USD 700 million of market intervention (Djiwandono, 2005).

The basic difference of the arguments and theories about the Asian crisis centers on the question of whether the causes of the crisis originated domestically – as weak fundamentals, cronyism and faulty policies – or externally, with abrupt changes in perception that triggered capital flow reversals, and which were exacerbated by a herd instinct mentality in the financial markets. It is my contention that the Indonesian crisis was caused by the combination of an external shock and domestic institutional weaknesses, and complicated further by inconsistent responses from the stakeholders, including the government, the private sector and the International Monetary Fund (IMF or the Fund). I like to use the phrase "home grown, but not home alone" to describe the causes and the process of the Indonesian crisis of 1997–1998.

An Indonesian crisis

In spite of the fact that what happened in the economies of the region is indeed a part of an Asian contagion, I would argue that over time, and with more careful assessment of what happened, one would find more differences in countries' experiences such that the Asian crisis could be considered country-specific. I would even go further and say that despite the fact that Indonesia's crisis is definitely part of the Asian contagion, it is also unique.

Academics are still debating about how to explain this phenomenon. It is also curious to note that recently the debate has turned in a different direction. In the midst of rampant domestic dissatisfaction about the slow process of reform and recovery, some have been pleasantly surprised to notice that Indonesia actually experienced a negative growth rate only in 1998. Since then it has been steadily growing to the present growth rate of close to 6 percent. The pleasant surprise comes from the fact that this has been achieved together with a democratic political process, which runs well. As some have argued, even though all crisis countries have experienced political changes, Indonesia's experience has been the most substantial (Hill and Shiraishi, 2007).

Both the similarities of Indonesia's initial conditions with other affected countries before the crisis as well as its worst position immediately after the crisis can be seen in Tables 4.1 and 4.2. The list of vulnerability indicators, including the ratio of short-term debts to GDP, and the non-performing loans in banking, show that crisis countries are similar. In some indicators, such as

Table 4.1 Vulnerability indicators

	Indonesia	*Korea*	*Thailand*	*Malaysia*
Dom debt/GDP (1992–1996)	50	50	87	82
Corp debt/equity				
1991	190	480	170	90
1996	200	640	340	200
Family controlled Cos	67.3	24.9	51.9	42.6
State Cos	15.2	19.9	24.1	34.8
Bank credits (1992–1996)	12	15	37	38
Property loans	25–30	15–25	30–40	30–40
NPLs 1996	8.8	0.8	7.7	3.9
(1998)	40	20	34	19
ST debt/res	188.9	217	121.5	45.3
Export (1996)	9.1	–2.8	–4.5	0.9
Cu Acc 1991–1995	–2.4	–1.8	–7.7	–7.6
Cu Acc 1996	–3.2	–4.4	–8.9	–4.4

Source: rearrangement of Table 2, Asian Crisis Countries: Vulnerability Indicators, Andrew Berg, "The Asia Crisis: Causes, policy responses, and outcomes," *IMF Working Paper* no. WP/99/138, p. 8 and Table 5, Assets of Corporate Relations with Banks and States, Qaizar Hussain and Clas Wihlborg, "Corporate insolvency procedures and bank behavior: A study of selected Asian economies," *IMF Working Paper*, WP/99/135, October 1999.

Table 4.2 Impacts of crisis (June 1997–March 1998, percent changes)

	Indonesia	*Korea*	*Thailand*	*Malaysia*
Nominal ER	–75	–41	–38	–33
Real EER	–63	–33	–27	–23
Nominal IR	32	12	8	3.5
GDP growth	–13.7	–5.8	–9.4	–6.7
Stock Mkt ($)	–50	–46	–58	–79
Stock Mkt (local cur)	–27	–38	–18	–38

Source: Adapted from Table 5, Andrew Berg, "The Asia Crisis: Causes, policy responses, and outcomes," *IMF Working Paper*, no. WP/99/138.

current account deficits, Indonesia's is even better. Maybe the indicator of company ownership as a proxy for cronyism is the only sign which definitely shows Indonesia as much larger in comparison to the others. Table 4.2 clearly shows that Indonesia suffered the most in terms of the immediate impacts of the crisis as seen by the negative GDP growth rate, the currency depreciation and the performance of the capital market.

The Indonesian crisis is in a way unique. Despite exhibiting similar initial conditions or vulnerabilities with other crisis countries and despite generally being recognized for coming up with prudent policy responses initially, it ultimately became a basket case, suffering the worst and taking the longest time to recover. At present, ten years after the crisis, most Asian economies with the exception of China, still exhibit lower economic growth rates and lower levels of investment compared to the pre-crisis levels. Despite much improvement after the crisis, the exchange rates of the Asian currencies are still worse than their pre-crisis levels. Indonesia is also experiencing continuing improvements, however it has been performing worse among the former crisis countries in most of the above indicators.

Some have argued that Indonesia fared the worst in the crisis due to government policies and Bank Indonesia actions. This argument is either unfair or incorrect. Many policies and steps were adopted by Bank Indonesia both as part of and independent from the Government of Indonesia's efforts to address the crisis and beyond. Some of the prominent policies to address the crisis included the decision to free float the rupiah in mid-August 1997, the policy to provide liquidity supports to all banks suffering from liquidity mismatches, the closure of 16 banks in early November 1997, and the debate on the possible introduction of a rupiah peg with a currency board – popularly known as the currency board system (CBS) in January 1998.

The government decision to free float the national currency on August 14, 1997 caught the Indonesian business community off-guard. It was hailed by many as pre-emptive when it was issued, but it was also accused by others of being unwarranted. The currency was depreciating rapidly afterward, partly due to business and public responses to government policies to address the crisis, which included the business community's action to buy dollars either to cut losses or to fly to safety with their financial assets. The government's and Bank Indonesia's policies to tighten the fiscal and monetary stance in response triggered the domestic contagion. And thus contagion spread from a currency shock into a banking crisis, then to a general economic crisis which led to the collapse of banks and the corporate sector through the balance sheet effects. With the benefit of hindsight, the doubling of interest rates by the central bank on its certificates (Sertifikat Bank Indonesia or SBI), the government instruction for state banks to transfer their deposits to central bank certificates, and the curtailment of routine budgetary expenditures that were meant to strengthen the exchange rate in a situation where banks were in distress, were indeed too stringent. This may explain why the policy actions failed.

The decision to invite the International Monetary Fund (IMF) in early September 1997 was made with the aim of propping-up market and public confidence in the economy and to bolster the management of the economy. This led to various actions, including comprehensive bank restructuring and the closure of insolvent banks. In fact, bank closures were a prior action program which served as a precondition for the IMF to agree to providing a standby loan.

Unfortunately for Indonesia, the bank closures were not just failing to bring back market confidence, they actually triggered bank runs and brought the banking sector near to total collapse. It turned out that the bank closures, in combination with tightening the monetary and fiscal stance, wound up pushing distressed banks into a real banking crisis.

There have been many discussions on the merits and demerits of the bank closures, including who is to blame as in other issues. On the debate about why the bank closures did not succeed different arguments have been raised. Many have argued that the bank closures failed because Indonesia did not have deposit insurance when the closures were made (Radelet and Sachs, 1998). Others have argued that more banks should have been liquidated (Goldstein, 1998). I do not agree with the argument about the absence of a deposit insurance scheme as the culprit. Most deposit guarantee schemes only cover small depositors, which Indonesia provided at the time of the closures. The problem arose from the big depositors, not from small ones, which a normal deposit guarantee scheme would not cover. It seems plausible that, if only Indonesia introduced an overall guarantee as the one introduced toward end of January 1998 (blanket guarantee), the bank closures of November 1997 might not have caused bank runs. I should add that if only all owners of the liquidated banks were behaving well, instead of protesting the closures by waging a public campaign criticizing the bank closures policy and suing the Minister of Finance and Bank Indonesia's governor in court, bank runs might have been avoided.

The most controversial policy was the provision of Bank Indonesia liquidity supports (BLBI) to banks experiencing liquidity mismatches during the crisis. It was controversial in several aspects. This policy caused the bank restructuring program to be estimated at close to 50 percent of the nation's GDP, the highest among the crisis countries with a huge amount of public money to finance it. Furthermore, the policy has been associated with cases of corruption by officials and bank owners. Even today, the public perception has predominantly been that BI liquidity supports were a mistake, which unfairly put the burden onto taxpayers, and that the onus should be borne by Bank Indonesia since it introduced the policy. For sure, there have been corruption cases involving bankers. Three of my colleagues, all former Bank Indonesia managing directors, were jailed – curiously, not for corrupting money but for violating internal measures and acting imprudently in the decision to provide BLBI. The story has not come to a close yet, and up to the present there are still accusations being leveled at current and former Bank Indonesia officials on these issues. BLBI has become a "scarlet letter" for Bank Indonesia and its officials.

I have been writing in different places on these issues (Djiwandono, 2004). I will only put down a few brief notes here. First, the findings of the audit by the supreme audit board (BPK) showed that the total amount of the BI liquidity supports to banks up to January 1999 was 144 trillion rupiah (close to USD 70 billion at the current rate). Some consider this amount equivalent to the loss to the state finance, without any consideration given to the amount of repayments by some of the banks and the revenues generated from the sales of assets of the recipient banks or even the sales of these banks themselves by the Indonesian Bank Restructuring Agency (BPPN). Second, the public generally perceived that the number of banks receiving the liquidity supports is only the number of banks managed by BPPN, i.e. 54 banks. However, the actual number of banks receiving the liquidity supports during the crisis was over 130. But not all recipient banks became problem banks that had to be managed by BPPN.

Arguments have been very strong that the total amount of the liquidity supports as mentioned before was the same as the total amount of the losses. Only a few seem to go back to economics and the alternative cost concept, like what would have been the cost to the economy had there been no liquidity supports provided to banks during the crisis. Would the government (BPPN) still have any right to sell privately owned banks after the crisis if there were no liquidity supports? In terms of policy, the liquidity supports for banks provided by Bank Indonesia were completely acknowledged by the recipient banks, which justified the government's claim to these banks. Would there still be 136 banks now in operation, which are relatively in good condition, had there been no liquidity supports during the crisis? Isn't there any difference between cost and loss? For sure, a thorough analysis would have to make this distinction to be able to come up with the actual figure of the economic and financial loss of the policy.

Bank Indonesia liquidity support certainly incurred costs and losses to the nation's economy. However, it is curious that almost no discussions were ever made on the cost of bank recapitalization, which cost more than four times the amount of the liquidity supports. And out of the total cost of bank recapitalization the biggest amount was recapitalization of state-owned banks. It is my view that the liquidity supports that the central bank provided during the crisis and the bank recapitalization of 1999 are similar in character; the former was designed to help banks facing a liquidity mismatch, while the latter sought to help banks facing a "capital mismatch" which could lead to solvency problems.

I should also give a proper explanation here on the debate about the rumor of President Soeharto's intention in January 1998 for returning to a peg system with the creation of a currency board and the rumor of my disagreement with that intention, as well as the perceived reasons for my dismissal as central bank governor. I did not support the idea of a peg system with a currency board then. But the main reason was the concern that I could not see a consistent implementation of a currency board system under the current conditions at the time. It was hard to see President Soeharto allowing the system to go on its course without his high propensity to intervene or tinker. A CBS is sometimes called "an auto-piloted system" whereby nobody should be allowed to tinker. I was also concerned that our reserves were not sufficient to back a currency board. But ultimately the idea was discarded in my opinion due to the mounting pressures from leaders of many Western countries against the plan, in addition to a Bank Indonesia memorandum to the President which basically showed that the adoption of a currency board was not feasible at that time.

Be that as it may, the Indonesian crisis is indeed very complex. There were both external and domestic factors at work to ultimately cause the Indonesian crisis. I do not subscribe to a single factor explanation to describe the crisis. However, if I were to mention the most important factor in explaining how the crisis developed into a multifaceted contagion, I have to pick inconsistency as the main problem. In fact, inconsistencies between different programs, between the programs and their implementations, and inconsistencies committed by the government, the private sector as well as the IMF in its involvements in the Fund-supported programs (Djiwandono, 2003). Basically, inconsistencies destroyed market confidence, which fueled contagion in the national economy, then spread to the social structure and the political system, and culminated in the toppling of a strong regime that ruled for more than three decades.

Is Indonesia facing a repeat of the 1997 crisis?

Have Indonesians learned from the past crisis? Actually the question should be addressed to all parties involved in the crisis and its resolution. Stan Fischer (Fischer, 2001) reminded us just before leaving the Fund that all parties, including the national governments, the multilateral institutions and private sector actors from lender as well as borrowing countries, have to make adjustments and reforms in order to be able to cope with another crisis.

With respect to Indonesia, much has been done, yet much more still needs to be done for the country to be effective in avoiding a repeat of the 1997 crisis and to face new challenges. Rather than looking at what has been done in terms of building up and maintaining proper institutions for policies to work effectively in avoiding another financial crisis and maintaining stability for future development of the national economy, I would conjecture that recent developments in the Indonesian financial system show that the danger of a repeat of the 1997 crisis is insignificant indeed.

The recent high volume of short-term capital inflows, as reported in the capital market performance, in tandem with strong property development resemble the developments shortly before 1997, and have raised concerns among government officials, including the Minister of Finance, of a possible repeat of a financial crisis. However, I think a repeat of the 1997 financial crisis is not highly likely at the moment since both the conditions of the Asian economies in general as well as domestic conditions, including Indonesia, have not generated strong motivations for market players to make moves that would trigger a shock which could develop into a contagion of the 1997 type.

The Asian economies are generally in better shape compared to the conditions in 1996/1997. The most important factors have been the accumulation of foreign reserves by almost all economies in Asia. The total reserves of East Asian economies are around USD 3.5 trillion with China alone holding USD 1.2 trillion. Even Indonesia holds more than USD 50 billion of reserves. The current accounts of most East Asian economies have been in good shape. In addition, despite no standard pattern or well-established cooperation among Asian economies, the exchange rate system in most economies in East Asia is more flexible compared to the past, generally closer to a floating system than fixed. Because of these two favorable factors in most East Asian economies, I do not see that there are enough incentives for market players to make a move for profit-taking that would trigger a contagion.

Furthermore, Indonesia's domestic conditions in terms of the banking system and other institutional structures are also less prone to a contagion as compared to the pre-1997 conditions. The banking sector is not as weak as in the past. The average capital adequacy ratio (CAR) of Indonesian banks is currently around 20, while just before the crisis in 1997 it was substantially less than the required eight. The average loan to deposit ratio of banks in Indonesia is currently around 60 percent, while in 1996 it was over 80 percent. At present, banks' foreign short-term exposures are much smaller than in the past, and private sector foreign exposures are also much less. The prudential measures and their compliance as well as the conduct of monetary policy and the lender of last resort by Bank Indonesia have undergone much improvement after the crisis. In addition, both social and political infrastructures are more robust now than in the past. I do not think that if a financial shock struck Indonesia today it would cause a second type of contagion that would cause financial crisis.

Thus, from both external as well as domestic environments, it is my conjecture that despite the fact that the financial sector continues to face a variety of risks, the danger of a repeat of the crisis is not imminent. However, this should not make Indonesia and indeed Asian economies complacent. The world economy is facing new and different challenges: the presence of unsustainable global imbalances which imply the presence of a huge risk for dealing with the implications of their unwinding to name one of the obvious dangers.

The most recent financial problems, originating from the collapse of some subprime mortgages, have raised valid concerns that if we are ready for addressing a crisis, it may only be for the last battle – that is no guarantee against new challenges, which may be completely different in nature from the past Asian crisis.

References

Berg, A. (1999) "The Asian Crisis: Causes, Policy Responses, Outcomes," *IMF Working Paper*, WP/99/138, Washington, DC: International Monetary Fund.

Bernanke, B.S. (2005) *The Global Saving Glut and the US Current Account Deficit*, Remarks at Sandridge Lecture, Virginia Association of Economics, Richmond, VA. Online, available at: www.federalreserve.gov.

Djiwandono, J.S. (2003) "Role of the IMF in Indonesian Financial Crisis," in H. Soesastro, A. Smith and H. Mui Ling (eds.) *Governance in Indonesia*, Singapore: Institute of Southeast Asian Studies.

Djiwandono, J.S. (2004) "Liquidity Support to Banks During Indonesia's Financial Crisis," *Bulletin of Indonesian Economic Studies* 40, no. 1: 59–75.

Djiwandono, J.S. (2005) *Bank Indonesia and the Crisis; An Insider's View*, Singapore: Institute of Southeast Asian Studies.

Fischer, S. (2001) "Asia and the IMF," Remark at the Institute of Policy Studies, Singapore. Online, available at: www.imf.org/external/np/speeches/2001/060101.htm.

Goldstein, M. (1998) *The Asian Financial Crisis: Causes, Cures, and Systemic Implications*, Washington, DC: Institute for International Economics.

Hill, H. and Shiraisi, T. (2007) "Indonesia after the Asian Crisis," *Asian Economic Policy Review*, Volume 2, Issue 1: 123–141.

Hussain, Q. and Wihlborg, C. (1999) "Corporate Insolvency Procedures and Bank Behavior: A Study of Selected Asian Countries," *IMF Working Paper*, WP/99/135, Washington, DC: IMF.

Ito, T. (2007) "Asian Currency Crisis and the International Monetary Fund," *Asian Economic Policy Review*, Volume 2, Issue 1: 16–49.

Radelet, S. and Sachs, J. (1998) "The East-Asian Financial Crisis: Diagnosis, Remedies, Prospects," *Brookings Papers on Economic Activity*, Washington, DC: The Brookings Institution.

Rajan, R.G. (2006) *Perspective of Global Imbalances*, Remarks at the Global Financial Imbalances Conference, London. Online, available at: www.imf.org.

Wolf, M. (2007) "Global Capital Flows; Who Are the Villains and Victims?" *The Straits Times*, June 14.

5 The Asian financial crisis ten years later

What lessons have we learned?

Anwar Ibrahim

The task before us today is daunting indeed. So much has been written and said about the Asian financial crisis that one runs the risk of flogging a dead horse. The academic discourse on this too has been as phenomenal as the crisis itself. We run the risk of hair-splitting, or getting drowned in a sea of statistics or having our vision blurred by the dazzling display of multicolored pie charts and towering graphs. But while it is very easy to be an armchair critic, learning the lessons from the crisis is much more difficult. I am reminded of the saying by the late John Kenneth Galbraith that this is not the age of doctrine; it is the age of practical judgment, the world of intelligent thought and action, not of adherence to controlling doctrine (Galbraith, 1996). There is only that much that theory can offer. We are after all talking about real situations here, as real as the fact that even as we sit here today, the world's financial markets are again in turmoil because of the crisis in US sub-prime mortgages. We are again seeing central banks, particularly in Southeast Asia, defending their currencies against panic selling, dumping millions of US dollars in market interventions.

I need not revisit the stark facts of this crisis but being a student of literature all my life and a firm believer that life can actually imitate art, let me begin with a short verse from Dante in his *Divine Comedy*:

> *A heavy clap of thunder! I awoke*
> *From the deep sleep that drugged my mind – startled,*
> *The way one is when shaken out of sleep.*

Sure enough, on the morning of July 2, 1997 a heavy clap of thunder reverberated across the financial markets of East Asia, shook us out of our slumber and signaled the start of a financial crisis unparalleled since the Great Depression. From Thailand, the turmoil spread to the Philippines, Indonesia, then Malaysia and Singapore. The other Asian countries followed suit, then Russia and Latin America. GDPs tumbled and unemployment rose to 18 million at the end of 1998. The speed of the contagion was totally unexpected, but can anyone of us deny that the writing was already on the wall? Ten years later, the question remains: have we learnt anything?

First, I think no one seriously disputes that there should be a major change in the principles and policies on which the Bretton Woods institutions work. A one-size-fits-all policy has been proven to have greater chances of failure than success under the global system. The need for diversity becomes all the more pressing. Hence, I make no apologies about criticizing the neo-liberal Washington Consensus and the IMF's standard formulae for borrowing countries. We are told that the IMF has already addressed this fundamental issue but it appears that neither sufficient thought nor serious commitment has been given to it. We are still left asking the question ten years after: Where is that new global financial architecture that was to come about after this wave of creative destruction?

The IMF prescription for privatizations is now recognized to be not only undemocratic but economically unsound. This is especially so where the pre-requisites are not in place. Among them are good governance, transparency and accountability. Just recently the Malaysian government unveiled a series of development projects which are so massive that the word "mega" doesn't even come close to describing their magnitude. Obviously, my concern is not against development per se, but when you have an undertaking three times the size of Singapore that would incur tens of billions of ringgit of taxpayers' money, the parceling out of projects and the awarding of contracts is surely a matter of great concern. Without the prerequisites that must be fulfilled for such a colossal enterprise, privatization will be a passport for plundering. That such banditry can happen is not a mere possibility but a near certainty.

Friendly policies and "pro-growth initiatives" may generate an even bigger pie but without those prerequisites this pie will be devoured only by the select few at the expense of the more deserving majority. And when a crisis breaks out, it is this majority who will bear the brunt. One of the most enduring lessons, therefore, is that in a financial crisis of the kind that we are talking about, the cronies and friends of the powers that be get away unscathed or, if they do get into trouble, they will be the first to be bailed out. The lifeboats are reserved for them in times of trouble. In good times, they get the icing on the economic cake and this applies across the board: water services, waste disposal, telecommunications and ports (speaking of which, at the time of writing, in Malaysia, a 5 billion ringgit port scandal is about to explode and it goes back to the issues of good governance, transparency and accountability).

Another lesson perhaps is the lesson about prudence or more accurately the lack of it. We also call it moral hazard. At the outbreak of the crisis, public investment expenditure in Malaysia surged, pushing the total investment to GDP ratio to 46 percent in 1997, the highest in the region. Through the 1990s, there had been a continuous increase in the share of investment in domestic aggregate expenditure, from about 35 percent early in the decade to over 46 percent in 1997. Mega projects required mega borrowings. Bankers were intimidated by the political connections of the big borrowers. Through such intimidation, "moral suasion" and collusion of interests, the entire banking system became hostage to a handful of borrowers whose debts made up more than half of the entire lending of the banking system. This was vintage moral hazard. There's much wisdom in Polonius's dictum that one should "neither a borrower nor a lender be for loan oft loses both itself and friend and borrowing dulls the edge of husbandry."[1] Of course, adopting this advice would mean the collapse of the entire banking and financial system but the truth remains that excessive leverage was one of the key causes of the crisis. One should not be faulted for erring on the side of caution.

Third, as regards managing the economy, my view is this: There must be flexibility and common sense. The rule should be Hayekian free enterprise with a dose of Keynesian fiscal remedy every now and then. This is the middle path. It has been said that Aristotle's recommendation of the Golden Mean was an attempt to evade the inadequacy of absolute maxims. There must not be too much of anything, even of the virtues. Just as too much courage is rashness, too much generosity is extravagance and too much accuracy is hair-splitting (Barzun, 1983: 94). In Islam we call it the *awsatuha*, just as we are familiar with the *chung yung* of Confucius. Translated into practical terms, it means that when the economy is underperforming below its potential, increased public expenditures would be needed. Obviously, fiscal discipline must be maintained to ensure that the consequent fiscal imbalance remains within manageable levels at all times.

As Finance Minister, I had on occasions endorsed pump-priming programs geared toward stimulating the economy. I had committed major expenditure for projects clearly underlined with the agenda for social justice: public health, education and human resource training, basic infrastructure and industry, public housing and rural development. Direct fiscal action such as tax reduction, public job creation, and other fiscal measures to expand demand is the hallmark of a caring state based on the humane economy, and should be recommended. But I must immediately lodge a caveat here: At the level of implementation, pump-priming measures, unless executed transparently and with an even hand, will be misused. In the hands of unscrupulous and corrupt leaders and politicians, such measures become a mere metaphor for the siphoning of taxpayers' money to line the pockets of their cronies and relatives.

Fourth, and this flows from the preceding issue, social justice must remain a long-term objective. So, how does that leave my professed belief in the free market? Adam Smith's laissez-faire economy postulated the invisible hand to maximize individual welfare and economic efficiency. With David Hume, and then fine-tuned by the Austrian school, Hayek being the most ardent of the exponents, the doctrine was that economies must be allowed to develop by spontaneous order.[2] The injunction is that state intervention should be avoided like the plague. But while the spirit may be willing, the flesh could be weak and in this regard the invisible hand has invariably demonstrated its fragility under the crushing weight of monopolist suppliers and rent-seekers alike. The dictum against state intervention is valid to prevent the overbearing tendency toward totalitarianism. But it has been shown time and again that the free market capitalist system has generated externalities that have led to gross inequalities of income distribution. So I am not totally with him either. Enough has already been seen in the history of free market that points to the exploitation of the poor by the rich whether they are individuals, corporations or countries. Unemployment goes up, wages remain stagnant or worse still, fall, while prices go up. Neo-liberals will tell us that price inflation is inevitable in a well-functioning economy and given time things will find their equilibrium; intervention will only worsen the situation. But my view is that the invisible hand should start making itself seen to ensure that such inflation is within limits. Disparities in purchasing power are real and cannot be analyzed purely from the halls of academia or the detached corridors of power. Governments must be committed to the principle that a more equitable distribution of income is a fundamental precept for the realization of social justice. They should undertake, with full conviction, integrated plans for poverty reduction in the long run while ensuring a comprehensive support system for the poor and economically marginalized. In other words, we can subscribe to Hayek only up to a point at which neo-liberalism must make way for the paternalism of Keynes. Some call this Dr. Jekyll and Mr. Hyde economics. I call it humane economics.

Fifth, regardless of whether the economy is developing or developed, or in the Rostovian sense, at the stage of take-off or high mass consumption, the right of workers to associate and protect their interests must be central. I subscribe to the view that income distribution is very much an issue of political power as it is of economic power. Such power must be checked by the principles of governance and accountability. Ten years after the crisis, we see the deterioration in the fabric of the institutions we have empowered to represent us. Politicians in public office are not just reneging on their promises of social justice, but are scandalizing the institutions of power with abuse and corrupt practices.

Yet another lesson that may be drawn concerns the issue of the liberalization of the capital account. I know this is stirring up a hornets' nest. Let me be the first to say that it is not the be-all and end-all. We are familiar with the negative impact of short-term capital on an economy with weak financial sectors. Countless tomes have been written about this. Nevertheless, as I had advocated before, I believe there is a case for such a measure to be introduced in phases, taking into account the macroeconomic situation, the stage of development of its financial institutions, and the impact of existing controls. We will recall that recently, the Malaysian Central Bank embarked exactly on this course by first unpegging the ringgit to the dollar and substituting it with a mixed managed float instead. Indonesia, for instance, successfully liberalized its capital account very early in the reform process.

We need to acknowledge, therefore, that imposing capital outflow controls to deal with a short-term crisis may be tempting but the long-term consequences are likely to be adverse. It would undermine the systemic ability to respond to a changing environment. To my mind, imposing capital controls was to treat only the symptoms. The lesson therefore is: in as much as the Bretton Woods institutions need reform, the respective governments in the region here are also in need of structural reform in the economic and political spheres.

It has often been argued that the emphasis on political freedom, liberties and democracy is a specifically Western priority. Economic development, it is said, must precede freedom. Empty stomachs do not shout for liberty, but for food. But why should development become a trade-off for un-freedom? Why should fundamental liberties be eroded and dissent muzzled in the name of development? If development is to enlarge freedom, then substantial development enlarges freedom substantially, for "it is hard to think that any process of substantial development can do without very extensive use of markets" (Sen, 1999: 7). The difference is clear: extensive use of markets does not mean letting market forces go out of control in as much as freedom cannot be absolute. In the words of Nobel laureate Amartya Sen: "Statecraft, which will necessarily warrant social support and public regulations, cannot be precluded when they can enrich – rather than impoverish – human lives."[3]

The claim that Malaysia has emerged triumphantly out of the crisis is empty. As the numbers show, Malaysia is significantly falling behind its Southeast Asian neighbors. We would have thought that among the most important lessons learnt is that unstable debt/GDP dynamics is a glaring red flag for the onset of financial crisis. It would appear that this basic lesson has not been learnt.

South Korea and Singapore are still leading the pack in showing budget surpluses over GDP. Thailand posted small surpluses in 2003 and 2004 and currently registers balanced budgets whilst Indonesia has been incurring deficit budgets year after year since the crisis. But Malaysia chalks up the highest deficit/GDP ratio among the countries affected by the crisis with low sovereign rating.

I am aware I will be accused of being the proverbial dog in the manger. But let me put this to rest. I will say that much good has come out of this and great strides have been made in various areas which will help to fortify the economies in the region when crisis strikes again. Various reputable studies show that in the area of trade, for example, intraregional exports have almost tripled, China being at the center and the rest are riding piggy-back. Ten years after, considerably much more has been expended on research and development while higher education has come on in leaps and bounds. The same is said about resource allocation, reduction of systemic risk and the gaining of financial depth.[4] But invariably this perspective is only useful when talking in general terms. Some countries are lucky to be endowed with oil and so they get oil money and this may be the primary thing sustaining the economy. Yet other economies have had a headstart even before the crisis, and with their infrastructures intact, have been able to recover faster. However, if we go beyond this veneer, reality bites hard.

For most Southeast Asian countries, there is little to show in the manufacturing sector, key industries and in the production of services to enhance global competitiveness. Malaysia, for example, needs a new economic agenda to propel the country to meet the challenges of global competition.

And finally, in the context of a regional free market, the efforts within ASEAN are more palpable even though unfortunately no intraregional financial integration appears in sight in the near future. But that should only strengthen our resolve to work for greater cohesiveness. Deeper integration means better capacity and preparedness to counter the fluctuations of capital inflows and we cannot talk about integration without mentioning liberalization again. But liberalization must be mutual, collective and coterminous.

When Caesar came upon the land and uttered those three famous phrases what was left unsaid was his immaculate game plan, iron resolve and practical judgment to achieve his ends. Recalling Galbraith's dictum that this is indeed the age of practical judgment and not of adherence to controlling doctrine, let me end by saying that with intelligent thought and action, a deep resolve to learn from the lessons of history and, most importantly, a profound commitment to the principles of accountability and good governance, we would be better placed to face the future ten years from now.

Notes

1 *Hamlet*, Act I, Scene III.
2 Hayek, 1972; also 1988.
3 Sen, ibid.
4 See Khara, 2007.

References

Barzun, J. (1983) *A Stroll With William James*, New York: Harper & Row.
Dante, A. (1985) *The Divine Comedy*, New York: Oxford University Press.
Galbraith, J.K. (1996) *The Good Society – The Humane Agenda*, Boston: Houghton Mifflin.
Hayek, F.A. (1972) *The Road To Serfdom*, Chicago: The University of Chicago Press.
—— (1988) *The Fatal Conceit – The Errors of Socialism*, Chicago: The University of Chicago Press.
Khara, H. (2007) "Ten Years After the East Asian Crisis: A Resurgent and Restructured Region," Washington, DC: The Brookings Institution.
Sen, A. (1999) *Development As Freedom*, New York: Oxford University Press.
Shakespeare, W. (1987) *Hamlet*, New York: Oxford University Press.

6 Ten years from the financial crisis

Managing the challenges posed by capital flows

Khor Hoe Ee and Kit Wei Zheng

Ten years ago, what started off as a currency crisis in Thailand quickly evolved into a much broader economic, social and political crisis engulfing the whole region. Although the crisis only directly affected four countries – Thailand, Indonesia, Malaysia and Korea – few countries in the region were left unscathed. As the crisis unfolded, the collapse of stock markets, currencies and banks, widespread bankruptcy and unemployment brought about social unrest and the overthrow of longstanding political leaders across the region. So in many ways, the Asian financial crisis proved to be a watershed event in the history of the region. The tenth anniversary of the crisis has provided an opportunity to take stock on how Asia has fared since and assess the new challenges posed by the return of capital flows into the region.

This chapter will not go into detail on the causes of the crisis, on which there is already a massive pool of literature.[1] Rather, the chapter focuses on a relatively narrow but central aspect of the crisis, that is, the ability of countries in the region to manage capital flows and their resilience to financial shocks. In the authors' view, the immediate cause of the crisis was a classic case of investor panic that triggered a massive withdrawal of capital from the region, leading to a liquidity crunch that evolved into a broader financial and macroeconomic crisis. Nonetheless, it is also clear that the crisis would not have become as severe as it did, if the fundamentals were stronger. Excessive investments in properties and mega infrastructure projects led to large and persistent current account deficits, which were funded mostly by short-term foreign currency denominated bank loans. These excesses were aided and abetted by weaknesses in institutional and governance structures. Once the crisis started, the dynamics and the management of the crisis further deepened its severity. The international community was not prepared for such a crisis and scrambled to put together rescue packages and programs which were not totally credible and effective. These factors interacted with each other in a malignant fashion, causing the initial liquidity crisis to spiral into a broader solvency, economic and eventually a political crisis.

This chapter is organized as follows. The first section reviews how Asia has fared since the crisis, focusing on different aspects of income and output. This will be followed by an examination of the challenges posed by the return of capital flows to the region, and Asia's ability to cope with these challenges. The chapter then assesses some of the other prevailing risks, as well as benefits arising from large capital inflows, and concludes with a summary of the main findings.

One decade after the crisis – a stocktake

As the financial crisis was marked by a collapse of regional currencies, a useful starting point is to see how Asian currencies have fared since then. Figures 6.1 and 6.2 show the performance of Asian currencies against the US dollar. While Asian currencies have generally appreciated in recent years, most, with the exception of the Korean won, are still well below their pre-crisis levels.

An examination of real income *levels* in Asia paints a rather positive picture. After falling by between 7–13 percent in 1998, real GDP in all the four crisis-hit economies had recovered to their 1997 levels by 2003, and were 22–45 percent higher than their 1997 levels by 2006 (Figures 6.3 and 6.4). Korea's recovery proved to be the swiftest amongst the crisis-affected economies, with real GDP recovering to its pre-crisis level as early as 1999. For the other economies, real incomes are more than 40–50 percent higher than in 1997, with China having more than doubled its real GDP over the past decade.

The recovery in income levels is just as impressive when measured in US$ terms (Figures 6.5 and 6.6). For most countries, this largely reflects the real GDP growth and appreciation of their currencies against the US dollar, especially in the past three years. For Indonesia, which suffered the most severe fall in real income, this also reflects the higher wage growth and inflation rates. Interestingly, for Hong Kong, Taiwan and Singapore, nominal GDP in US dollar terms appears to have increased more moderately, because of deflation or very low inflation rates. In terms

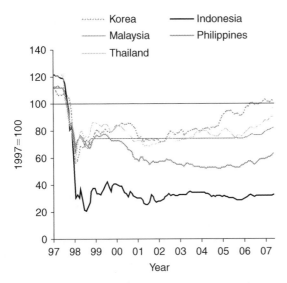

Figure 6.1 Bilateral exchange rate against the US dollar– crisis four (source: CEIC Data Company Limited).

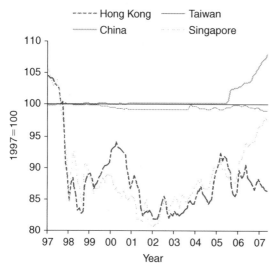

Figure 6.2 Bilateral exchange rate against the US dollar – other Asia (source: CEIC Data Company Limited).

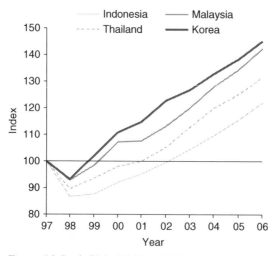

Figure 6.3 Real GDP (1997 = 100) – crisis four (source: CEIC Data Company Limited).

of per capita incomes, countries are also well above their 1997 levels, whether measured in purchasing power parity (PPP) terms, or in nominal US$ terms.

Despite the strong recovery in output *levels*, the *growth rate* of real output has generally been lower during the post-crisis period, suggesting that the region's recovery, while impressive, may not be fully complete. Table 6.1 shows real GDP growth rates since the 1980s. After growing between 7–10 percent in the early 1990s, growth collapsed in 1998. Indonesia was the worst affected, as real GDP contracted by more than 13 percent in 1998, as the collapse of the currency, run on the

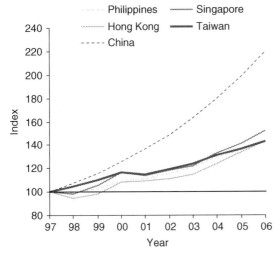

Figure 6.4 Real GDP (1997 = 100) – other Asia (source: CEIC Data Company Limited).

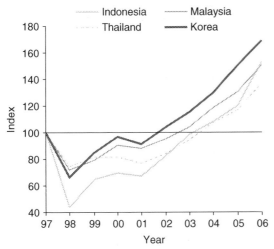

Figure 6.5 US$ nominal GDP – crisis four (source: CEIC Data Company Limited).

banking sector and ensuing social and political unrest took their toll on domestic demand. Real GDP growth in most of Asia has recovered to the 4–6 percent range but remains about 2–3 percentage points below the growth rates of the 1990s.

The slower real GDP growth rates in the post-crisis period partly reflect the sluggish recovery in fixed investments. Although the levels of fixed investments have recovered from the trough, investment-to-GDP ratios are still 5–20 percentage points below 1997 levels in all the Asian economies except in China (Figures 6.7–6.10). The lower rates of investments may not necessarily be bad, as the pre-crisis rates were obviously too high and not sustainable, especially since a

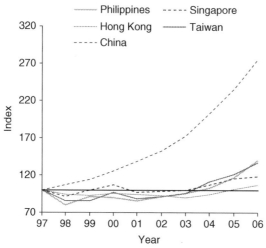

Figure 6.6 US$ nominal GDP – other Asia (source: CEIC Data Company Limited).

Table 6.1 Average annual real GDP growth

	1980–1990	1991–1996	1997	1998	1999–2006
Hong Kong	7.2	5.4	5.1	−5.5	5.3
Korea	7.8	7.7	4.7	−6.9	5.7
Taiwan	7.9	7.0	6.6	4.5	4.0
Indonesia	5.9	7.4	4.7	−13.1	4.4
Malaysia	6.2	9.6	7.3	−7.4	5.6
Philippines	2.1	2.8	5.2	−0.6	4.6
Thailand	7.6	8.1	−1.4	−10.5	5.0
Singapore	7.7	8.7	8.3	−1.4	5.7

Source: IMF WEO April 2006.

significant proportion was invested in non-productive sectors. Thus, the slow recovery in fixed investments is partly an adjustment to the excess capacity built up during the pre-crisis period. Other factors contributing to the slow recovery could be the stricter credit policy of the banks and the decline in foreign direct investments in some of the economies. Even so, the adjustment period appears to have been unusually prolonged, and supply-side bottlenecks, for example in infrastructure, have already started to appear. For growth to be sustained at a higher rate, it may be necessary for fixed investments to recover more fully.

Coping with the challenges posed by capital flows

The region's economic recovery and the prospect of earning attractive returns on Asian assets have led to a massive resurgence of foreign capital inflows in recent years, not unlike the situation in the early 1990s. Figure 6.11 shows that the

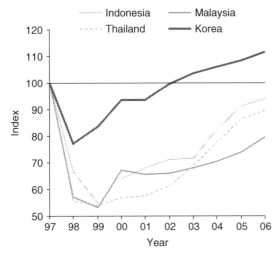

Figure 6.7 Real gross fixed capital formation – crisis four (source: CEIC Data Company Limited).

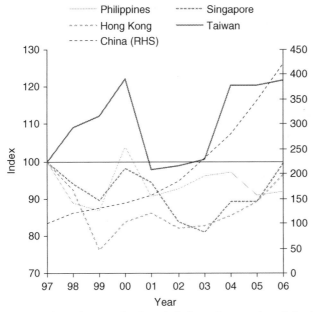

Figure 6.8 Real gross fixed capital formation – other Asia (source: CEIC Data Company Limited).

surge of gross foreign capital inflows in early 1990s was followed by massive outflows in 1997–1998. However, since 2002 foreign capital has once again returned to these countries. Indeed since 2005, the value of such flows has exceeded the pre-crisis peaks. As a proportion to GDP, these foreign capital inflows are now close to the peak of 5.5 percent in 1996.

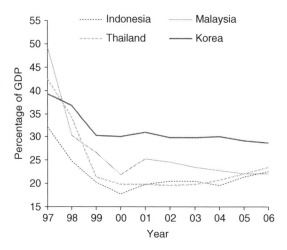

Figure 6.9 Fixed investments to GDP ratio – crisis four (source: CEIC Data Company Limited).

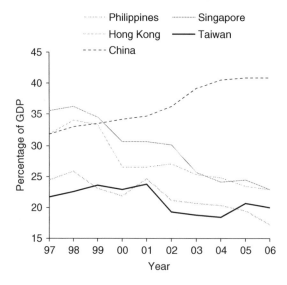

Figure 6.10 Fixed investments to GDP ratio – other Asia (source: CEIC Data Company Limited).

The present resurgence of capital inflows should be seen in the broader historical context of the post-Bretton Woods period, when capital accounts were liberalized in the industrialized countries. Figure 6.12 shows that net private capital flows to emerging markets first experienced a large upswing in the 1970s, especially to Latin America, before reversing in the early 1980s during the Latin America debt crisis. There was another sharp cyclical upswing in capital flows from 1990 to 1996, especially to developing Asia,

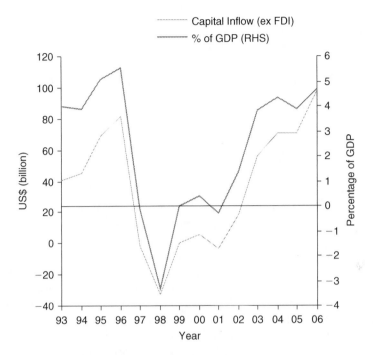

Figure 6.11 Gross capital inflows, excluding FDI – ASEAN-4, Korea and Taiwan
(source: CEIC Data Company Limited).

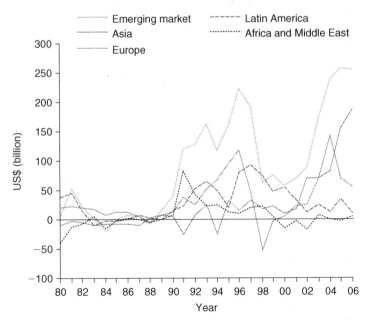

Figure 6.12 Net private capital inflows to emerging markets (source: IMF WEO).

which subsequently reversed following the Asian financial crisis. The current wave of private capital flows to emerging markets started sometime in 2002, driven by the search for yields as interest rates in the developed countries were at record lows.

Besides the larger volume of private capital flows, the post-Bretton Woods period has also been characterized by increased *volatility* of such capital flows, as shown in Table 6.2. In the 1980s, this was mainly due to volatility of net flows to Latin America. In the 1990s, it was Asia that experienced greater volatility of capital flows, especially during the Asian financial crisis. Volatility of capital flows to Asia has also been high in the more recent period.

The situation in the post-Bretton Woods period can thus be characterized as one whereby smaller emerging economies have had to manage the increased volatility of capital flows originating from industrialized countries. The increased magnitude and volatility of capital flows can be thought of, in some sense, as an exogenous shock imposed on emerging markets' economies. Boom–bust cycles in emerging economies have historically accompanied each wave of capital flows. This point has been made in a paper by Kaminsky *et al.* (2004),[2] which argues that capital flows tend to be pro-cyclical. This means that the direction of capital flows can exacerbate economic – or financial distress – "when it rains, it pours." A natural question that arises is whether a reversal of the current tide of inflows would result in a financial crisis in the region, similar to that seen in 1997/1998.

On the whole, the authors' assessment is that a banking or balance of payments crisis similar to that in 1997/1998 is unlikely even if these capital flows were to reverse. Macroeconomic and institutional frameworks in Asia are much stronger today than before the pre-crisis period, increasing the region's resilience to financial shocks. Additionally, there have also been changes in the financial landscape which have mitigated against the risks of such a financial crisis occurring. We elaborate on these factors next.

Table 6.2 Coefficient of variation of net private capital flows to emerging markets

	1880–1913	1970–1979	1981–1990	1991–1996	1997–1998	1999–2006
Total net private capital flows to emerging markets	1.71	0.29	1.90	0.26	0.72	0.55
Asia	1.65	0.67	0.72	0.53	−24.74	1.01
Western Hemisphere	1.97	0.67	2.27	0.47	0.16	0.58
Eastern Europe	7.04	−1.12	−1.60	5.07	0.39	0.76

Source: IMF.

Increased resilience of the financial system

First, the various structural reforms undertaken in the aftermath of the financial crisis have strengthened the resilience of Asia's financial systems to shocks. Following the crisis, non-performing loans were carved out or written off, banks were recapitalized, and the corporate sector de-leveraged (Figures 6.13 and 6.14). With the authorities' active encouragement of development of bond markets, the corporate sector has also started to issue bonds and reduce its reliance on bank borrowing.

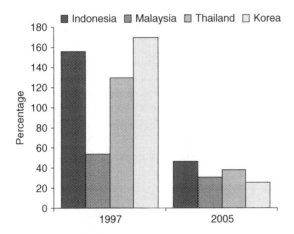

Figure 6.13 Listed non-financial corporates median debt-to-equity ratios (source: Thomson Financial).

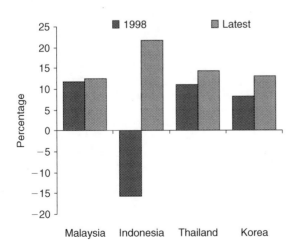

Figure 6.14 Commercial banks' capital adequacy ratios (source: CEIC Data Company Limited).

Beyond balance sheet restructuring, regulators have strengthened their prudential framework for supervision of banks and other financial institutions with the adoption of a more risk-based approach. Operational restructuring has also made progress with the improvement in risk management capabilities, and corporate governance has been strengthened. Improvements in these areas have also been helped by the injection of foreign management expertise in many cases. In many countries, steps have been taken to reduce the relationship-based lending practices that were the norm before the crisis. These developments have been complemented by enhanced surveillance of financial systems by regional central banks.

To be sure, restructuring is an ongoing process, and there is room for further improvement. For example, recent studies have pointed to continued weaknesses in enforcement, which limits the gains achieved through tightening accounting standards.[3] Nonetheless, compared to 1997, much progress has been made. On the whole, the present situation is quite unlike during the pre-crisis period, where balance sheet weaknesses meant that financial shocks were quickly amplified and transmitted to the real economy. For instance, where balance sheet vulnerabilities are present, a sharp rise in the interest rate or fall in the exchange rate can lead to a sharp increase in bad loans, greater risk aversion amongst banks, reduction in bank lending and a credit crunch for the corporate sector.

Improved credibility of macroeconomic policies and greater exchange rate flexibility

Second, Asian authorities have also made great efforts to improve the effectiveness and credibility of their macroeconomic policies. Although the cost of banking sector restructuring had led to large fiscal deficits in the immediate aftermath of the crisis, fiscal deficits have since narrowed or swung to surpluses, in most countries leading to a significant decline in public debt.

Another important development has been the adoption of inflation targeting by a number of regional central banks in order to establish a new nominal anchor for price stability (Table 6.3). Inflation targeting commits the central bank to an explicit inflation target and requires it to be more transparent and accountable. The greater transparency, and other institutional reforms that come

Table 6.3 Inflation targeting in Asia

	IT adoption date	*Current inflation target (percent)*	*Publishes forecast*
Thailand	2000Q2	0–3.5	Y
Korea	2001Q1	2.5–3.5	Y
Philippines	2002Q1	4–5	Y
Indonesia	2005Q3	6 (+/–1)	Y

Source: Various national central banks.

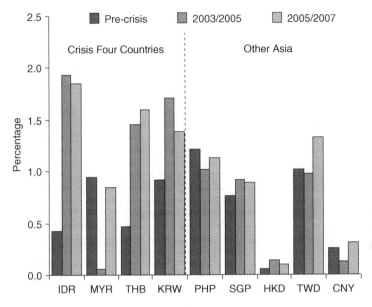

Figure 6.15 Monthly standard deviation of bilateral exchange rate movements (source: Bloomberg, authors' calculations).

with an inflation-targeting framework, will, over time, enhance central bank credibility and help to anchor price stability more firmly. With price stability more firmly anchored, the pass-through effects of exchange rates to domestic prices are likely to weaken, and central banks would be able to allow greater flexibility in their exchange rates.

Indeed, most Asian currencies have exhibited greater flexibility in the post-crisis period (Figure 6.15). The move toward greater exchange rate flexibility is also important, as relatively fixed exchange rate regimes were regarded as one of the main vulnerabilities behind the financial crisis. Greater exchange rate flexibility will encourage greater hedging by domestic agents of their foreign currency exposures, whilst also allowing for greater flexibility of the domestic economy in response to external shocks.

Stronger external positions

Third, Asia's external position has improved markedly since 1998. Unlike in the mid-1990s, Asia is not faced with the problem of financing large current account deficits. In fact, almost all Asian countries ran large current account surpluses in the immediate post-crisis period, as a result of the collapse in investments even as saving rates remained fairly stable (Figure 6.16). Without the need to finance large current account deficits, most countries have been able to reduce their external debt. Indeed, external debt in the four crisis-hit countries has been

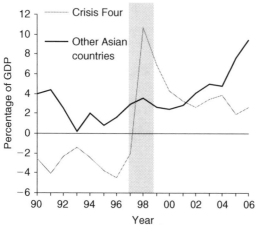

Figure 6.16 Current account positions (source: CEIC Data Company Limited).

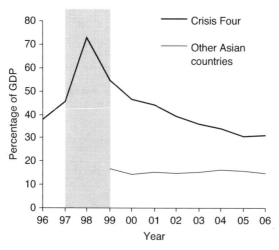

Figure 6.17 External debt positions (source: CEIC Data Company Limited).

reduced from a peak of over 70 percent of GDP in 1998, to around 30 percent currently (Figure 6.17). Moreover, the crisis-hit countries have all repaid their debts to the IMF ahead of schedule.

Asia's external resilience is further bolstered by the substantial stock of foreign reserves held by Asian central banks, reflecting the current account surpluses and capital inflows. These reserves were accumulated mostly through sterilized interventions and can be seen as an attempt by Asian central banks to purchase self-insurance against the risk of "sudden stop" in capital flows (see Box 6.1).

Box 6.1 Is Asia pursuing a mercantilist export-led growth strategy?

One view that has become quite popular among economists and market analysts in recent years is the idea that Asia is pursuing a mercantilist export-led growth strategy. The main thrust of this view is that despite the rhetoric of a move towards more flexible exchange rate regimes, Asia has effectively returned to a system of fixed exchange rates, in other words, the emergence of Bretton Woods II (BW2). Bretton Woods II is a description coined by David Folkerts Landau *et al.* of Deutsche Bank some years ago to characterize the economic model followed by the Asian countries that aims to promote exports and suppress domestic demand via an undervalued exchange rate.

While it is true that manufacturing sectors in Asian economies are generally highly dependent on exports for growth, it does not follow that the Asian economies are suppressing domestic demand. The fact that the Asian manufacturing sectors are oriented toward exports simply means that their manufacturing sectors are closely integrated into the global economy and the global division of labor. They produce for the global markets and in turn earn foreign exchange which is used to finance imports to meet their domestic consumption and investments. The strength of their domestic spending has little to do with the export orientation of their manufacturing sector.

Indeed, Figures 6.18–6.21 show that domestic demand has been the dominant contributor to growth in most of the Asian countries. While exports do account for a substantial share of aggregate demand, once imports are netted out, domestic

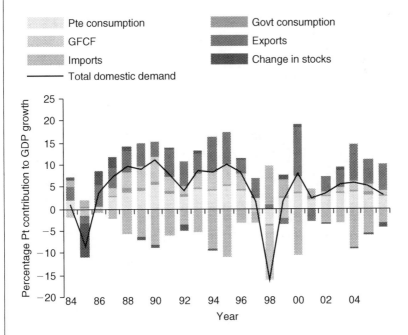

Figure 6.18 Contribution to real GDP growth – ASEAN-4 (source: CEI Data Company Limited, authors' calculations).

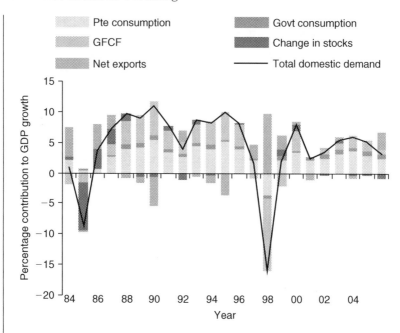

Figure 6.19 Contribution to real GDP growth – ASEAN-4 (source: CEI Data Company Limited, authors' calculations).

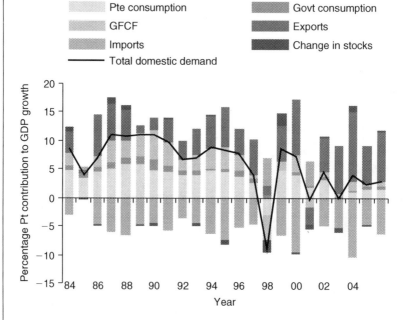

Figure 6.20 Contribution to real GDP growth – NIEs (source: CEI Data Company Limited, authors' calculations).

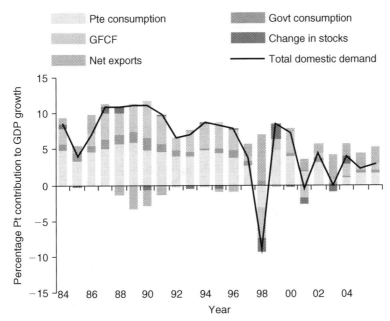

Figure 6.21 Contribution to real GDP growth – NIEs (source: CEI Data
Company Limited, authors' calculations).

demand constitutes the dominant component of growth in expenditures. Indeed, it
was excessive domestic demand via excessive investments that resulted in the
Asian financial crisis. While the immediate post-crisis period in 1999–2000 was
characterized by large positive net exports, since 2001, domestic demand has
again been the main contributor to growth in the ASEAN-4 economies, as private
consumption has been supported by strong growth in consumer credit and rural
incomes reflecting high commodity prices. In the case of the NIEs, domestic
demand was the major contributor to growth from 1999–2002, reflecting the
strength of private consumption in Korea before the collapse of its credit card
bubble in 2003.

For China, again domestic demand has accounted for the bulk of its growth
(Figure 6.22). Although gross exports constitute a large share of GDP, net exports
have been relatively small. Unlike the rest of Asia, however, the high domestic
expenditures have been mainly due to high rates of investments, rather than consumption. Going forward, the challenge for China is to rebalance growth by
raising the contribution of private consumption to overall growth.

The importance of domestic demand in driving Asia's growth weakens the
argument that Asian central banks were intervening in currency markets to pursue
a mercantilist export-led growth strategy. Rather, Asian central banks' interventions have been aimed at preventing the exchange rates from becoming misaligned
and curbing excessive exchange rate volatility. Given the large size and inherent
volatility of capital flows, and the small size of Asian foreign exchange markets,
movements in capital flows can cause the exchange rates to overshoot and become
overvalued, eroding the competitiveness of their manufacturing exports and

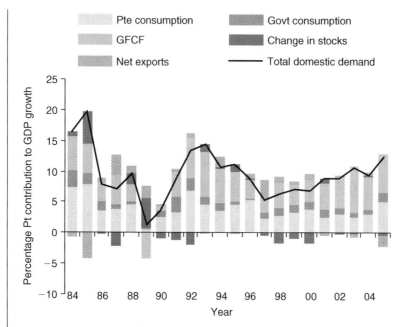

Figure 6.22 Contribution to real GDP growth – China (source: CEI Data
Company Limited, authors' calculations).

resulting in lower growth. Excessive volatility of the exchange rates can also lead
to uncertainty for investors. Hence the intention is to smooth out excessive volatility in exchange rates and avoid currency misalignment, rather than to keep
exchange rates artificially weak in order to gain export shares.

Changes in the composition of capital flows

In addition, changes in the composition of capital inflows may also be an important mitigating factor. Unlike in the pre-crisis period when the capital inflows
were mostly in the form of short-term bank loans, most of the capital inflows in
the recent period have been in the form of portfolio investments (Figure 6.23).

While portfolio flows can also be highly volatile, they are less risky compared to
bank lending. First, prices in capital markets adjust to changes in perceived risk
automatically, and in ways that can pose less systemic risk than foreign currency-
denominated short-term loans. Second, portfolio inflows also involve larger
numbers of creditors and investors, reducing the problem of relationship lending
and problems associated with bank-centered financing, which precipitated the crisis.

The exception to this has been in Korea, where bank liabilities increased substantially in 2006, due to requirements by the Bank of Korea for the shipping
industry to hedge their future foreign currency receipts (Figure 6.24). In addition,
foreign banks have been increasing their exposure to Korean banks since 2002, in
tandem with improvements in their creditworthiness. The historically low interest
rates in Japan have also given a strong incentive for SMEs to borrow in yen. As a

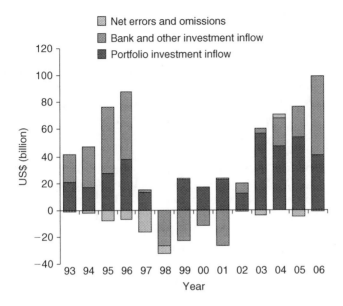

Figure 6.23 Capital flows (ex FDI) into ASEAN-4, Korea and Taiwan (source: CEIC Data Company Limited).

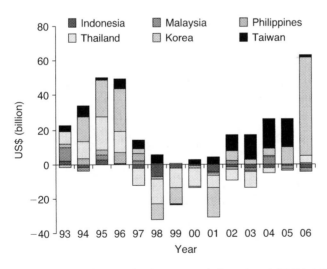

Figure 6.24 Bank and other investment inflows into ASEAN-4, Korea and Taiwan (source: CEIC Data Company Limited).

result, the country's short-term external debts rose to a record level of US$129.8bn at the end of the first quarter of 2007, exceeding the previous peak in 1997. In response to the rising currency and interest rate risks facing retail customers, the authorities have instructed banks to adopt stricter requirements for yen-denominated lending.

Changes in the global financial landscape

There have also been dramatic changes in the global financial landscape since the crisis, which has changed the level and profile of risk in the system.

First, there has been a sharp proliferation in the number and variety of financial instruments and players. Financial innovation has allowed for risk in the system to be dispersed amongst different players, reducing concentration risk within the system. On the other hand, the dispersion of risks may have actually increased the aggregate demand for it, thereby contributing to higher risk appetite in financial markets in recent years, as seen in compressed credit spreads and lower volatility of asset returns (Figure 6.25).

Second, there have also been significant changes in the hedge fund industry. In general, there appears to be a wider range of hedge fund players now, employing a greater diversity of strategies, as compared to 1997–1998. For example, a recent paper by the Federal Reserve Bank of New York has shown that while correlation of hedge fund returns has increased recently, this has been due to lower volatility of returns, rather than an increase in covariance of hedge fund returns, as was the case in 1998.[4] Indeed, covariance of returns is currently significantly lower compared to the long-run average. This reduces the possibility of many hedge funds recording losses simultaneously, and the adverse consequences for market stability and liquidity.

Risks

While the risk of a banking crisis or a balance of payments crisis may be smaller than before, large and volatile capital inflows have nonetheless brought with them other forms of risks and challenges.

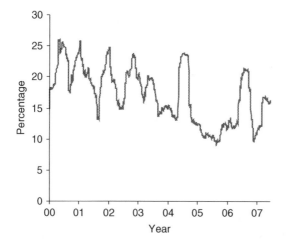

Figure 6.25 MSCI Asia-ex Japan 90-day volatility (source: Bloomberg, authors' calculations).

Excess liquidity and asset bubbles

The resurgence in capital inflows had led to strong acceleration in liquidity and broad money growth in many Asian countries recently. For example, M2 growth has accelerated well above nominal GDP growth for a number of countries in the region. However, the correlation is not perfect. The acceleration in monetary growth has not been uniform across all the countries. For example, monetary growth in Taiwan and Thailand was in the single digits and, for Singapore, it was also in single digits until last year when it began to accelerate sharply. On the other hand, monetary growth has been in double digits in China for the longest time, even in the early 1990s.

Strong capital inflows have manifested themselves in higher asset prices. For example, until recently, foreign buying had driven the stock markets to record highs in several economies, some as much as twice the level of the previous peak (Figures 6.28 and 6.29). However, again the run-up in the market has not been uniform. China has experienced a sharp spike but Thailand has been straggling behind the other markets. Also, although high, the valuations of the market in terms of price-to-earnings ratios are not excessive. In other words, the run-up in prices has been driven more by earnings growth than pure speculation. Hence investors seem to be quite discerning and not entirely irrational. Similarly in the property markets, there is some evidence of speculative activities and an asset bubble in some countries (Figures 6.30 and 6.31). This is particularly the case for high-end residential properties which has become an asset class and has become popular with foreign investors.

A key risk is that asset prices could fall sharply in the event of a sudden reversal of foreign capital inflows. As Figure 6.32 suggests, there is a reasonably

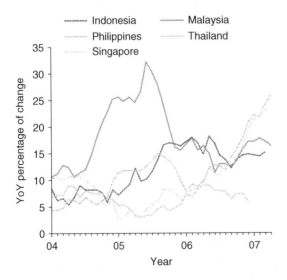

Figure 6.26 M2 growth – Southeast Asia (source: CEIC Data Company Limited).

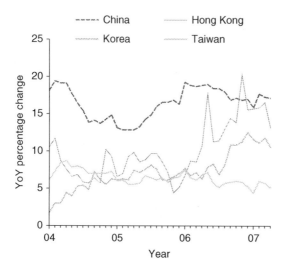

Figure 6.27 M2 growth – Northeast Asia (source: CEIC Data Company Limited).

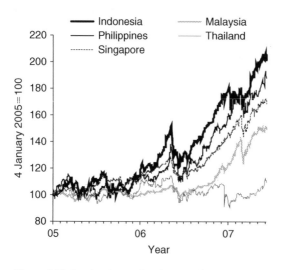

Figure 6.28 Stock prices – Southeast Asia (source: CEIC Data Company Limited).

strong correlation between foreign net purchases of Asian equities and stock price movements. Downside surprises in incoming economic data could trigger a broad-based re-pricing of Asian assets by foreign investors, spikes in risk premiums and a sharp correction in regional equity markets. Sporadic episodes of such heightened risk aversion and market volatility cannot be ruled out, especially if incoming economic data surprises on the downside.

Given the strength of the external balance, regional central banks should be able to accommodate the capital outflows and it is less likely that the capital out-

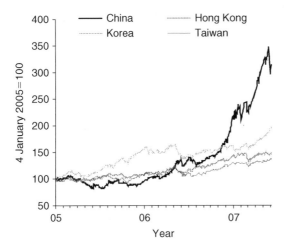

Figure 6.29 Stock prices – Northeast Asia (source: CEIC Data Company Limited).

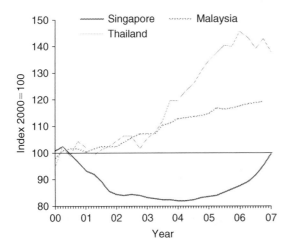

Figure 6.30 Residential property prices – Southeast Asia (source: CEIC Data Company Limited).

flows will result in a liquidity crunch or balance of payments difficulties, although it is possible for individual corporates to experience difficulties reflecting losses from their hedging or funding operations. Asset price corrections should, under normal circumstances, not cause significant damage to the banking sector unless asset purchases are financed heavily by bank borrowing, which does not appear to have been the case so far. Since the start of 2006, there have been three such significant corrections in the asset markets and, so far, the impact on the economy appears to have been contained.

Notwithstanding the small direct impact, asset price corrections could affect the economy through other indirect channels. For example, a sharp correction in

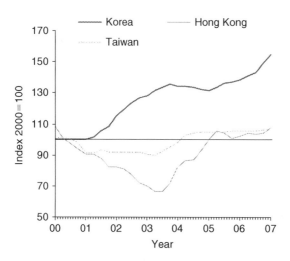

Figure 6.31 Residential property prices – Northeast Asia (source: CEIC Data Company Limited, Bloomberg, Author's estimates).

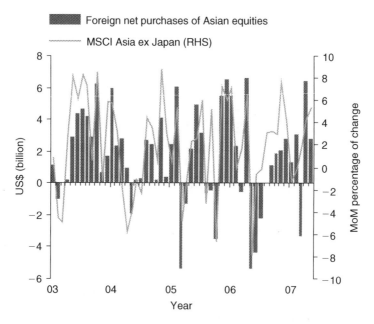

Figure 6.32 Foreign net equity purchases and stock prices (source: CEIC Data Company Limited).

asset prices could dampen consumer spending through a negative wealth effect, or simply by lowering consumer confidence. Domestic banks could also be affected in a global asset market correction, via their holdings of risky overseas assets, for example, collateralized debt obligations (CDOs) linked to subprime mortgages. Whilst not underestimating the consequences of such occurrences, they are nonetheless distinct from a currency and banking crisis induced by capital flow reversals from the region.

Some observers have also argued that the underlying cause of the capital inflows and asset price inflation is the foreign exchange intervention by Asian central banks to moderate the appreciation of their currencies. Incomplete sterilization of these interventions has led to an increase in the monetary base and broad money supply via the money multiplier process. However, even some industrial countries such as Australia, New Zealand, the UK and Iceland, which are on floating exchange rate regimes, have been unable to stop the surge of capital inflows and asset price inflation. In these cases, despite the absence of intervention and relatively stable money supply, capital inflows have nonetheless led to an acceleration in broad money growth, fueling asset price inflation. In short, the root cause of asset price inflation is perhaps less an issue of the exchange rate regimes and the excess liquidity stemming from foreign exchange intervention per se, but primarily one stemming from strong capital inflows, driven by attractive returns on investments.

Rising sterilization costs

Another commonly cited risk is the rising cost of sterilizing interventions in the foreign exchange markets. To avoid excessive volatility and overshooting of the exchange rates while retaining a meaningful degree of monetary policy independence, a number of Asian countries have engaged in sterilized interventions. Sterilization helps mop up excess liquidity resulting from interventions and rein in credit growth.

However, sterilization is becoming increasingly difficult because of the large size of capital inflows relative to the size of the money markets. As a result, some central banks have run out of instruments to mop up the liquidity and have had to resort to issuing their own bills, administrative measures, or partial sterilization. The problem is compounded if domestic interest rates are higher than foreign interest rates, as this implies that the interest cost of servicing sterilization bonds is higher than the returns on investments of the foreign reserves. These costs could become prohibitive and result in losses on the central banks' balance sheets. In addition, central banks are likely to suffer translation losses on their foreign exchange reserves should their currencies appreciate.

One consequence of this is that further sterilized foreign exchange interventions become increasingly difficult politically, forcing central banks to resort to other measures, including the imposition of capital controls. While such measures may be understandable based on domestic political considerations, they also come with their own set of costs, such as the negative impact on investor confidence. This may affect not just short-term foreign portfolio investors, but also long-term direct investors as well, since capital controls inevitably increase the risk and costs of doing business in a country. These costs can be quite significant, particularly in a world characterized by stiff competition for foreign investments.

At this point, however, sterilization costs remain manageable for most countries in the region. The cost of servicing sterilization bonds appears to be fully offset by the interest income earned by central banks' investment of foreign reserves. With the exception of Indonesia, the yield gap between a one-year Asian government bond and the US equivalent, turned negative around 2005 for most Asian countries, and has been widening since (Figures 6.33 and 6.34). With the yield differential now between 90 to 300 bps, it would take a significant spike in Asian interest rates and/or a sharp fall in US interests before sterilization costs become prohibitive. While unlikely at this point, such a scenario could materialize if Asian central banks are forced to hike interest rates sharply in

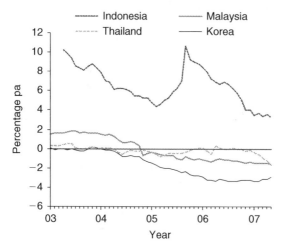

Figure 6.33 Yield differentials between one-year government bonds (Asia–US Treasury) (source: CEIC Data Company Limited).

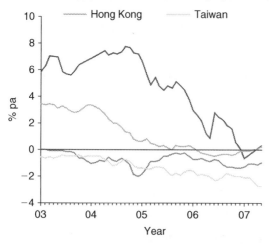

Figure 6.34 Yield differentials between one-year government bonds (Asia–US Treasury) (source: CEIC Data Company Limited).

response to a sharp rise in inflation in Asia, or if a hard landing of the US economy leads to a sharp cut in interest rates by the US Federal Reserve.

Benefits of capital flows

The size and volatility of capital flows pose major challenges for Asian central banks. However, such inflows have also brought about substantial benefits to recipient countries.

First, the self-insurance that Asian countries have purchased via the foreign exchange reserves accumulated in the course of their interventions has strengthened their external positions, improved their resilience, and reduced their vulnerabilities to balance of payments crisis. This, in turn, has led to a reduction in risk premia, improvement in credit ratings, lower domestic interest rates, and reduced the cost of capital for domestic firms (Figure 6.35). For the central banks, the greater degree of self-insurance has given central banks greater confidence to operate a more flexible exchange rate regime, since a larger war-chest of reserves will allow central banks more leeway to effectively counter speculative attacks on their currencies.

Second, capital inflows have also indirectly encouraged countries to develop their financial markets. In particular, the painful experience of the 1997/1998 banking crisis has given regional governments a strong incentive to develop local currency bond markets, and to reduce the reliance on bank-centered financing (Figure 6.36). Many countries have also attempted to offset the impact of capital inflows on their exchange rates, through the liberalization of restrictions on capital outflows. The opportunities offered by such liberalization measures could spur domestic financial institutions to broaden the range of services

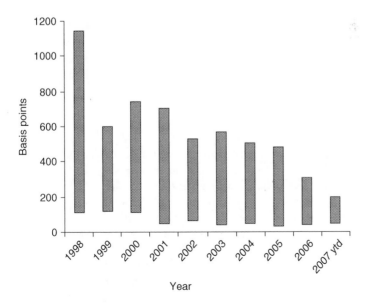

Figure 6.35 EMBIG spread range (source: J.P. Morgan).

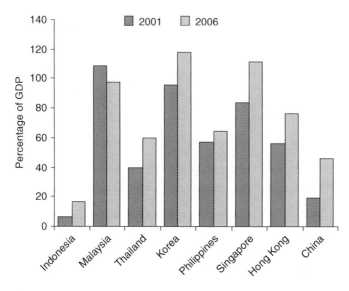

Figure 6.36 Local currency bond market capitalization (source: Asia Bonds Online).

offered to customers. More broadly, whilst contributing to market volatility, capital inflows have also increased market liquidity, an essential condition for further financial market developments.

Lastly, the potential impact on financial stability caused by these inflows has also catalyzed efforts to strengthen regional financial cooperation, for example through the bilateral swap arrangements under the Chiang Mai Initiative, and more recently, regional reserve pooling initiatives. Regional financial surveillance has also been stepped up, through fora such as the ASEAN+3 and EMEAP. Such regional financial cooperation efforts could be further enhanced.

Conclusion

On many measures of income and output, Asia has made a remarkable recovery since the Asian financial crisis. Economic output and growth have recovered, the financial system has been reformed, the external position has been strengthened, and the macroeconomic policy framework has been enhanced. However, it is also clear that the recovery may not be complete, as growth and investment rates in many countries are still significantly lower than the 1990–1997 levels.

The resurgence of large-scale capital flows into the region, drawn by the reflation story in Asia, raises questions as to whether another financial crisis could occur if there were a massive reversal of these capital flows. In our view, the structural reforms and stronger macroeconomic fundamentals of the economies have made the economies more robust and resilient to financial shocks and a balance of payments or banking crisis of the nature of 1997/1998 is therefore unlikely.

Nonetheless, this does not preclude the possibility of other kinds of risk scenarios materializing, including financial market distress in the event that investor confidence takes a hit and capital flows reverse.

Ultimately, the challenges Asian central banks face arise from the free flow of capital and the globalization of finance in the post-Bretton Woods period. There is no ideal solution to the difficulty of coping with capital inflows while retaining adequate control over exchange rates and monetary conditions. The best thing that the emerging economies of Asia can do under the circumstances is to continue to manage the inflows by enhancing the robustness of their financial system, pursuing sound macroeconomic policies, judiciously building up reserves, and allowing a greater degree of flexibility in their exchange rates to avoid major misalignments.

Notes

1 See Corsetti and Roubini (1998) and Radelet and Sachs (1998) for two excellent, if somewhat contrasting, discussions on the primary causes of the Asian financial crisis.
2 See Kaminsky *et al.* (2004).
3 See Ball *et al.* (2003).
4 See Adrian (2007).

References

Adrian, T. (2007) "Measuring Risk in the Hedge Fund Sector," *Current Issues in Economics and Finance*, Federal Reserve Bank of New York.

Ball, R., Robin, A. and Wu, J.S. (2003) "Incentives versus Standards: Properties of Accounting Income in Four East Asian Countries," *Journal of Accounting & Economics*, Vol. 36, nos. 1–3, pp. 235–270.

Corsetti, G. and Roubini, N. (1998) "What Caused the Asian Currency and Financial Crisis? Part I: A Macroeconomic Overview," NBER Working Paper series.

Kaminsky, G.L., Reinhart, C.M. and Veigh, C.A. (2004) "When it Rains, it Pours: Procyclical Capital Flows and Macroeconomic Policies," NBER Working Paper series.

Radelet, S. and Sachs, J. (1998) "The Onset of the East Asian Financial Crisis," NBER Working Paper series.

7 The Asian financial crisis ten years later – lessons learnt

The private sector perspective

Manu Bhaskaran

This chapter looks at the lessons learnt from the Asian financial crisis of 1997–1998 from the perspective of the private sector, which we take to be Asian-based companies, investors and banks. Since there is not likely to be a single "private sector" perspective that can capture the divergent views of each of these components of the private sector in Asia, one cannot pretend to speak on behalf of all private sector perspectives, particularly on an issue as complex and as emotive as the Asian financial crisis. So, what this chapter will do is to give a personal view on the crisis and the lessons learnt.

In doing so, we are conscious that the reason we want to study the lessons learnt from the crisis must be to produce improvements in key areas including (a) crisis prevention, i.e. to avoid a repetition of the crisis or any other similar painful disruption to economic development; and (b) crisis mitigation and resolution – i.e. so as to better contain the effects of future crises and to manage more efficiently the process of returning the affected economies to stability and growth. Given this approach, what this chapter will do is to investigate the major changes in the region and international environment since the crisis and make a judgement on how effectively these two objectives have been met. From this, we can then assess whether the lessons learnt have been sufficient or not.

Summary of key points

In essence, our view is that:

- Asian policymakers have made substantial improvements in the macroeconomic frameworks and financial sectors. These are probably sufficient to prevent the recurrence of a crisis of the enormous scale of that in 1997–1998. But the changes made – and by implication the lessons learnt – have probably not gone far enough to prevent disruptions of economic activity in future which, while falling short of crisis proportions, could still be painful.
- Similarly, the international economic environment has also seen encouraging improvements in growth momentum and stability. But we do not believe it has changed fundamentally enough to prevent a recurrence of disruptive shocks to emerging market countries. A major concern we have is that the

international financial architecture has yet to be refashioned to prevent irrational investor behavior that could precipitate substantial disruption to the global economy.

In short, we do not believe that sufficient lessons have been learnt and we would not be surprised if another crisis or period of material dislocations recurred in Asia and/or other emerging market regions in coming years.

The chapter is organized as follows. The following section will look at what has changed in the crisis-affected countries since 1997 while the section after will assess how the international environment has changed. Finally, these changes will be assessed to understand what lessons have been learnt – by governments in Asia as well as by those responsible for the global environment in which emerging or developing economies operate.

What has changed in Asia?

This section will first sketch out some key insights from the Asian financial crisis and then describe the changes in the crisis-affected countries since the crisis. These changes have been significant in several areas:

- Economic performance has slowed in most countries.
- Resilience to external shocks has improved.
- While there have been considerable improvements in the underlying economic structure, such improvements have not gone as far as they should and much work remains to be done.

The Asian financial crisis – likely causes

The Asian financial crisis started on July 2, 1997 with the devaluation of the Thai baht. The sharp plunge in the baht immediately affected the currencies of Thailand's neighbors who were either important trading partners or had economic structures that seemed similar. Thus, the currencies of Malaysia, Indonesia, the Philippines and Singapore all depreciated at a speed that investors, businessmen and other economic agents had not expected.

The resulting re-appraisal of risks by investors then caused precipitate outflows of capital from these countries, further reinforcing the currency depreciation and also triggering off sharp interest rate increases as central banks worked to protect currencies and as the fall in available liquidity forced up rates. As confidence sank and economic growth looked like collapsing, panic set in – domestic and foreign banks pulled credit lines and ordinary citizens pulled money out of banks, especially in Indonesia. Not surprisingly, political tensions rose sharply as senior political leaders squabbled over appropriate policy responses and ordinary citizens protested higher prices and loss of jobs.

As Southeast Asia suffered, investors began to reappraise risk elsewhere, causing banks to stop rolling over credit lines to Korean companies. By

October/November 1997, the crisis had spread to Korea as well with precipitate declines in the Korean won and massive outflows depleting foreign exchange reserves. At the same time, speculators spying an opportunity in Hong Kong mounted speculative attacks on the Hong Kong dollar while simultaneously shorting the stock market, calculating that they could only win by such "double play" – even if the Hong Kong dollar peg held, interest rates would rise, causing stock prices to fall, as they did.

This chapter is not meant to provide an analysis of the causes of the crisis but a number of conclusions need to be drawn as a basis for the chapter. First, Asian economies had made themselves vulnerable to shocks in several ways:

- Capital account liberalization had produced massive inflows of portfolio equity and debt capital as well as foreign bank lending to the region. These inflows helped to fund current account deficits which had risen sharply on account of increased investment rates. Thus, long-term investment was being funded by easily reversible inflows which later turned out to be largely of short-term maturities.
- As many currencies were managed as quasi-pegs or as predictable crawling pegs to the US dollar, domestic banks and companies felt safe to borrow in foreign currencies since the interest costs were lower. Thus, there were currency mismatches in addition to the maturity one.
- Domestic banks also created a vulnerability by operating more as pawn shops, offering loans in exchange for collateral, which was usually land or real estate or shares in companies. Banks also often lent on the basis of name lending rather than proper credit assessment and in many cases were lending to companies affiliated in some way to their shareholders.
- With managed exchange rates ensuring that currencies were undervalued initially and with the actual cost of capital to domestic borrowers kept low by lower-cost foreign money, domestic investors assumed that returns on investment would be very high. This produced a substantial rise in investment rates (investment to GDP ratios). It soon became clear in many countries that substantial excess capacity was being created, especially in real estate.
- Political leaders compounded the problem in some cases by creating a sense of hubris, promoting grand projects and giving economic agents the sense that governments would somehow ensure that returns on investment would be high and that there would not be a problem with excess capacity.

However, the crisis was not entirely caused by domestic weaknesses. There were also weaknesses in the international environment:

- Easy monetary conditions prevailed in the global economy in the early to mid-1990s even with the tightening of monetary policy in the US in 1994–1995. While monetary policy may well have been optimal when viewed from a single country perspective, such as that of the US, the global monetary conditions thus created may not have been optimal from the perspective of emerging markets or the global economy as a whole. Huge increases in capital flows occurred and asset markets performed strongly, despite warnings from the Chairman of the Federal Reserve Bank of the United States that there was "irrational exuberance" in asset markets.

• The crisis showed a tendency for herd behavior in financial markets. Banks and portfolio investors moved capital on the basis of fairly superficial understandings of the emerging markets they invested in. For instance, the underlying view in Asian investing was that since Asian economic growth was high and would remain high, earnings growth in companies would produce strong returns for equity investors and low risk for bank lenders or investors in emerging market bonds. When these doubts surfaced about such superficial assumptions, there tended to be a simultaneous rush for the exits. Thus, small changes in asset prices or currencies or assumptions about policy led to disproportionate and self-reinforcing flows of capital which turned out to be highly disruptive.

This chapter will assess whether these domestic and international vulnerabilities have really been reformed.

Economic performance: slower economic growth

As shown in Table 7.1, economic growth has mostly slowed in the crisis-hit countries. Although per capita GDP growth slowed elsewhere as well, the performance in Indonesia, Malaysia and Thailand was much worse than the deceleration in the OECD economies and stood in marked contrast against China's acceleration. The Philippines stands out, however, as an economy that had substantially accelerated growth in per capita income but this is mainly because the performance before the crisis was pulled down by multiple political crises.

A major reason for this slowdown appears to be the decline in investment's role in the economy. As Table 7.2 shows, investment rates (gross fixed capital

Table 7.1 Per capita GDP growth

	1976–1996	2002–2006	Change
OECD	2.3	1.8	–21.7
China	8.0	8.9	+11.2
Korea[1]	10.4	5.9	–43.6
Indonesia	5.2	3.5	–32.7
Malaysia	5.0	3.0	–40.0
Philippines	0.4	2.9	+625
Thailand	6.3	4.6	–28.1

Source: World Bank, East Asia Update, April 2007.

Note
1 Korea's pre-crisis figure is for the period 1983–1986.

Table 7.2 Investment–GDP ratios

Country	1990	1995	2000	2005	2005/1995
China	25.3	40.2	32.9	42.0	+4.5
Hong Kong	26.1	34.8	26.4	20.9	−40
India	22.9	26.2	22.7	28.1	+7.3
Indonesia	28.3	31.9	19.9	23.6	−26
Korea	36.9	37.0	28.2	30.1	−18.6
Malaysia	33.0	43.5	25.6	20.0	−54
Philippines	23.1	21.6	21.2	14.9	−31
Singapore	32.9	33.7	30.6	22.3	−33.8
Taiwan	22.3	23.7	23.9	20.5	−13.5
Thailand	40.4	41.6	22.0	29.0	−30.3

Source: Asian Development Bank, *Asian Development Outlook*, various issues.

formation/GDP) have fallen sharply in all the crisis-hit countries – in contrast with the outcomes in China and India where investment rates have risen significantly.

In other words, the bottom line on all the changes in these economies post-crisis is that they failed to attain the conditions needed to achieve high enough investment rates to produce GDP growth rates as high as in pre-crisis years.

Resilience to shocks has improved

Figure 7.1 shows our measure of economic resilience. In general, economic resilience has improved substantially since the middle of the crisis in 1998 but the improvement on the pre-crisis level in 1996 is not impressive. Our measure of resilience is composed as a weighted sum of several key indicators of external and domestic financial, economic and policy strength, some of which are shown in Table 7.3 below.

Essentially, the crisis-hit countries have improved their stability indicators: external balances are now in surplus compared to sizable deficits pre-crisis while the cushion provided by foreign exchange reserves has become considerable. The leeway for fiscal policy responses in a crisis has been improved by reduced fiscal debt, with fiscal deficits contained at reasonable levels. Financial sectors are stronger and foreign direct investment inflows have started to recover, in some cases exceeding pre-crisis levels.

What has hurt resilience is the loss of growth momentum: countries that are growing rapidly usually have a greater capacity to absorb shocks – it takes a very large shock to cause a rapidly growing economy to stall. A second reason is that foreign investment inflows have also diminished in relation to the size of the economy – meaning that an important and less reversible form of funding growth is less available than before.

This analysis of resilience suggests that Asian economies are unlikely to experience a crisis similar to 1997–1998. The foreign exchange reserve cushion

Table 7.3 Indicators of economic resilience

	Year	*Indonesia*	*Korea*	*Malaysia*	*Philippines*	*Thailand*
Current account/	1996	−3.4	−4.1	−4.4	−4.8	−7.9
GDP	2006	2.6	0.7	17.1	4.3	1.6
FDI inflows/GDP	1996	2.8	0.4	5.1	1.8	1.3
	2006	1.9	0.4	3.0	1.1	4.5
Foreign portfolio	1996	6.6	11.2	19.0	13.6	5.3
investment/GDP	2006	12.1	38.9	31.3	22.2	23.3
NPL ratio	1996	6.60	4.50	3.20	2.80	8.25
	1998	48.60	7.40	13.60	10.37	45.02
	2006	7.00	0.70	4.80	5.66	4.15
Fiscal balance/GDP	1996	1.2	0.2	0.7	0.3	0.9
	1998	−2.9	−3.9	−1.8	−1.9	−2.8
	2006	−0.7	0.4	−3.5	−1.0	1.0
External debt/	1996	56.7	28.2	38.6	48.1	65.9
GDP ratio	1998	158.5	47.4	60.0	70.8	69.9
	2006	34.2	29.6	32.8	45.4	33.0
Official foreign	1996	17,820	33,236	26,156	9,930	37,192
exchange reserves	2006	40,696	23,838	81,724	19,891	65,147
Growth momentum[1]	1996	8.0	8.1	9.9	5.3	7.6
	2006	5.6	4.6	5.5	5.2	4.7

Source: Collated by Centennial Group from CEIC Database and other official sources.

Note
1 Growth momentum is measured as the average growth in the two years preceding the year shown.

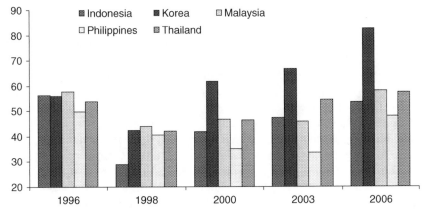

Figure 7.1 Resilience among major AFC victim economies has improved significantly (source: collated by Centennial Group).

is massive and, anyway, the need for external funding is limited since countries are mostly running current account surpluses. The analysis is also borne out by recent experiences, of which two in particular stand out:

- First, Indonesia experienced a mini-currency crisis in July 2005. Failure to tighten monetary policy in the face of rising inflation and reluctance to reform fuel subsidies which were undermining fiscal stability led to a sharp depreciation of the Indonesian rupiah at the end of July 2005. However, as soon as Bank Indonesia raised interest rates and the government indicated a firm willingness to reform fuel subsidies, the crisis subsided. The Indonesian economy continued to demonstrate reasonably high growth in both 2005 and 2006 – despite the interest rate and currency shocks. The acceleration in inflation caused by the currency depreciation and the cut in fuel subsidies also turned out to be a lot more muted than expected.
- Thailand has been experiencing a series of political convulsions since late 2005, culminating in a military coup in September 2006 and a sharp rise in separatist violence in southern Thailand. Despite this, economic growth has been maintained at above 4 percent and the currency, if anything, has been too strong for policymakers' comfort.

Underlying economic structure has not changed sufficiently

But the changes go beyond just per capita incomes. Table 7.A1 in the appendix outlines some of the changes in key areas of the economy since the crisis. In short, we would argue that:

First, the financial economy has seen significant changes. Banks have been restructured – the number of banks has been reduced, non-performing loans have been reduced to pre-crisis levels and new frameworks for regulation and supervision have been introduced.

Second, economies are far more open than before, with trade in goods and foreign investment liberalized. The role of exports in the economy is larger, restrictions on foreign ownership in key sectors have been relaxed and capital accounts are more liberalized. The ASEAN Free Trade Area is now in effect for the core ASEAN economies, so Indonesia, Malaysia, Thailand and the Philippines have cut tariffs for fellow core ASEAN members to a maximum of 5 percent. Nevertheless, even the limited requirements of the ASEAN Free Trade Area have not been fully implemented in some sectors because governments have been reluctant to completely give up protecting these sectors.

Third, policy regimes have changed. Fixed exchange rate regimes have given way to more flexible ones based on some form of inflation targeting. However, central banks continue to intervene, sometimes aggressively, in order to prevent their currencies from appreciating too rapidly, giving the impression that policymakers are not fully committed to the inflation-targeting framework. Fiscal policy is more cautious, with governments having succeeded in bringing down public debt/GDP ratios which soared as a result of the crisis.

Fourth, corporate sectors have seen significant changes. There has been some privatization, thus reducing the role of state enterprises but the progress overall has been slow, especially in Indonesia. There has been more financial restructuring to improve balance sheet strength than operational restructuring to improve underlying competitiveness and profitability. The influence of Korean chaebols in the economy has been reduced but they remain highly influential. Corporate governance regulations have been introduced but compliance and enforcement leave much to be desired in Southeast Asia.

Fifth, capital markets have developed considerably. Bond markets are bigger and more active while equities markets have also grown in size and liquidity. In addition, an Islamic finance sector is developing rapidly in some countries, especially Malaysia.

While much has changed, Table 7.A1 in the appendix also highlights that there remain many areas where change has been slow:

- First, despite some progress towards greater democracy, some of the characteristics of the political economy which created vulnerabilities remain. The influence of vested interests remain entrenched in many countries, preventing necessary reforms such as further trade opening, privatization and effective enforcement of corporate governance strictures that have been passed into law. The unhealthy nexus between political leaders and businessmen remains, but in different forms.

- Second, policymaking remains a source of risk. While exchange rates have been made more flexible, policymakers are still reluctant to allow them to appreciate too rapidly or too much. The sudden imposition of capital controls in December 2006 by the Bank of Thailand when the Thai baht was appreciating rapidly is an example. Yet, they do not have the tools of policy needed to manage the liquidity and other consequences of their efforts to prevent currency appreciation. Although this dilemma is not as risky for stability as that prevailing in the run-up to the 1997 crisis, it is still a source of risk.

- Third, the domestic corporate sector remains a potential point of vulnerability. As discussed above, corporate governance is not being enforced as rigorously as it should.

Competitiveness under pressure

In addition, competitive positioning appears to have shifted against many of the crisis-hit countries. First, their share of world exports (Figure 7.2) has largely stagnated or declined a little, except in Korea where its share of world exports has risen. This is in marked contrast to the performance of China whose share of world exports has soared.

Second, their ability to attract FDI has also weakened. As Figures 7.3 and 7.4 show, their share of FDI flows to developing countries fell sharply after the crisis erupted and has yet to fully recover to pre-crisis levels.

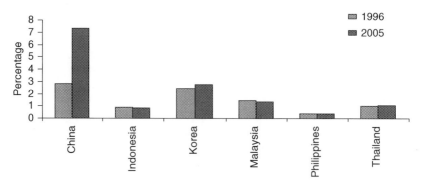

Figure 7.2 Shares of global exports for AFC victims stagnant (source: collated by Centennial Group using IFS Database).

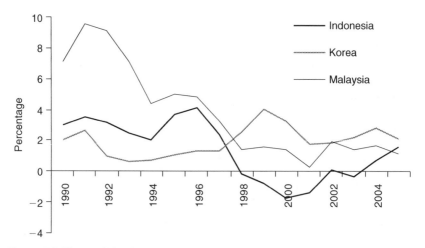

Figure 7.3 Shares of developing countries' FDI recovering (source: collated by Centennial Group using World Investment Report 2006).

Third, their rankings in various surveys of competitive positioning have fallen or remained relatively low, as seen in Table 7.4 which shows the survey rankings conducted by the World Economic Forum, IMD and AT Kearney.

What has changed in the international environment?

In this section, we will first review a number of developments in the international economic environment and then look at the international financial architecture. Finally, we will assess whether the changes in the international financial architecture have gone far enough for us to say that sufficient lessons have been

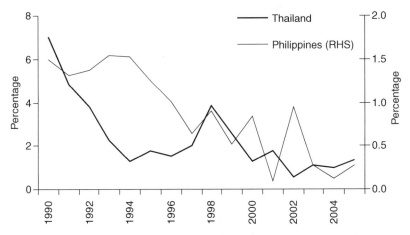

Figure 7.4 Shares of developing countries FDI falls short of pre-crisis levels (source: collated by Centennial Group using World Investment Report 2006).

Table 7.4 Global competitiveness rankings

Country	WEF growth competitiveness index rankings		IMD world competitiveness yearbook rankings		AT Kearney FDI confidence index	
	2000	2006	2000	2006	2002	2005
China	40	54	30	19	1	1
India	48	43	39	29	15	2
Indonesia	43	50	44	60	N/A	N/A
Korea	28	24	28	38	21	23
Malaysia	24	26	27	23	N/A	N/A
Philippines	36	71	37	49	N/A	N/A
Thailand	30	35	35	32	20	20

Source: Collated by Centennial Group using WEF, IMD and AT Kearney reports (various years).

learnt about the role the international environment plays in generating and resolving crises.

What has changed in the global economy?

The period since the Asian crisis has been marked by several major changes in the global economic landscape, most of which have been positive:

* World economic growth has accelerated, with most parts of the world enjoying the highest economic growth rates in about 30 years. Growth has also

been far more broad-based than it has been for several decades. Global output grew by 4.9 percent in 2006, the fastest pace since 1977 except for 2003's 5.3 percent rate. China's economic growth has accelerated while the size of its economy has reached a point where it is able to significantly affect key global variables such as commodity prices, world trade and pricing in key manufactured goods and the competitive positioning of smaller economies all across the globe. India's economy has also taken off, meaning that the two most populated countries are now rising in importance to the world economy.

• Asset markets have been particularly strong all over the world. Real estate prices have soared in most parts of the developed world except Japan and Germany. Bond prices have risen sharply, producing unusually low yields. Equity prices have soared, most recently in China but also in Brazil, Russia, India and even in Vietnam's fledgling market. Liquidity for financial asset markets has been substantial.

• This strong performance was achieved despite several major economic shocks or headwinds: a massive three-fold spike in oil prices between 2003 and 2006, the global war on terror and other wars in the Middle East, gyrations in major currencies, the bursting of the technology bubble and subsequent corporate bankruptcies and scandals, weak corporate sector fixed asset investment and the threat of pandemics such as SARS and avian flu.

• Such global resilience was evident in how easily the world economy absorbed more recent emerging market crises – in Argentina and Turkey for example.

Such dynamism and resilience has led many commentators to conclude that there has been a fundamental improvement in the functioning of the global economy.

What has changed in the international financial architecture?

Much discussion of the international financial architecture (IFA) takes a narrow definition. For example, the World Bank[1] sees it as the "range of initiatives to help prevent crises and to manage them in the event that they nevertheless occur" that were put in place after the Asian financial crisis. These include the Financial Stability Assessment Programme (FSAP), Reports on the Observance of Standards and Codes (ROSC) and various efforts to reform and strengthen domestic financial sectors. Some excellent academic assessments of the changes in the IFA have adopted a somewhat broader definition. For example, Barry Eichengreen[2] identifies several improvements in the IFA but these essentially relate to changes in policies in emerging market countries themselves – longer maturity structures of foreign debt, improved current account balances, stronger foreign exchange reserves, exchange rate flexibility and more prudent fiscal policies. He also looks at the role of international institutions such as the IMF and technical issues such as bond covenants.

We agree with the latter approach but would propose an even broader definition of the IFA for the purposes of assessing the Asian crisis. By the IFA we mean the global financial system comprising:

- The processes by which pools of liquidity are created and deployed such as the operations of central banks and private lending institutions as well as those of savings institutions and proprietary trading desks of banks and companies. This component of the IFA is critical in our view as it includes key issues relating to risks in the global financial system:

  a The global impact of a multiplicity of single country monetary policies.
  b One major risk is the rapid and expanding flows of capital especially into emerging markets which are often not well equipped to manage their consequences.

  It also includes issues such as the herd behavior of such investors and the potential damage that this can unleash on developing economies in particular.

- The regulatory and oversight institutions which include:

  a global institutions such as the World Bank, the International Monetary Fund (IMF), the Bank for International Settlements (BIS) and smaller and less formal groups such as the Financial Stability Forum;
  b regional development banks and mechanisms such as the Asian Development Bank (ADB), the Chiang Mai Initiative and the Manila Framework in Asia; and
  c national level agencies such as central banks, financial regulatory institutions and sovereign wealth management institutions.

- The financial markets in which such pools of liquidity are allocated – markets for equities, bonds, derivatives, commodities and real estate where international liquidity can trade with relative freedom of access. The IFA would include how these markets are set up and technical issues which affect their processes such as bond covenants and other factors which affect the resolution of a financial crisis.

- Structural weaknesses in the global economy and at single country levels.

Our major concern is that not enough is being done to address these components in our broader definition of the IFA – the way in which large amounts of capital can flow in and out of emerging markets, creating bubbles – and potentially busts – in their wake. We examine how the IFA has changed since the Asian crisis in Table 7.5.

Implications – lessons learnt and not learnt

Important lessons have been learnt

The good news is that much has been learnt and implemented. Tables 7.4 and 7.A1 in the appendix summarize important changes that have reduced risks. Important groups have taken to heart the lessons of the Asian crisis:

- Crisis-hit countries and other emerging market countries have probably learnt the most. As a result, domestic policy regimes are less likely to produce a

Table 7.5 Assessment of changes in IFA

Component of IFA	Changes since Asian crisis
Creation and deployment of liquidity	
Monetary policy and liquidity creation	Still set according to single country needs with no surveillance or regulation of the impact on global liquidity conditions. Result is frequent episodes of ultra-easy global monetary conditions which promote the creation of bubbles and busts.
Leverage	Anecdotal evidence suggests that considerably more leverage is now being used by investing and trading institutions. Not clear how much of a pyramid of debt has built up as a result.
Transparency	New standards for national statistics and disclosure have been implemented but the quality of developing country data is still questionable, particularly in relation to capital flows data and corporate sector financials. Timely data showing the extent of portfolio capital or leverage used by key investing institutions is unavailable.
Surveillance	Has improved with the IMF's regular Global Financial Stability Report and the Financial Stability Assessment Programme. But the approach is still country-focused and does not look sufficiently at highly leveraged investing institutions such as hedge funds or at proprietary trading desks of banks.
International institutions	
IMF	Is more transparent and has modified its approach to managing crises as seen in its more flexible approach to Brazil and Turkey in recent years. Understands better the need for domestic ownership of stabilization policies. Not clear if the substantial amounts of money needed to rapidly restore confidence can be assembled and deployed in time by the IMF.
Other institutions	New groupings such as the Financial Stability Forum and other small but focused groups do help in surveillance.
Financial markets/operations	
Bond covenants	The World Bank has noted that the greater use of collective action clauses in debt securities can help facilitate more orderly debt restructuring should similar crises recur but it was not confident that such changes had gone far enough.
Structural weaknesses	
Emerging markets	Stronger and less vulnerable: • Longer maturity structures • Massive foreign exchange reserves cushion • More flexible exchange rates • Monetary policies are better anchored • Fiscal policies more prudent • Current account balances improved
Balance of payments imbalances	Large deficits in the US and other OECD countries such as Australia. China's surplus is large and growing rapidly.
Distortion in key relative prices	• US dollar reportedly overvalued • Risk may be mis-priced currently judging by unusually low spreads for higher risk bonds over low risk ones.

Source: Prepared by Centennial Group.

crisis. Most policymakers understand that macroeconomic frameworks need to be credible and transparent. Exchange rates are now more flexible. Monetary policy is better anchored, giving central banks greater credibility in containing inflation. Fiscal policy is less marked by large deficits. Self-insurance against external shocks has been put in place through a large build-up in foreign exchange reserves. Considerable progress has been made in improving the supply side of emerging market economies through trade opening, domestic deregulation and corporate sector restructuring.

• International institutions such as the much-criticized IMF have also felt chastised by their failures during the crisis. They have improved their surveillance so that they are less likely to be taken by surprise by a crisis again. The IMF and World Bank are taking a more nuanced approach to managing crises, acknowledging the need for more customized stabilization policies and for securing domestic ownership of such stabilization policies. However, there are still many areas where not enough has been learnt.

Political reforms have not gone far enough

First, it is not a coincidence that the most dramatic improvement in economic resilience and in the underlying economy has been in Korea. This probably shows the importance of having a reasonably mature political system. This can be defined as one where:

1 the political leadership is able to secure and institutionalize a legitimate national consensus on policies needed for stabilization in a crisis; and
2 where an effective administrative machinery exists which can implement reforms effectively and consistently. It is not clear at all that other developing economies have achieved this level of political development.

Second, some unhealthy dimensions of the nexus between the political class and business continue to exist. In some countries, business groups whose cozy relationships with governments created vulnerabilities in the economy which eventually contributed to the economic collapse have made a comeback by exploiting their relationships with key political personalities. Worse still, these relationships continue to create distortions in policies for private gain – in ways which may well create new vulnerabilities. Efforts to enforce newly established rules on corporate governance have come to grief as a result of such a nexus. In other words, cronyistic relationships between government and business continue to be a weakness in many parts of Asia.

Third, at the international level, resistance from the big powers, especially the United States, has meant that there has been little fundamental overhaul of the IFA. While the IMF has commendably reformed itself internally, the major powers who control the IMF have not shown a willingness to allow reforms to the overall IMF structure – either in terms of voting powers or in the IMF's capacity to mobilize and deploy funds rapidly in times of crisis.

The result is that future crises will continue to be managed in an ad hoc manner. This means that countries with strategic value to powerful nations (such as Korea and Mexico) will have a better chance of being helped than those that have less value (as Thailand found when its August 1997 rescue package was judged too small to help and provoked a further decline in the currency and asset markets).

Risk of policy errors remains

Policymakers continue to make errors of judgment which could create instability in future. A key risk is that while exchange rates are more flexible, some policymakers are not reconciled to the logic of such systems – which is that they have to accept that exchange rates may well appreciate a lot faster than they had anticipated. As the Bank of Thailand's imposition of capital controls in December 2006 showed, policy-related risks remain when policymakers want to have their cake and eat it as well. As appreciating pressures continue to rise in emerging Asian currencies over coming months, we believe that this tendency could well produce a lot more policy-related shocks in financial markets.

International financial architecture is still disposed to occasional panics

There are two issues in particular which concern us:

- First, large inflows of capital can complicate macroeconomic policies which in developing countries are mainly geared toward growth. When capital flows increase hugely, either currencies appreciate or central bank intervention to prevent appreciation causes a large increase in foreign exchange reserves and then in domestic liquidity which then threatens domestic price stability. Or if sterilized intervention is undertaken, the costs can be quite high and in many cases, countries are unable to sustain sterilized intervention for long. Eventually countries are forced to allow their currencies to appreciate in order to accommodate flows of portfolio capital which may not be sustained in the longer term. But when the currency appreciates, the export sector may suffer a loss of competitiveness and this could well undermine economic growth prospects.
- Second, the IFA in 1997–1998 saw several financial panics that severely damaged economies. When investors lost confidence in one country and ran for the exits, the currency of that country fell sharply. But in falling sharply against its neighbors' currencies, the neighbors lost export competitiveness since many of them were trade competitors. This caused neighbors' currencies to fall as well, which then sparked a further fall in the first currency, which then fed through to even greater falls in the neighbors' currencies. Nothing in economic fundamentals could justify the plunging values of the Indonesian rupiah, for instance, in late 1997 and January 1998.

Thus our major worry is that nothing we have seen in terms of changes to the IFA have addressed this occasional tendency for the IFA to descend into a sheer panic.

Concluding thoughts

This analysis leads us to the following conclusion.

First, enough lessons have been learnt to reduce the chances of a crisis on the same scale and form as the Asian financial crisis of 1997. In particular, the bottom line on the crisis-hit Asian economies is that while they are growing more slowly since the crisis, their resilience to external shocks has improved of late. They are therefore unlikely to go into a free fall as in 1997.

Second, however, key areas of domestic policy and the IFA remain unreformed. There is consequently still a tendency for the creation of inappropriate levels of global liquidity and for this liquidity to flow in undisciplined ways that create speculative froth – and in some cases asset price bubbles.

Third, there remain structural weaknesses in the global economy and in investor behavior which can in some circumstances cause the correction of asset prices that will occur from time to time to become exaggerated and produce disproportionate damage to financial markets and the real economy, either in single countries or in regional economies.

Appendix

Table 7.A1 Key changes in crisis-hit countries

	Indonesia	Korea	Malaysia	Philippines	Thailand
Ownership/ sectoral deregulation	Food distribution deregulated with BULOG's monopoly removed. Permits for forestry and plantation sector simplified. Oil and gas refining and distribution opened up. 100 percent foreign equity in the distribution and retail sectors allowed.	Liberalization of land ownership, including move to mortgage-based payment system and easing of rent controls. Shipping sector progressively deregulated with foreign flagships now allowed to carry trade.	Rules regarding foreign versus indigenous (Bumiputera) ownership eased. Complete relaxation of rules for foreign investment in manufacturing sector. Relaxation of affirmative action rules for foreign investment in services sector, only allowed in Iskandar Development Region. Policymakers have suggested greater foreign participation in local banks on a case-by-case basis. Resistance towards foreign ownership of key industries, such as national car maker Proton.	Foreign ownership in crisis-hit banks allowed up to 100 percent later reduced to 70 percent. Omnibus Electricity Bill. Retail trade: bill to allow foreign ownership in Congress. Mining sector: foreign firms now allowed to run domestic mines (December 2004). Relaxation of price controls in electricity sector (2005)	Foreign ownership in finance sector eased. Foreign ownership in key urban areas permitted. Leasehold tenures for foreigners increased from 30 years to 50 years.
Investment	Foreign Direct Investment (FDI) rules streamlined. Rise in number of export processing zones (EPZs) e.g. Batam Island	FDI rules liberalized. Hostile foreign takeovers now eligible for tax breaks and incentives.	FDI rules eased. Since 2003, restrictions on foreign exchange rules eased.	Streamlined.	Some easing but investment had already been deregulated as far back as 1990.

Trade regulation	Easing of trade restrictions: • Gradually reducing tariffs on non-agricultural products to maximum of 10 percent. • ASEAN Free Trade Area: tariffs on ASEAN goods imports cut to a maximum of 5 percent. • Export taxes on timber and minerals cut. • Many formal non-tariffs barriers were dismantled. • Export permits reduced and simplified. • Ended several credit programs that offered subsidized loans to agriculture and SMEs to support exports.	Market opening measures: Elimination of trade-related subsidies. Improvements of import certification procedures.	ASEAN Free Trade Area: tariffs ASEAN goods imports cut to a maximum of 5 percent.	Average nominal tariff reduced to 9.5 percent except for ASEAN FTA member countries where maximum rate is 5 percent. Quota allocation procedure made more transparent. Simple average Most Favoured Nation (MFN) tariff rate fell from 9.7 percent in 1999 to 5.8 percent in 2003, rose to 7.4 percent in 2004 – with strong opposition to free trade from lobby groups (e.g. Agriculture). A blanket ban on rice imports still remains.	Already quite open. ASEAN Free Trade Area: tariffs ASEAN goods imports cut to a maximum of 5 percent.
Privatization	Slow, political will lacking but new state enterprises minister has promised accelerated privatization. Three out of four largest banks in the country remains state-owned (as of Sept 2006). Large stakes in Jakarta airport, Aneka Tambang and Indosat planned to be sold in 2007/2008 fiscal year.	Privatization of POSCO (2001), KEPCO (Apr 2001), Korea Telecommunications (May 2002).	Pre-crisis Malaysia had already privatized significantly.	Limited progress	Under Premier Thaksin, strong impetus for privatization of state companies, especially in energy industry. Electricity Generating Authority of Thailand (EGAT) was privatized, and then renationalized. Strong anti-privatization

(continued)

Table 7.A1 Continued

	Indonesia	Korea	Malaysia	Philippines	Thailand
					petitioners (e.g. Confederation of Consumer Organisations, Free Trade Area Watch, etc.) inhibits privatization movement. Privatization further impeded by allegations of corruption.
Capital markets	Longer tenure (one-year and three-year) bonds to be issued. Move to auction based issue of short-term government securities. Bond market capitalization in 2001 = IDR90 tr; 2004 = IDR5,300 tr	Loosened restrictions on: • Forex transactions and derivatives trade. • Foreign ownership of various assets. • Foreign equity ceilings in non-listed companies. • Korean companies' access to foreign capital markets. By 2006, most regulations on foreign exchange transactions removed. New policy framework includes won internationalization, liberalization of overseas investment by Koreans. Bond market capitalization: 1996 = KRW175 tr; 2006 = 778 tr won.	Bond markets developing more quickly now as bank and corporate restructuring increases supply. To ensure that efforts to develop the bond market are well coordinated, a high-level National Bond Market Committee (NBMC) was established by the government in 1999. • Malaysian Capital Market Masterplan launched in 2001. • Islamic finance sector developing rapidly. Bond market capitalization 1996 = 118 bn ringgit; 2005 = 383 bn ringgit	Authorities able to sell bonds globally so less needed to tap domestic market. Central bank revised rules on foreign portfolio investments, allowing investors to convert the peso proceeds of their stock investments into dollars, removing any restrictions on the outflow of dollars from the stock market. Bond market relatively underdeveloped. Government-issued bonds available – market capitalization	Bond markets developing more quickly now. • Outstanding domestic bonds totaled THB 4 tr up 600-fold from THB 546.8 bn in 1997. • Baht denominated foreign bond debuted in 2005 when the Asian Development Bank (ADB) issued THB 4 billion worth of domestic bonds on 24 May 2005. • Government promoting

	development of secondary mortgage market. • Credit rating agencies set up. Bond market capitalization 1996 = 519 bn baht; 2006 = 3.9 tr baht.		2002 = PHP909 b; 2006 = PHP1.5 tr	Capital adequacy ratios increased to international standards by 2000.
Bank regulation	Number of banks reduced from 238 before the crisis to 131 in 2006. Prudential standards raised. Phase out of full deposit guarantee scheme, deposit insurance reduced to IDR5 bn in Mar 2007.	Prudential regulations raised to international best practice standards: • Higher degree of banking sector disclosure to meet international accounting standards. • Improvement in BIS capital ratio calculation. • Full disclosure in the management of trust accounts. • Revision of loan classification to reflect capacity to repay and not just past performance. • Prudential rules for foreign exchange liquidity and exposure. • Introduction of mark-to-market for securities. • Debt-equity ratio 200 percent become a de facto limit in provision of loans. • Prohibition of new loans with guarantee by affiliated firms.	• International best practice regulations being introduced. E.g. The classification period of NPLs was reduced from six to three months.	New capital requirements with increase in general loan loss provision to 2.0 percent by Oct 1999. Prudential regulations governing lending to related interests expanded in Mar 2004 to include subsidiaries and affiliates. Exposure limits also introduced, as well as stiffer penalties for non-compliance. Phasing in Basel II and adopting risk-based supervision for the country's commercial banks. From end-2005, financial statements of banks have to be prepared in line with International Financial Reporting Standards.

(continued)

Table 7.A1 Continued

	Indonesia	Korea	Malaysia	Philippines	Thailand
Failure resolution frameworks	Key institutions set up for debt and bank restructuring. In addition, the Jakarta Initiative and Private Sector Debt Settlement Teams addressed corporate sector debt.	Key institutions set up: • Korean Asset Management Corporation (KAMCO). • Financial Supervision Commission.	Exemplary action: Danamodal to recapitalize. Danaharta to clean up bank balance sheets. Corporate Debt Restructuring Committee.	Monetary Board examines troubled bank – if deemed unable to be rehabilitated, will be closed and placed under Philippine Deposit Insurance Corporation (PDIC) receivership.	Foreclosure law passed. Bankruptcy court set-up, bankruptcy law updated. Financial restructuring agency and asset management corporation were also set up.
Macroeconomic management	More flexible exchange rate regime. Inflation targeting regime from 2005.	Shift in policy stance: • Counter-cyclical to pro-cyclical. • Pro-growth to pro-stability.	Shifted to flexible exchange rate Jul 2005.	Interest rate-oriented policy continues, exchange rate has been flexible.	Shifted to inflation targeting. Exchange rate flexible but central bank intervenes aggressively.
Corporate governance	Authorities have tightened disclosure standards.	Oversight functions of corporate boards of directors increased. Introduction of consolidated financial statements. Obligation of establishing election committee for the assignment of outside auditors for listed companies and affiliated firms.	Major strides in establishing world standard governance structures but enforcement is lacking.	From Jan 2005 onwards, adoption of accounting and financial reporting standards based on the International Accounting Standards (IAS) and International Financial Reporting Standards (IFRS).	SEC tightening up standards for listed companies, enforcing tighter disclosure standards by delisting recalcitrant companies.

| Corporate restructuring | Substantial restructuring of former politically connected conglomerates but many of them seem to have reincarnated themselves despite their massive debt defaults. Raising of environmental regulation standards, especially in the mining sector. | Substantial reform of chaebols:
• Top chaebols swapped businesses for greater focus.
• Number of subsidiaries reduced.
• Sales of subsidiaries to foreign partners.
• Debt equity ratio of listed companies fell from 330 percent in 1997 to 110.9 percent in 2005 (lowest since 1966). | Has gathered pace under the new prime minister. Govt now reforming remaining government-linked companies. | Largest companies restructured operations and saw improving profitability. | Significant balance sheet restructuring. Some operational restructuring: in a few large companies – selling non-core businesses, mergers to reduce excess capacity. |

Source: Collated by Centennial Group.

Notes

1 World Bank, *The International Financial Architecture*, Internal Discussion Note, July 2005.
2 Barry Eichengreen, Plenary address to 3rd Annual PECC Finance Conference, Sheraton Santiago Hotel and Conference Center, Santiago, Chile, June 21, 2004.

8 Politics, policy, and corporate accountability

Peter Gourevitch

The Asian financial crisis (AFC) is, from the point of view of social science, a natural experiment: countries experienced the same shock, but responded differently. We learn what is distinctive about countries by comparing their varying responses to that same stimulus – like pouring a chemical into several beakers and watching them turn different colors. We also learn something about causality: what variables matter in shaping important social outcomes?

Corporate governance has come to be seen as among the most important micro institutional variables that shape economic growth and development. Before the AFC, the Asian model was held up for its ability to sustain vigorous growth rates in several countries. After the AFC, the East Asian Miracle[1] became dubbed as "crony capitalism:" insider networks; close bonds among firms; resistance to a market for control; weak protections for minority shareholders.

This shift of labels is surely pejorative. It reflects the Washington Consensus – that the US model is superior, that other countries need to conform if they expect to grow, and certainly if they expect foreign capital to flow in. International associations and institutions (the OECD, TIAA CREF, CalPERS) around the world have developed standards of "shareholder protection" which embody the patterns found in the US and UK. They differ in detail but are quite similar in calling for a regime of strong protection of external minority shareholders from abuse by internal management and large blockholders. Countries and firms are under pressure to adopt these standards. Many have adopted codes of conduct, some by private associations, others by law. The driving logic of these codes is to end crony capitalism and create the new world of "arm's length transparency." Wade, in Chapter 11 of this volume, critiques this drive for uniformity as another form of pressure by the richest countries on the less developed ones.

While codes have spread and some laws changed, it is hard to tell how much behavior has changed. Has the system of corporate governance changed in deep ways, or do we have a familiar pattern of verbal compliance but behavioral difference? And do we really have consensus on the utility for change, the desirability of it? There is plenty of reason to doubt that codes change behavior by themselves. Codes and norms change behavior if there is support for doing so. That support lies in institutions, interest groups, political processes, and the norms that influence each of these. Without strong internal support, we may have cosmetic change, what Walter (2006) calls "mock compliance" – change in the formal rules, but not change in actual practice, or "substantive compliance," a distinction raised as well by Chapters 7 and 11 in this volume.

For the formal rules to produce substantive compliance, political support needs to exist. Many of the advocates of international standards assume that these are somehow "self-enforcing," that they will spread by the power of normative convergence, training of elite civil servants, and the demands of international capital to converge on the new pattern of regulation. And yet, researchers find severe limits to these instruments of change. These researchers note the resistance of well-rooted habits, interest groups, organizations, and ideas to change. To understand what actually happens and what reforms are really adopted, we need to understand the mechanisms within countries that lead to adopting effective change. It is perhaps too soon to provide definitive conclusions on the extent of change. But we can explore the analytic issues that underlie the process of rule change and rule compliance. We can do this by exploring the way political factors encourage or inhibit these processes. The divergence or convergence of corporate governance has been alternatively explained by the channel of:

1   legal tradition;
2   political institutions;
3   interest groups;
4   informal networks and norms.

Mixed in are debates about convergence: is there a single best practice, around which market economies converge? Or are there different paths to efficiency, and profitability, which can attract different "types" of capital?

This chapter briefly describes some features of East Asian corporate governance, then examines some of the conflicting interpretations for these patterns, and then explores some implications of this for understanding the impact of the AFC.

Comparing governance systems: East Asia in a global context

The standard instrument for comparing corporate governance systems is shareholder concentration: the more concentrated the shares among few investors, the more firm governance is one of blockholder control; the more diffuse the shareholding, the more the firms are supervised by markets of external minority shareholders acting through boards of directors. A second indicator is the strength of "MSPs" – Minority Shareholder Protections, a set of rules and regulations concerning: information (disclosure and audit), oversight (board independence), control rules (voting processes), and managerial incentives (executive pay). Countries differ on the strength of MSPs. A key causal argument in the literature is that the quality of MSP drives the level of diffusion: the higher the MSP the more likely countries have *diffuse* shareholding, the lower the MSP the greater the concentration, thus the *blockholding* pattern. Overall there is some support for this idea; there is also a lot of variance, strong examples which don't fit (Gourevitch and Shinn, 2005).

In comparison with a sample of 39 countries, those of East Asia fall toward the middle and the bottom of the shareholder concentration and shareholder protection lists; that is, they have high concentration and low MSP. In Table 8.1, Hong Kong and Indonesia lie between France and Chile at the bottom of the concentration index; South Korea lies a bit below Australia and New Zealand in the upper third; Malaysia, Taiwan, Singapore, the Philippines, and Thailand fall in the middle with Finland, Austria, Sweden, and India. China and Japan don't fit. For China, this is an artifact of the high level of public ownership in the Chinese economy; the data includes only public firms without a state blockholder, which consist of only 5 percent of the economy. In Japan, MSP is high, but cross shareholding renders it meaningless as the system has been de facto bloc dominated (though some experts argue this is now changing, e.g. Schaede, 2007). On MSP, Singapore is the highest in our group, followed by Hong Kong; Indonesia is close to the bottom, with Thailand, Taiwan, and Korea a bit above in the thirties on an index of 100.

This table is static, measuring a single point in time. A recent IMF study (De Nicolò *et al.*, 2006) provides some rough way of tracking change over time. Instead of looking at MSP (or other legal regulations), this study looks at indicators of

Table 8.1 Shareholder diffusion and Minority Shareholder Protections

	Concentration	*MSP*
China	5.0	11
Taiwan	45.5	35
Philippines	46.4	35
Japan	4.1	37
Korea	31.8	37
Venezuela	49.0	41
Norway	38.6	48
Argentina	72.5	50
New Zealand	27.0	52
Malaysia	42.6	67
Hong Kong	71.5	70
Australia	27.5	71
Singapore	44.8	84
US	5.0	97
Mean	46.9	45.6

Source: Gourevitch and Shinn, 2005, table adapted for Peter Gourevitch, "Containing the Oligarchs: the politics of corporate governance systems in East Asia," in John Ravenhill *et al. East Asia Ten Years After the Crises*, Cornell, forthcoming.

Notes
Concentration: tells us the percentage of total shares in publicly traded firms without primary government owner, held by the top group of owners; thus a low number means a high degree of shareholder diffusion.
MSP: Minority Shareholder Protections are a composite index of several indicators including control, compensation, board composition, etc.

behavior. It constructs an index they call CGQ (Corporate Governance Quality) out of three variables: Accounting Standards (AS) – how much information companies report; Earnings Smoothing (ES) – the extent to which managers may obscure earnings by adjustments over time to make them smoother; Stock Price Synchronicity (SPS) – the extent to which stock prices vary together or independently. Low accounting information, obscure earnings reports, and low independence of stock price movement are all behavioral indicators of poor corporate governance patterns. This measure has the advantage of getting past the difficulty of knowing if the formal MSP actually are enforced (Berglof and Claessens, 2004). The study finds shifts that are not large, but they show some change, confirming the impression of modest improvement:

So some modest change appears to be taking place in East Asian corporate governance. What can we say about the process of change, the causal mechanisms?

Channels of change: the causal mechanisms

Specialists in corporate governance have been debating sharply contrasting explanations for the variance in CG systems around the world. In these debates about explanation, three arguments contend for primacy:

1   the *formal rules of law (legal family)*, where common law is argued to provide stronger support for MSP than does civil law;[2]
2   *political institutions* where constitutional government subject to accountability produces better results than authoritarian ones; or *de jure*, parchment institutions, associated with constitutions;[3]

Table 8.2 Change in "corporate governance index" 1995–2003

	1995	1998	2003	AvGroRa
Korea	0.584	0.615	0.592	0.002
China	0.559	0.547	0.507	−0.012
Hong Kong	0.586	0.568	0.712	0.024
Taiwan	N/A	N/A	N/A	N/A
Japan	0.572	0.620	0.640	0.014
Australia	0.661	0.680	0.727	0.012
Malaysia	0.521	0.529	0.613	0.020
New Zealand	0.470	0.562	0.651	0.041
Singapore	0.605	0.571	0.648	0.009
Argentina	0.523	0.510	0.536	0.003
Venezuela	0.525	0.532	0.487	0.031
Philippines	0.535	0.561	0.663	0.027
Norway	0.698	0.691	0.681	−0.003

Source: Di Niccolo, Laeven, and Ueda, and from IMF Report, 2006. "The CGQ index is a simple average of three proxy measures of *outcomes* of corporate governance in the dimensions of accounting, disclosure and transparency."
(Table drawn from Gourevitch paper for Ravenhill *et. al.* volume, op. cit.)

3 *social forms of power*, where elements of civil society, such as interest groups, social class, media, and professional associations, balance to produce good policy outcomes (Acemoglu and Johnson, 2005).

These three approaches differ on the answer to this question: if law and regulation protect investors from exploitation by insiders, *what explains the supply of these laws and regulations?*

1 Legal family – the formal rules approach

For shareholder diffusion to occur, blockholders must be willing to sell down and outside investors must accept a minority position in the firm. To do so, argues a rich literature, they must obtain some kind of protection from insider abuse. Law and regulation provide this – Minority Shareholder Protections.[4] These measures include: *information* (disclosure and audit), *oversight* (board independence), *control rules* (voting processes), and *managerial incentives* (executive pay). The higher the level of MSP, the more supervision of managers, the more reassured are investors (who buy) and blockholders (who sell to diversify) and the deeper will markets become – at least that is the core assumption of the "law matters" school.[5] Laws about insider trading, the composition of boards, the issuance of shares, providing information about the firm's finances, takeovers, and the market for control – these allow outsiders to judge the value of their investment and take action: buy, sell, or take over.

The prediction of this approach is that where MSP is strong, diffusion occurs. Table 8.1 above provides a summary of an index from Gourevitch and Shinn of MSP and diffusion. Figure 8.1 (also from Gourevitch and Shinn) below tests the prediction, correlating blockholding with MSP.[6]

So, MSP and corporate governance patterns do connect, as expected. Some relationship exists – though the correlation is not strong, which suggests other variables are at play. To the extent MSP (law and regulation about shareholders) accounts for diffusion, what explains the provision of MSP?[7] La Porta *et al.* argue it is "legal family:" common law systems, they suggest, have higher MSP than do civil law countries. The major common law countries – the UK and its former colonies, including the US, are heavily grouped in the shareholder diffusion and high MSP quadrant, while France, Spain, and their former colonies tend toward the blockholder and low protection pattern. This is a striking pattern, which has given the legal family interpretation wide currency.

And yet, closer inspection reveals problems with the legal family explanation. On the empirical side, we observe substantial variance in corporate governance patterns within countries over time, while their legal family stays constant. In their important paper, "The Great Reversals,"[8] Rajan and Zingales (2003) track within-country change extensively, showing France and Japan developing considerable stock markets prior to World War II, then showing a sharp swing toward bank dominance. The US looked much like Germany prior to World War I, but policy changes created the regulatory system of anti-trust, banking regulation, and MSP

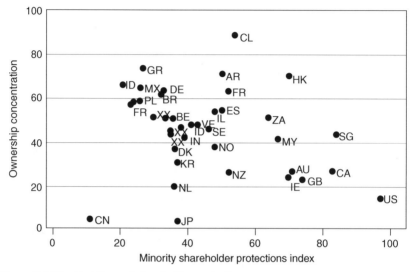

Figure 8.1 Blockholding and shareholder protections.

Note
For the definitions of country abbreviations see Gourevitch and Shinn, 2005.

which produced the system we know today (Roe, 1994). Berkowitz *et al.* (2003) show a "transplant effect" that local conditions influence considerably how countries alter efforts to import legal structures from outside. Within the same legal family, considerable variance exists among countries, with Germany and Sweden showing stronger protections than France and Spain.

On the conceptual side of the legal family argument, the mechanism of causality remains unclear: just why does the legal family produce the claimed effect? Legal family, a formal characteristic, does not explain the content of the actual laws which are passed, nor the pattern of enforcement. Nothing about common law guarantees that countries will enact vigorous MSPs, nor that they will enforce them. Nothing about civil law systems prevent countries from enacting strong MSPs, nor from enforcing them. Laws are passed and sustained because of political processes: the demands of various groups in society and the institutions that process them. It is to these we turn.

2 *Political institutions* – de jure *power*

Laws are made, and enforced, by political systems. Variation in the content of laws, regulation, and enforcement might then be the product of variation in political systems. In this respect, formal legal system (civil vs. common law) can be differentiated from political institutions and from social structures. Acemoglu and Johnson (2005) call the legal systems "contractual institutions," while labeling political structures as "property rights institutions."[9] Contractual processes, they argue, do differ according to legal family, but do not predict economic development. Property protection institutions don't correlate with legal family and do correlate with economic growth. Similar problems arise with legal family for results on corporate governance (Roe, 2003; Gourevitch, 2003; Gourevitch and Shinn, 2005).

What are property-protecting institutions? In formal terms, they are the structures which organize power in political systems. Here Acemoglu and Johnson make another quite important distinction: between *de jure* institutions, formal structures that shape the way "preferences" (interests, ideas, goals) are aggregated,[10] and de facto institutions (forms of power in civil society, such as land, guns, money). We know that different methods of counting the votes yield different outcomes because of cycling and agenda control. The same applies to other aspects of political system. This insight generates an important literature comparing countries along different dimensions of their political institutions, including electoral laws, the structure of the executive and the legislature, federalism, courts and the independence of the judiciary, free speech and press. Countries are compared with categories such as presidential vs. parliamentary systems, majoritarian vs. consensus systems, high or low number of veto gates or veto players. Important World Bank research by Beck, Kiefer and others has made an important contribution to this literature, for a number of years, building a valuable database (Acemoglu *et al.*, 2001; North, 1981; Haber *et al.*, 2003); other research projects have added substantially to our knowledge (Beck *et al.*, 2001; Lijphart, 1999; Persson and Tabellini, 2003; Shugart and Carey, 1992; Haggard and McCubbins, 2001).

The institutionalist approach – the focus on *de jure* institutions – provides leverage in accounting for variance in MSP provision and corporate governance outcomes. In stable democracies, for example, Gourevitch and Hawes (2002) and Gourevitch and Shinn (2005) show that MSP and corporate governance outcomes correlate with the majoritarian/consensus distinction. Majoritarian systems are more likely to have high MSP and diffuse shareholder patterns. The logic has to do with the impact institutions have on the bargains among groups in each system. Majoritarian systems have wider policy swings, which undermines the corporatist foundations of a particular set of arrangements around blockholding, which then induces actors to seek autonomy through arm's length economic relationships, and thus to MSP and shareolder diffusion; conversely, "consensus" systems reinforce the bargains in corporatism and sustain blockholding arrangements (Hall and Soskice, 2001; Iversen and Soskice, 2001, 2006; Mares, 2003). Pagano and Volpin (2001, 2005a, and 2005b) stress the impact of electoral systems: countries with proportional representation are more likely to have high shareholder protection rules and diffuse shareholding patterns than are countries with once-past-the-post single member plurality districts.

The impact of veto players and stable institutions may be different between stable democracies and authoritarian regimes. Strong regimes can enforce rules but can also predate on economic life, undermining incentives to invest; weak regimes can't enforce rules, which also undermines incentives. Blockholding may arise out of either extreme. Having many veto points can create policy paralysis. Having few veto points lessens the chances of policy paralysis, but increases the threat of predation. The confidence of investors may be highest at some intermediate point on a U-shaped curve, some "just right" balance, between inaction and too much. We do know that for some periods, investment in authoritarian regimes can be high; such regimes are able to signal some kind of commitment to investors that predation will be limited (Gourevitch and Shinn, 2005; Fisman, 2001; McIntyre, 2001).

3   Social forms of power, de facto power

In contrast to this stress on *de jure* political institutions, another literature looks at de facto forms of power – control of land, guns, people, votes – which enables social groups to manipulate the political process to their advantage (Acemoglu and Johnson, 2005). Constitutions seek to constrain later generations by structuring the political game on behalf of whoever is writing the documents; the constitution is thus a commitment technology. But groups with social power are able to undermine these restrictions, capturing the formal structures, altering their usage, or even changing the constitution. The histories of Latin America, Africa, and even Europe and the US, are full of examples of this kind.

Stasavage critiques the influential North and Weingast essay on the English political settlement of 1688 by noting the limits on the crown came not only from formal changes in parliamentary oversight, but from the goals of the particular majority that dominated parliament at that time, so that a different majority would have led to a different outcome, as in France (Stasavage, 2002). These examples suggest that to understand just how formal institutions work, we need to know who uses them and for what purposes (Rajan and Zingales, 2003).

In the case of corporate governance, these considerations compel a look at the interest group politics that surround policy toward MSP. Laws regulating corporations and shareholders express the demands of groups acting through politics, whose support politicians and bureaucrats need in order to create and enforce legislation. Who wants strong MSP?

One line of reasoning assumes investors want strong MSP, while workers or employees oppose it: a classic pairing of right (the side of capital) vs. left (the side of labor). Roe (2003) provides evidence that where labor-related groups are politically strong, we have weaker MSP, and where conservative pro-market groups prevail we have stronger MSP. This mirrors the frequently made argument that capital movement forces convergence around high MSP, as investors demand legal protections for their stock purchasing (MacAvoy and Milstein, 2003; Hansmann and Kraakman, 2001).

The second way of seeing the political divide sees conflict by sector, across class lines. In some situations workers, managers, and inside owners support a mutually reinforcing regime of blockholding. The coalition members prefer the stability of existing arrangements of employment, investment, and leadership to the fluid relationships of the high MSP systems. Minority shareholders are seen as outsiders, seeking to uproot stable relationships built up over time. That stability sustains a distinctive pattern of production which saves in transaction costs and specializes in high-quality products and producer goods (Kester, 1996; Hall and Soskice, 2001). Germany is the most well-known example of this corporate governance pattern. It involves extensive collaboration among members of the system through a set of arrangements frequently labeled as corporatist. There is some research evidence for the existence of such patterns (Pagano and Volpin, 2005a; Gourevitch and Shinn, 2005; Carney, 2004, 2005, and 2006; Pinto and Pinto, 2006).

A third form of cleavage on corporate governance allies minority shareholders with workers to support high levels of MSP and transparency, generally against inside managers and blockholders who want to insulate the firm from hostile takeover and market pressures. Pension funds are a key ingredient of this coalition reversing the expectation that workers and investors are in conflict. The growth of pension funds may be causing an historical shift in the coalitional patterns around public policy concerning MSP and corporate governance.[11] Employee pension funds see MSPs as a way of protecting an investment, and they lobby political parties dependent on labor support to get them. The result is a pattern of "left" governments doing more for investors than do the supposedly capital friendly right-wing governments which are more beholden to insiders and managers (Hoepner, 2003; Cioffi and Hoepner, 2004). An example is Germany, where the SPD supported legislation that strengthened shareholder protection and lowered the tax on capital gains from selling shares, while the supposedly more business friendly CDU opposed these moves (Cioffi and Hoepner, 2004).

The greater the share of a country's pension funds in private hands, rather than in public systems, the higher the level of MSP (Gourevitch and Shinn, 2005), and the more likely we will see demands to strengthen them further. Just how actively pension funds use MSP powers to impact corporate governance can be substantially affected by the micro-institutional details of financial inter-mediaries: who controls the funds; do the institutional investors have a conflict of interest between their shareholders and those who invest with them; how much competition among funds; what control do investors have over the funds and their money; what powers do institutional investors have to challenge man-agement? These details influence both the rate of return and the impact of priva-tized funds on corporate governance (Gourevitch and Shinn, 2005; Gourevitch and Allen, 2006; Lefort and Walker, 1999).

The role of institutional investors in the corporate governance system deserves more attention (Gourevitch, 2007). They impact the rate of return to privatized systems: Chile, for example, which received substantial attention for privatizing social security early on, is now the object of controversy as the rate of return has fallen below that of people who stayed in the public PayGo system: a substantial reason is the size of the fees taken by the private AFPs which administer the funds. In the US, mutually owned Vanguard drives down the fees, but with weak competition, as will be likely in many countries, the fees remain high (Bogle, 2005; Swenson, 2005). Can government policy create low fee AFPs? Do the AFPs actually play a role in monitoring the managers, or are they captured by the large blockholders in the Chilean economy (Gourevitch and Allen, 2005)?

These three patterns of political cleavage involve three different coalitions: what brings these coalitions together, causing some to win at some points and lose at others? Institutionalists stress the role of formal structures in shaping the way clusters of preferences aggregate: thus the argument that it is the electoral law or majoritarian structures which shape the victory of different coalitional patterns among countries. The de facto power approach looks instead at the resources various groups have to mobilize for political action (votes, organizations, the ability to strike). Variance among countries in outputs expresses differences in the political strengths of these various interest groups.

The interest group approach can help clarify the role of historical context and path dependence in shaping outcomes. The demands of interest groups vary across countries in part because of incentives shaped by prior choices in public policy and the results of earlier conflicts. Rajan and Zingales' (2003) description of the "great reversals" (countries switching policy directions) notes the impact of interest groups to economic dislocations after 1914. Domestic groups reacted against the disruptive effects of free trade and sought stability via regulation. Among the effects was a shift toward bank influence and away from open equity markets. Similarly, the "transplant effect" analyzed by Berkowitz *et al.* (2003) can be interpreted as the impact of interest groups within each country toward the costs (and benefits) of adopting foreign practices. Roe (2006) explores the impact of war on interest group alignments; countries which experienced considerable damage from the World Wars shifted toward blockholding. Perotti and von Thadden (2005, 2006a, and 2006b) look at the impact of hyperinflation during the 1920s: countries whose middle-class investors were wiped out shifted toward preferring the regulatory bank-centered model. Rogoswki (1989), Hiscox (2002), Frieden (2006), and Gourevitch (1986) examine the impact of world trading patterns on policy choices: contractions in the economy produce demands for protection, while prosperity prepares the ground for free trade.

Policy choices, once made, influence the politics of subsequent disputes. They generate mutually reinforcing patterns of regulation and interest groups' preferences. Hall and Soskice (2001) show labor and capital ally or conflict depending on earlier policy choices. Labor vs. capital (investors) may conflict in the neo-liberal economic structures of the US and the UK (which they call Liberal Market Economies (LMEs), which have fluid labor relations, vigorous anti-trust, general skill-oriented educational systems, strong product market competition, and diffuse shareholder-oriented corporate and governance systems). Conversely, alliances or bargains between labor and capital can be found in Coordinated Market Economies (CMEs), which have highly structured labor relations, limited domestic competition, price and market coordination, specific skill-oriented educational training, and blockholding governance systems. "Institutional complementarity" (Milgrom and Roberts, 1990) among components of the economy generates political support for these bargains. Firms may invest in worker training, which makes sense if there is low labor market fluidity which is in turn more likely in the blockholding financial structures with patient capital and low market for control. Once systems of this kind start, at some point in the past, the pieces reinforce each other. Management, blockholders, and labor generate reasons to cooperate around preservation of the firm. The interests and politics of each production factor are thus strongly influenced by context. What labor, management, or capital want depends in part on which national production system they operate in.

Institutional complementarity helps explain the weaknesses of MSP levels as an explanation of corporate governance outcomes (Hall and Soskice, 2001; Gourevitch and Shinn, 2005; Roe, 2003). So far, we have emphasized alternative explanations of the provision of MSPs – legal family, formal political institutions, and interest group politics. But investors may look at variables other than MSP alone. The conditions in labor relations, product market competition, price setting, and labor training all influence the risks investors take in buying shares. Roe notes where labor is strong in the firm and in the political system, investors may prefer blockholding to maintain stronger bargaining posture with labor, and labor in turn may sustain militancy to deal with blockholding management. Power relationships and policy regulation outside the strict domain of corporate governance as defined by MSP thus have an impact on corporate governance patterns.

Another critique of the MSP approach moves away from regulation and law altogether. Shareholder diffusion began, argue several specialists, before regulations: the listing requirements of the London and New York stock exchanges provided "private bonding" reassurances (Cheffins, 2001, 2002a, and 2002b; Franks *et al.*, 2005a, 2005b; Morck *et al.*, 2005). In the UK, mergers occurred among local elites, who knew each other well. The demand for formal shareholder protections occurred later, as shareholding spread. In addition to the historical evidence for this pattern, it is reinforced by a political logic: who would lobby for shareholder protection if there were no shareholders? The social foundations of markets can be quite important and are worth further analysis (Greif *et al.*, 1994; Greif, 1993).[12]

The non-legal and regulatory processes are particularly important for understanding governance outcomes in many emerging market situations. The MSP approach assumes good governance can only arise out of strong law. But much of the world lacks strong law of this kind, and yet many countries do rather well in economic growth. China is surely a strong example, but so are Indonesia, Vietnam, and other places. These countries do not rank high on measures of quality of law and legal enforcement, that is contractual fairness noted above (Djankov, 2002). Several of them do not rank high in indicators of political accountability: that is, in security of property rights that comes from checks and balances in political institutions (the *de jure* distinction made above). How then to explain vigorous growth, the substantial flow of investment into these countries, and considerable internal investment?

Several answers emerge. Most of them have to do with various forms of "bonding," or informal modes of guarantee. First, governments are more accountable to investors than a focus on formal institutions suggests. Governments respond to pressures other than votes. They care about the general level of discontent, the creation of wealth, the ability to support the costs of military and police, their own wellbeing and the wellbeing of the various groups that keep them in office, or could overthrow them. These mechanisms can be quite powerful in their constraints on governments. They can provide strong incentives to worry about both capital and labor. They can induce policies friendly to investors, both foreign and domestic. These may be less fully institutionalized than formal legal authority, but can be quite real. China attracts substantial capital and investment without any clearly accountable democratic political system. Singapore does not comply with the Westminster model of accountability; yet capital feels quite secure here, unfearful of predation by the government. Foreign investors, and local ones, accept as their guarantee against predation the dependence of the government on sustaining a good economy, thus the goodwill of investors. Governments that don't signal that kind of dependence lack the guarantee: that could be particularly authoritarian governments as with North Korea and Myanmar, where mass discontent is ignored.

Second, private bonding mechanisms can substitute for formal rules. Family, ethnicity, religion, and region – these affective ties often provide information that facilitates coordination among units in an economic system. They provide the grounds for a kind of contracting based on private sanctioning, where the family, religious, or ethnic leaders carry out the punishment, rather than formal courts. These mechanisms of trust can be quite effective. They involve ways of gathering information, transmitting reliability or violations from previous practice, which can solve coordination problems (McMillan and Naughton, 1992; Johnson *et al.*, 2002; McMillan and Woodruff, 1999). They act like institutions, without being formal political ones and without the formal institutions of coercion (police, courts, law) associated with political systems.

These social and private mechanisms seem particularly prevalent in Asia. Migration patterns provide one source: overseas Chinese in many parts of Asia are well known for this, a modern example of a pattern going back to Phoenicians, Armenians, Jews, Magrhebi traders and other groups for centuries.

As one moves toward social and private bonding mechanisms in explaining economic relationships such as corporate governance, it is likely the analysis moves against large cross-national patterns. Countries generate distinctive micro-institutions that specify incentives. The more varied these are according to local conditions, the more variance across countries which do not scale easily in cross-national measures: we get rich networking accounts, but we don't get strong cross-national tests (Herrigel, 2008; McDermott, 2007).

Lessons from the AFC: the role of politics

The varying and mixed impact of the AFC on corporate governance reflects the strength of political variables in shaping national responses. As the strength of groups differs, so will the response to common pressures. The policy prescription implied by seeing the importance of variety is to reject uniformity or mono-cropping. The Washington Consensus against crony capitalism assumes uniformity of conditions. It assumes, as Wade critiques, that a model based on American and to some degree British practices is best for everyone, but the world is too hetero-geneous. The efficiency of markets is partly about specialization. It is likely that governance structures are a form of production process, in which firms and coun-tries can specialize, and therefore differ. The debates over corporate governance reveal an abundance of forms that work in varying conditions. Obligating countries to adopt MSP rules in a strict way regardless of local circumstances runs against what we have been learning about variety (Easterly, 2006). Why impose MSP when countries lack the structures to use them effectively? Blockholding makes a lot of sense when legal regimes are weak, or the political conditions for containing corruption are absent, or where many uncertainties prevail, or where various private bonding mechanisms are strong (Samphanthanarak, 2007; Bertrand *et al.*, 2007). This quarrel resembles the one concerning the "transition problem" – as the USSR unraveled and China chose to marketize, was "big bang" the best way (the Russian choice), or a gradual process of learning through experimentation (the Chinese choice)? The record favors the latter (McMillan and Naughton, 1992).

Policy choices at a given moment reflect the interaction of interest group preferences, ideology, and political institutions. The relationship among these can shift with shocks – like the AFC – or changing conditions in the economy, or the international political environment. How countries respond to these shifts and pressures is likely in each case to be mediated through political processes.

Notes

1 The World Bank's 1994 volume *The East Asian Miracle: Economic Growth and Public Policy* explored the debate over causes of the East Asian miracle; the contest was between a state-led vs. "natural market" model. Wade (2004), Haggard (1990), and others sustained this debate; Johnson (1982) stated the Japanese version. The debate has evolved: was it ministerial leadership of key sectors which constituted the government's role, or the regulatory environment that promoted "patient capital" and stable markets?

2 The problem of managers escaping the control of investors was famously observed by Berle and Means (1933). While country specialists knew the US pattern was by no means universal, La Porta *et al.* (1997, 1998, 1999, 2000, and 2002) helped develop recent awareness of the variance. For an extensive review of the literature see Becht *et al.* (2005).

3 This particular use of the terms *de jure* and de facto derive from Acemoglu and Johnson (2005). See also Acemoglu and Robinson (2006); Acemoglu *et al.* (2001, 2005); Acemoglu (2005).

4 This passage draws on Gourevitch and Shinn (2005), especially Chapters 2 and 3.

5 Historical research questions the causal sequence: do shareholders precede MSP or does MSP come ahead of shareholder? Private bonding arrangements via stock exchanges or mergers may have created a group of shareholders who then demanded MSPs. That makes political sense (why create something for which there is no con-stituency), and may be historically accurate, but it is not clear how it handles the present: can formal MSP regulations and their enforcement induce shareholding? See Cheffins (2001, 2002a, and 2002b), Morck (2006), and Coffee (2001).

6 Gourevitch and Shinn (2005: 51), and Table A-4, p. 301. The correlation is strongest for developed countries, at –0.42 ** (p < 0.05) at significance of 0.03 , while reversed in sign and weak significance for developing countries (0.29).

7 This section draws on Gourevitch (2006).

8 See Rajan and Zingales, *Saving Capitalism from the Capitalists*, for further exploration of the role of interest groups in producing the "rent-seeking" that shapes financial systems.
9 Also see Woodruff (2006) and Laeven and Woodruff (2005).
10 Glaesar *et al.* (2004) make important warning about the need to be sure measures of institutions are independent from those of the outputs they produce.
11 Predicted by Peter Drucker (1976).
12 For an evaluation of how decision-maker understanding of their options shapes behavior, see Culpepper (2005).

References

Acemoglu, D. (2005) "Constitutions, Politics and Economics; A Review Essay on Persson and Tabellini's 'The Economic Effects of Constitutions'," *Journal of Economic Literature* 43: 1025–1048.

Acemoglu, D. and Johnson, S. (2005) "Unbundling Institutions," *Journal of Political Economy* 113: 949–995.

Acemoglu, D. and Robinson, J. (2006) "The Persistence of Power, Elites and Institutions," mimeo.

Acemoglu, D., Johnson, S., and Robinson, J. (2001) "The Colonial Origins of Comparative Development: An Empirical Investigation," *American Economic Review* 91: 1369–1401.

—— (2005) "Institutions as the Fundamental Cause of Long-Run Growth," in *Handbook of Economic Growth*, vol. 1A, North-Holland.

Becht, M., Bolton, P., and Röell, A. (2005) "Corporate Governance and Control," in *Handbook of the Economics of Finance*, Boston: Elsevier/North-Holland.

Beck, T., Clarke, G., Groff, A., Keefer, P., and Walsh, P. (2001) "New Tools in Comparative Political Economy: The Database of Political Institutions," *World Bank Economic Review* 15: 165–176.

Berglof, E. and Claessens, S. (2004) "Corporate Governance and Enforcement," *World Bank Policy Research Working Paper 3409*, September: 1–49.

Berkowitz, D., Pistor, K., and Richard, J.-F. (2003) "Economic Development, Legality and the Transplant Effect," *European Economic Review* 47: 165.

Berle, A.A. and Means, G. (1933) *The Modern Corporation and Private Property*, New York: Harcourt, Brace and World.

Bertrand, M., Johnson, S., Samphantharak, K., and Schoar, A. (2007) "Mixing Family With Business: Study of Thai Business Groups and the Families Behind Them," mimeo.

Bogle, J. (2005) *The Battle for the Soul of Capitalism*, New Haven: Yale University Press.

Carney, R. (2004) "Corporate Governance and the Financial System: the Role of Politics," *Journal of Corporate Ownership and Control*, Vol. 2, Issue 2.

—— (2005) "Globalisation, Politics, and European Financial Integration," in C. Tisdell (ed.) *Globalisation and World Economic Policies*, Delhi: Serials Publications.

—— (2006) "Varieties of Capitalism in France: Interests, Institutions, and Finance," *French Politics*, Vol. 4, Issue 1.

Cheffins, B. (2001) "Does Law Matter?: The Separation of Ownership and Control in the United Kingdom," *Journal of Legal Studies* 30: 459.

—— (2002a) "Corporate Law and Ownership Structure: A Darwinian Link?," *University of New South Wales Law Journal* 25: 346.

—— (2002b) "Putting Britain on the Roe Map: The Emergence of the Berle–Means Corporation in the United Kingdom," in J. McCahery (ed.) *Corporate Governance Regimes: Convergence and Diversity*, New York: Oxford University Press.

Cioffi, J.W. and Hoepner, M. (2004) "The Political Paradox of Corporate Governance Reform: Why the Center-Left is the Driving Force Behind the Rise of Financial Capitalism," paper presented at the Annual Meeting of the American Political Science Association, September 2–5, in Chicago, Illinois.

Coffee, J. (2001) "The Rise of Dispersed Ownership: The Roles of Law and the State in the Separation of Ownership and Control," *The Yale Law Journal* 111: 1.

Culpepper, P.D. (2005) "Institutional Change in Contemporary Capitalism: Coordinated Financial Systems since 1990," *World Politics* 57: 173.

De Nicolò, G., Laeven, L., and Ueda, K. (2006) "Corporate Governance Quality in Asia: Comparative Trends and Impact," *IMF Research Department*, unpublished manuscript.

Djankov, S. (2002) "Courts: the Lex Mundi Project," *NBER Working Paper # 8890*.

Drucker, P. (1976) *The Unseen Revolution: How Pension Fund Socialism Came to America*, New York: Harper & Row.

Easterly, W. (2006) *White Man's Burden*, New York: Penguin.

Fisman, R. (2001) "Estimating the Value of Political Connections," *American Economic Review* 91: 1095.

Franks, J., Mayer, C., and Rossi, S. (2005a) "Spending Less Time with the Family: The Decline of Family Ownership in the UK," in R. Morck (ed.) *The History of Corporate Governance Around the World: Family Business Groups to Professional Managers*, Chicago: University of Chicago Press.

Franks, J., Mayer, C., and Wagner, H. (2005b) "The Origins of the German Corporation – Finance, Ownership and Control," mimeo, unpublished.

Frieden, J. (2006) *Global Capitalism: its Fall and Rise in the Twentieth Century*, New York: W. W. Norton.

Glaeser, E., La Porta, R., Lopez-de-Silanes, F., and Shleifer, A. (2004) "Do Institutions Cause Growth?," *Journal of Economic Growth* 9: 271.

Gourevitch, P. (1986) *Politics in Hard Times*, Ithaca: Cornell University Press.

—— (2003) "The Politics of Corporate Governance Regulation," *The Yale Law Journal*, Vol. 112, No. 7: 1829–1880.

—— (2006) "Politics, Institutions and Society: Seeking Better Results," in A. Palacio (ed.) *World Bank Legal Review: Law Equity and Development*, The Hague: Martinus Nijhoff.

—— (2007) "What do Corporations Owe Citizens?: Pensions, Corporate Governance and the Role of Institutional Investors," in H. Rosenthal and D. Rothman (eds) *What Do We Owe Each Other: Rights and Obligations in Contemporary American Society*, New Brunswick: Transaction Books.

Gourevitch, P. and Allen, J. (2005) "De-constructing Financial Institutions: Why the Variance Among Them Toward Corporate Governance?," UCSD, mimeo.

—— (2006) "Chilean Pension Reform and Corporate Governance," Graduate School of International Relations and Pacific Studies, UCSD, mimeo.

Gourevitch, P. and Hawes, M.B. (2002) "The Politics of Choice among National Production Systems," *L'Année de la regulation*, Presses de Sciences Po, 241.

Gourevitch, P. and Shinn, J. (2005) *Political Power and Corporate Control: The New Global Politics of Corporate Governance*, Princeton: Princeton University Press.

Greif, A. (1993) "Contract Enforceability and Economic Institutions in Early Trade: The Maghribi Traders' Coalition," *American Economic Review* 83: 525.

Greif, A., Milgrom, P., and Weingast, B. (1994) "Coordination, Commitment and Enforcement: The Case of the Merchant Guild," *The Journal of Political Economy* 102: 745.

Haber, S., Razo, A., and Maurer, N. (2003) *The Politics of Property Rights: Political Instability, Credible Commitments, and Economic Growth in Mexico 1876–1929*, New York: Cambridge University Press.

Haggard, S. (1990) *Pathways from the Periphery: The Politics of Growth in the Newly Industrializing Countries*, Ithaca: Cornell University Press.

Haggard, S. and McCubbins, M. (2001) *Presidents, Parliament and Policy*, New York: Cambridge University Press.

Hall, P. and Soskice, D. (2001) *Varieties of Capitalism: The Institutional Foundations of Comparative Foundation*, New York: Oxford University Press.

Hansmann, H. and Kraakman, R. (2001) "The End of History for Corporate Law," *Georgetown Law Journal* 89: 439–468.

Herrigel, G. (2008) "Corporate Governance," in G. Jones and J. Zeitlin (eds) *The Oxford Handbook of Business History*, New York: Oxford University Press.

Hiscox, M. (2002) *International Trade and Political Conflict: Commerce, Coalitions, and Mobility*, Princeton: Princeton University Press.

Hoepner, M. (2003) "European Corporate Governance Reform and the German Party Paradox," *Max-Planck-Institute for the Study of Societies Program for the Study of Germany and Europe Working Paper series* 03–1.

Iversen, T. and Soskice, D. (2001) "An Asset Theory of Social Policy Preferences," *American Political Science Review* 95: 875–893.

—— (2006) "Electoral Institutions, Parties, and the Politics of Class: Why Some Democracies Redistribute More than Others," *American Political Science Review* 100: 165–181.

Johnson, C.A. (1982) *MITI and the Japanese Miracle: The Growth of Industrial Policy, 1925–1975*, Stanford: Stanford University Press.

Johnson, S., McMillan, J., and Woodruff, C. (2002) "Property Rights and Finance," *The American Economic Review*, Vol. 92, No. 5: 1335–1356.

Kester, W.C. (1996) "American and Japanese Corporate Governance: Converging to Best Practice?," in S. Berger and R. Dore (eds) *National Diversity and Global Capitalism*, Ithaca: Cornell University Press.

La Porta, R., Lopez-de-Silanes, F., Shleifer, A., and Vishny, R.W. (1997) "Legal Determinants of External Finance," *The Journal of Finance* 52: 1131–1150.

—— (1998) "Law and Finance," *Journal of Political Economy* 106: 1113–1155.

—— (2000) "Investor Protection and Corporate Governance," *Journal of Financial Economics* 58: 3–27.

—— (2002) "Investor Protection and Corporate Valuation," *Journal of Finance* 57: 1147–1170.

La Porta, R., Lopez-de-Silanes, F., and Shleifer, A. (1999) "Corporate Ownership Around the World," *The Journal of Finance* 54: 471–518.

Laeven, L. and Woodruff, C. (2005) "The Quality of the Legal System: Firm Ownership and Firm Size," mimeo.

Lefort, F. and Walker, E. (1999) "Ownership and Capital Structure of Chilean Conglomerates: Facts and Hypotheses for Governance," *Revista ABANTE* 3.

Lijphart, A. (1999) *Patterns of Democracy: Governmnent Forms and Performance in Thirty-Six Countries*, New Haven: Yale University Press.

MacAvoy, P. and Milstein, I. (2003) *The Recurrent Crisis on Corporate Governance*, New York: Palgrave Macmillan.

McDermott, G. (2007) "The Politics of Institutional Renovation and Economic Upgrading; Recombining the Vines that Bind in Argentina," *Politics and Society*, March.

McIntyre, A. (2001) "Institutions and Investors: The Politics of the Financial Crisis in Southeast Asia," *International Organization* 55: 81.

McMillan, J. and Naughton, B. (1992) "How to Reform a Planned Economy: Lessons from China," *Oxford Review of Economic Policy*, Vol. 8, No. 1.

McMillan, J. and Woodruff, C. (1999) "Interfirm Relationships and Informal Credit in Vietnam," *The Quarterly Journal of Economics*, Vol. 114, No. 4: 1285–1320.

Mares, I. (2003) *The Politics of Social Risk*, New York: Cambridge University Press.

Milgrom, P. and Roberts, J. (1990) "The Economics of Modern Manufacturing: Technology, Strategy and Organization," *American Economic Review* 80: 511–528.

Morck, R. (ed.) (2006) *History of Corporate Ownership*, Chicago: University of Chicago Press.

Morck, R., Wolfenzon, D., and Yeung, B. (2005) "Corporate Governance, Economic Entrenchment and Growth," *Journal of Economic Literature* 43: 655–720.

North, C.D. (1981) *Structure and Change in Economic History*, New York: W.W. Norton.

Pagano, M. and Volpin, P. (2001) "The Political Economy of Finance," *Oxford Review of Economic Policy* 17: 502–519.

—— (2005a) "The Political Economy of Corporate Governance," *American Economic Review* 95: 1005–1030.

—— (2005b) "Workers, Managers, and Corporate Control," *The Journal of Finance* 60: 841–868.

Perotti, E. and von Thadden, E.-L. (2005) "Dominant Investors and Strategic Transparency," *Journal of Law and Economics* 21: 76–102.

—— (2006a) "The Political Economy of Corporate Control and Labor Rents," *Journal of Political Economy* 114: 145–174.

—— (2006b) "Corporate Governance and the Distribution of Wealth," *Journal of Institutional and Theoretical Economics* 162: 204–217.

Persson, T. and Tabellini, G. (2003) *The Economic Effects of Constitutions: What do the Data Say?* Cambridge: MIT Press.

Pinto, P. and Pinto, S. (2006) "The Politics of Investment: Partisanship and Sectoral Allocation of Foreign Direct Investment," paper presented at the annual meeting of the the Midwest Political Science Association.

Rajan, R. and Zingales, L. (2003) "The Great Reversals: The Politics of Financial Development in the 20th Century," *Journal of Financial Economics* 69: 5–50.

Roe, M. (1994) *Strong Managers, Weak Owners: The Political Roots of American Corporate Finance*, Princeton: Princeton University Press.

—— (2003) *Political Determinants of Corporate Governance*, New York: Oxford University Press.

—— (2006) *Legal Origins and Stock Markets in the Twentieth Century*, mimeo.

Rogoswki, R. (1989) *Commerce and Coalitions*, Princeton: Princeton University Press.

Samphanthanarak, K. (2007) "Internal Capital Markets in Business Groups," UCSD, mimeo.

Schaede, U. (2007) "Japan's Corporate Renewal: Business Strategies in the 21st Century," UCSD, mimeo.

Shugart, M.S. and Carey, J.M. (1992) *Presidents and Assemblies: Constitutional Design and Electoral Dynamics*, New York: Cambridge University Press.

Stasavage, D. (2002) "Credible Commitment in Early Modern Europe: North and Weingast Revisited," *Journal of Law, Economics, and Organization* 18: 155–186.

Swenson, D. (2005) *Unconventional Success: A Fundamental Approach to Personal Investment*, New York: Free Press.

Wade, R. (2004). *Governing the Market*, Princeton: Princeton University Press.

Walter, A. (2006) "Adopting International Financial Standards: Compliance and Regulatory Effectiveness in the Global Political Economy," mimeo.

Woodruff, C. (2006) "Measuring Institutions," in S. Rose-Ackerman (ed.) *International Handbook on the Economics of Corruption*, Cheltenham, UK and Northampton, MA: Edward Elgar.

Part III

Preparations for future problems

9 The Asian financial crisis revisited

Lessons, responses and new challenges

Masahiro Kawai and Pradumna B. Rana

Introduction: issues

The depth and the breadth of the Asian financial crisis, which is now ten years old, took everyone by surprise. Nobody had predicted it, at least not its severe impact. Initially there were two schools of thought. Some, focusing mainly on the relatively high current account deficit of Thailand, labeled it as a traditional current account crisis like the debt crisis of the 1980s in Latin America, while others argued that it was a new type of crisis associated with the increasing integration of Asian countries with global capital markets. Eventually, there was a consensus that it was a capital account crisis preceded by large private capital inflows and triggered by sudden shifts in market sentiment, which led to massive capital flow reversals. Shifts in market sentiments were in turn due to weaknesses in the financial and corporate sectors of these countries. The currency crisis also quickly led to a banking crisis.

The International Monetary Fund (IMF) was called in to help but some of its policies were criticized as being inappropriate for a capital account crisis. The 2003 report of the IMF's Independent Evaluation Office (2003) accepted some of these arguments. The report noted that in Indonesia IMF surveillance had identified the vulnerabilities in the banking sector that would later become crucial to the evolution of the crisis, but it had underestimated the severity and potential macroeconomic risks posed by them. In Korea, IMF surveillance had failed to adequately identify the risks posed by the uneven pace of capital account liberalization and the extent of banking sector weaknesses, owing to the adoption of its conventional approach that focused on macroeconomic variables. In both countries, the design of macroeconomic policies had turned out to be too tight given the outcome of aggregate demand and output, which collapsed sharply in 1998.

Given that the incidence of capital account crises was bound to increase in the future because of greater financial globalization, there were urgent calls to reform the international financial architecture and national policies, particularly those related to the financial and corporate sectors. Also, the fears that IMF resources were limited compared with the scale of cross-border capital flows, the inappropriateness of several policy recommendations of the IMF at that time, and risks of regional contagion led the East Asian countries to initiate self-help efforts in the area of regional monetary and financial cooperation. Slow progress in World Trade Organization (WTO) negotiations also led to the promotion of enhanced cooperation in the area of foreign trade and foreign direct investment (FDI). In some cases, regional arrangements go deeper than multilateral ones.

It is important to note that prior to the financial crisis, East Asia had experienced market-led integration as part of its outward-oriented development strategy. The financial crisis focused the region's attention on its interdependence and shared interests and East Asia became keen to supplement market-led integration with various policy efforts.

We organize the chapter in the following way. First, we summarize the lessons learned from the 1997–1998 financial crisis. Second, we review efforts being made for crisis prevention, management and resolution, to:

1   reform the international financial architecture at the IMF and World Bank;[1]
2   improve national policies and institutions; and
3   strengthen regional financial cooperation.

Third, we assess whether the ongoing efforts at the global, national and regional levels have sufficiently enhanced East Asia's resilience to future capital account crises and identify new economic and financial risks facing East Asia. Finally, we explore the potential for further deepening East Asian economic and financial integration and identify the next steps in moving the agenda forward.

Lessons from the 1997–1998 crisis

Twin crises: capital account and banking sector crises

The Thai baht devaluation in July 1997 was triggered by the investors' perceptions of deteriorating financial sector conditions and of unsustainable overvaluation of the currency. Once the baht declined sharply, currency speculation spread quickly to the Philippines, Indonesia, Malaysia and Korea within a matter of a few months. The speed and extent of the regional "contagion" of currency attack was remarkable. The strong contagion within East Asia suggested that the economic linkage through trade, FDI and finance was much more pronounced there than in other regions.

It is well understood now that the Asian financial crisis was a twin crisis – a combination of capital account and banking sector crises. It was a capital account crisis, as opposed to a traditional current account crisis, because the proximate cause was the rapid inflows and outflows of capital induced by progressive capital account liberalization and de facto fixed exchange rates. Pre-crisis capital inflows created the so-called "double mismatches," i.e. currency and maturity mismatches – short-term borrowing in foreign currency to finance long-term investment in domestic currency – and vulnerability in the balance sheets of debtors (banks and corporations), which exposed them to risks of sudden changes in currency values and interest rates. Rapid capital inflows had led to excess liquidity, overinvestment and asset market bubbles. Once the market started to lose confidence about the sustainability of the exchange rate, however, equally rapid capital outflows occurred, exerting large downward pressure on the currencies and putting sudden brakes on the overextended economic activities.

The crisis was also a banking sector crisis resulting from weaknesses in bank regulation and supervision and in corporate governance. Commercial banks had intermediated excessively large amounts of domestic savings as well as external funds for domestic investment and projects with often doubtful quality, thereby creating vulnerabilities that could lead to a banking crisis. The sharp currency depreciation led to a full-fledged banking crisis. Externally indebted banks and corporations faced difficulty in making repayments when the domestic-currency value of external debt inflated. Corporate sector difficulties magnified banking sector problems as corporations were also bank clients. The underlying factor behind the overextension of bank loans was weak risk management practice on the part of banks – reflecting inadequate prudential regulation and supervision over banks – and imprudent over-borrowing by corporations which aggressively expanded their operations.

Crises that initially seemed benign evolved into a full-blown financial and economic crisis in the affected countries in 1998. The crisis deepened because of pervasive weaknesses in the financial and corporate sectors in these economies. Indeed, GDP growth in the five crisis-affected economies of East Asia – Korea, Indonesia, Malaysia, Thailand and the Philippines – declined sharply from a pre-crisis average of positive 7.1 percent during 1990–1996 to negative 7.6 percent in 1998. The depth of the collapse in Indonesia, with GDP contracting by more than 13 percent in 1998, was among the largest peacetime contractions, excluding the experience of several transition economies in the early 1990s. The simultaneous economic contraction in the affected economies in 1998 was another sign of strong regional economic interdependence. The traditional first- and second-generation theories cannot explain the type of capital account crisis that Asian countries experienced, and newer third-generation theories have been developed to explain these crisis and their severe economic consequences (Allen *et al.* 2002; Ghosh 2006).

Lessons for crisis prevention, management and resolution

There are many lessons to be learned from the Asian financial crisis. Valuable are lessons from some alleged mistakes committed by national policymakers as well as by the IMF, which intervened in Thailand, Indonesia and Korea. The most important lesson learned is that "it is better to prevent a crisis than cure it." However, once a capital account crisis breaks out, efficient crisis management and resolution become important. Table 9.1 summarizes not only the national and global, but also regional dimensions of crisis prevention, management and resolution.

Table 9.1 Summary of policy lessons from the Asian financial crisis

Objective	National measures	Global measures	Regional measures
Preventing or reducing the risk of crises	*Adopt sound macroeconomic management (monetary, fiscal, public debt)*		
	• Pursue non-inflationary monetary policy • Maintain sound fiscal policy • Manage public debt prudently • Avoid large current account deficits • Reduce boom-and-bust business cycles • Improve data transparency (SDDS)	• Strengthen IMF surveillance and its policy advice • Utilize private sector monitoring agencies (rating, sovereign risk monitoring)	• Strengthen regional policy dialogue and monitoring • Develop regional early-warning system
	Avoid "double mismatches" in the balance sheets of public and private sectors		
	• Secure adequate foreign exchange reserves • Monitor short-term capital flows and restrain them if necessary • Sequenced capital account liberalization	• Remove regulatory biases to short-term external lending • Strengthen regulation to limit speculative activities by HLIs	• Strengthen monitoring of regional capital flows
	Adopt sustainable exchange rate regime		
	• Adopt a viable exchange rate regime • Ensure consistency between exchange rate regime and overall macroeconomic policy • Avoid excessive currency overvaluation	• Maintain stable exchange rates among major industrial countries	• Maintain regionally coherent exchange rate regimes through exchange rate policy coordination
	Build a robust and resilient financial system and corporate sector for adequate risk management		
	• Strengthen regulatory and supervisory frameworks over financial institutions • Improve information transparency and disclosure in financial and corporate sectors • Establish good corporate governance for financial institutions and corporations • Introduce greater competition to product, factor and financial markets • Develop capital market-based finance • Introduce limited deposit insurance	• Strengthen financial sector monitoring (FSAP) • Support implementation of international standards and codes (ROSCs) • Support best-practice corporate governance tailored to specific country conditions • Regulate tightly financial institutions that lend to HLIs	• Establish regional initiatives to improve regional regulatory and supervisory frameworks • Undertake regional initiatives for better corporate governance • Develop regional capital markets for mobilization of regional savings

	National level	Global level	Regional level
Managing crises	*Mobilize timely external liquidity of sufficient magnitude* • Restore market confidence through consistent policy packages • Reduce moral hazard problems	• Strengthen IMF liquidity support, including a new type of CCL	• Strengthen a regional liquidity support facility to contain crises and contagion
	Adopt appropriate macroeconomic and structural policies to reflect the specific conditions and reality of the economy • Adopt an appropriate monetary and fiscal policy mix contingent on the specific conditions of the economy	• Streamline IMF conditionality on macroeconomic and structural policies	• Strengthen regional capacity to formulate appropriate adjustment policies
	Involve private international investors • Impose official stand-stills • In extreme cases, allow involuntary PSI	• Establish the international rules of the game through PSI	• Involve international creditors from both inside and outside the region
Resolving the systemic consequences of crises	*Establish domestic mechanisms for resolving impaired bank assets and corporate liabilities* • Establish clear procedures for bank exits, recapitalization and rehabilitation • Establish legal and formal procedures for corporate insolvencies and workouts	• Provide international budgetary support for bank and corporate restructuring	• Finance regional programs to help accelerate bank and corporate restructuring
	Introduce international mechanisms for resolving public and private external debt • Introduce insolvency clauses in debt issuance	• Establish international frameworks for PSI in external debt resolution	• Involve international creditors from both inside and outside the region
	Cushion the effects of crises on low-income groups through social sector policies • Strengthen social safety nets and mitigate social consequences of crises	• Finance the activity through the World Bank and other international organizations	• Finance regional programs to help mitigate social impact through regional assistance

Source: Kawai (2007b).

Crisis prevention

The first key lesson is that crisis prevention is better than cure. The major preventive mechanisms required are:

1 establishment of a sound macroeconomic management framework (monetary, fiscal, exchange rate, and public debt management policies);
2 avoidance of double mismatches in balance sheets;
3 adoption of sustainable exchange rate regimes; and
4 building robust and resilient financial and corporate sectors, particularly banking sector.

Establishing a sound macroeconomic management framework is a fundamental requirement for crisis prevention. At the national level, this includes: pursuit of sound macroeconomic policies (non-inflationary monetary policy, disciplined fiscal policy and good debt management); avoidance of boom-and-bust cycles; and improved data transparency. At the global level IMF surveillance should be strengthened, and at the regional level regional policy dialogue should be improved and early-warning systems developed.

Avoiding double mismatches in the balance sheets of private sector debtors would require their prudent risk management as well as well-sequenced capital account liberalization. Monitoring of short-term capital should also be strengthened at the regional level. At the global level, speculative activities of highly leveraged institutions (HLIs) should be regulated and the regulatory biases to short-term lending be removed. With a relatively weak macroeconomic management framework and an inadequately supervised financial system, several precautionary measures can be used. One is a control on short-term capital flows of cross-border capital to prevent the volatility of capital flows from generating boom-and-bust cycles. The other is a set of self-help mechanisms such as the accumulation of sufficient foreign exchange reserves to cushion external financial shocks.

Adoption of viable exchange rate regimes that are consistent with the overall macroeconomic policy is needed. Excessive currency overvaluation should be avoided. Efforts to achieve stable exchange rates should be strengthened at the global and regional levels: at the global level, the major industrial countries should pursue stable macroeconomic policy to ensure mutual exchange rate stability, and at the regional level policy coordination should be explored to achieve intraregional coherence and stability of exchange rates.

Building a robust and resilient financial and corporate sector, particularly a sound banking sector, is the fourth requirement for crisis prevention. At the national level, the regulatory and supervisory frameworks over the financial systems should be strengthened and good governance promoted. Information transparency and disclosures should be encouraged, and limited deposit insurance provided. Regional initiatives to improve regulatory and supervisory frameworks should be introduced, and regional capital markets developed. At the global level, monitoring of financial sectors should be strengthened, standards and codes implemented and HLIs regulated.

Crisis management

Once a currency crisis breaks out, it is important to ensure that the crisis does not deepen or prolong. Crisis management mechanisms include:

1   mobilization of timely and adequate external liquidity;
2   adoption of appropriate macroeconomic and structural policies to reflect the specific conditions and reality of the economy; and
3   involvement of international private investors.

At the time of a currency crisis or contagion – particularly when resulting from irrational herding behavior – timely provision of large-scale international liquidity of sufficient magnitude is needed to prevent the economy from slipping into a serious economic contraction. For such a financing facility to be effective in restoring market confidence, its provision must be accompanied by an appropriate adjustment program – including macroeconomic (monetary and fiscal) and structural policies – as lending "conditionality." Such an adjustment program should be contingent on the particular conditions and reality of the economy.

Involving international private investors, in the form of a temporary suspension of debt payments, can constitute an integral part of crisis management. This procedure functions as a floodgate that helps stop the decline in the currency value and enables the authorities to buy time – while avoiding tight monetary policy – to put in place a credible adjustment program and to organize creditor–debtor negotiations.

Crisis resolution

Once a currency crisis evolves into a full-blown economic crisis, with systemic damages to the banking and corporate sectors, it is vital to quickly resolve the problem. Crisis resolution measures include:

1   establishment of domestic mechanisms for resolving impaired bank assets and corporate liabilities;
2   introduction of international mechanisms for resolving public and private external debt; and
3   social safety nets for low-income groups.

Essentially, domestic mechanisms for resolving impaired bank assets and corporate liabilities is the first priority. Resolution of non-viable banks (liquidation, closure, nationalization, merger and acquisition) and revitalization of viable banks (recapitalization, carving out of non-performing loans (NPLs) and their transfer to asset management companies) are two key strategies. This must be accompanied by frameworks to facilitate early corporate debt restructuring: creation of enabling environments by eliminating legal and tax impediments to corporate restructuring; strengthening of court-based bankruptcy, reorganization and foreclosure laws and legal protection of creditor rights; and establishment of voluntary, out-of-court frameworks for corporate restructuring based on the "London rules."

Establishing an international collective framework for orderly external-debt workout is useful. Its purpose is to encourage debtor–creditor negotiations to reach restructuring agreements while suspending payments on foreign debt. Such mechanisms can help minimize the risk of moral hazard by requiring both private – particularly international – creditors and debtors to share the burden of losses.

Capital account crises tend to have serious social impacts. It is, therefore, necessary for governments to develop social safety nets with regional and international support.[2]

Need for national, global and regional reforms

To sum up, it was the interaction between large and volatile capital flows – facilitated by global financial integration – and structural weaknesses in national banking and corporate sectors that made individual economies vulnerable to shocks and contagion and prone to capital account crises. Reforms of the international financial system, improvements in national financial systems and regional financial cooperation are the best protection against crises and contagion. Actions are required at the national, global and regional levels.

National reforms

There are at least two important lessons for national policymakers. First, economies that are integrated with international capital markets should manage their own financial globalization in a prudent way by taking into account the implications of volatile short-term capital flows for macroeconomic and financial-sector vulnerabilities. Policymakers should pay due attention to the right sequencing of capital account liberalization and the need for monitoring short-term capital flows and responding to rapid flows.

Second, economies need to strengthen domestic policy frameworks and capacities, particularly through the introduction of sound and consistent macroeconomic policy frameworks – including monetary, fiscal and exchange rate policies and debt management – and financial and corporate sector supervision. Effective financial sector regulation and supervision is required for better asset-liability management and stronger governance of financial institutions and corporations, backed by adequate accounting, auditing and insolvency procedures.[3] With a robust and resilient domestic economic system, a crisis could be prevented, or its impact on the economy could be mitigated even if a crisis occurs.

Essentially, each economy must manage the process of financial globalization by strengthening the domestic economic system in a way that makes it resilient to shocks emanating domestically and/or from abroad.

Global efforts: strengthening the international financial system

At the global level, various reforms for crisis prevention, management and resolution are necessary. Important reforms could include global initiatives to improve information transparency, functions of the IMF and private sector involvement.

First, the international community needs to encourage information transparency of emerging economies and important market players. Lack of accurate information on the economies and markets in question can create instability in investor perceptions and price and transactions volatility, by amplifying market responses and herd behavior. It is therefore important for the international financial institutions to encourage emerging economies to improve information transparency on macroeconomic development, financial sector conditions and future policy directions and institutional reforms. Similarly, enhancing information disclosure of systemically important market participants – such as HLIs including hedge funds – would also be important.

Second, the operations and functions of the IMF need to be strengthened. The IMF-IEO (2003) has argued that the availability of IMF short-term liquidity at the time of crises and contagion needs to be increased. Policy conditionality attached to IMF financial assistance to crisis countries needs to be streamlined, particularly with regard to the nature of macroeconomic stabilization programs and the scope and depth of structural policies. Recently, there has been a call to improve the governance of the IMF to reflect the new realities of the world economy.

Third, private sector involvement should be an important focus of reform, partly because of the need to reduce moral hazard on the part of private investors and partly because of the large volume of private resources relative to official resources. An important issue is to identify the role of private international creditors at the time of a crisis – such as a standstill. In the case of commercial bank debt, coordination between a limited number of international creditor banks and domestic debtor banks can relatively easily result in an agreement on temporary standstills on repayments as in Korea's external debt restructuring arrangement in late 1997.[4] In the case of corporate debt, agreements on standstills at times of emergencies would be more difficult as observed in Indonesia in 1998.

Regional financial cooperation

While individual economies and the global financial community should focus on national and global policy reforms, respectively, a well-designed regional framework can complement these efforts.

First, reform at the global level is either difficult or may result in only modest outcomes, and national reforms take time to become effective. To supplement the IMF resources, a regional financing facility can be used to head off currency crises and contagion.

Second, as economic contagion tends to begin with a geographic focus, a regional framework for financial cooperation to address crisis prevention, management and resolution is a logical way to proceed. The economies that are closely interdependent and, hence, face similar shocks and similar policy challenges, can benefit from regional policy dialogue and coordination at a relatively low transaction cost of communication. It enables them to internalize various types of spillover effects and externalities – including financial contagion – due to economic interdependence. To the extent necessary, these economies can take collective action in monetary and financial areas.

Reform of the international financial architecture

The Asian financial crisis heightened calls for the reform of the international financial architecture. Many academics put forward radical reform plans ranging from abolishing the IMF to transforming it into the international lender of last resort, or an international bankruptcy organization. Proposals were also made to establish a World Financial Organization to monitor and implement sound international practices in finance. Actual changes have been more modest, partly because the crisis turned out to be short-lived. Nevertheless, as a response to the Asian financial crisis and other emerging market crises in the 1990s, the IMF, World Bank and the Bank for International Settlements (BIS) have undertaken major efforts to reform the international financial architecture. These efforts have focused mainly on the issues of crisis prevention, crisis management and resolution and IMF governance reforms.

Crisis prevention

Standards and codes

Standards and codes refer to provisions relating to the institutional environment or "rules of the game" within which economic and financial policies are devised and implemented. The development, dissemination and adoption by countries of international standards is expected to assist countries in strengthening their economic institutions, inform market participants to allow for more effective market discipline and inform IMF surveillance and World Bank country assistance strategies.

The IMF, World Bank and BIS have established international standards in 12 areas, which are broadly categorized into three groups:

1   policy transparency;
2   financial sector regulation and supervision; and
3   market integrity.

Standards in policy transparency include data transparency, fiscal transparency and monetary and financial policy transparency. Standards on financial regulation and supervision cover five areas: banking supervision, securities, insurance, payments systems and anti-money laundering and combating the financing of terrorism. Standards of market integrity include corporate governance, accounting, auditing and insolvency and creditor rights.

A county's observance of standards in each of the 12 areas is assessed at the request of a member country by the IMF and the World Bank; the results of these assessments are then summarized in a Report on the Observance of Standards and Codes (ROSCs). The report is the principal tool for assessing members' implementation of these standards and codes. Publication of these assessments by member countries is voluntary, although the IMF and World Bank do encourage their publication. As of February 2008, nearly three-fourths of its 185 member countries had completed one or more ROSC modules, of which 76 percent had been published.

Data transparency

Data dissemination standards help to enhance the availability of timely and comprehensive statistics, which in turn contributes to designing sound macroeconomic policies. The IMF has taken several steps to enhance information transparency and openness, including the establishment and strengthening of data dissemination standards to help countries prevent future crises and diminish the effect of unavoidable ones.

The standards for data dissemination consist of two tiers. The first, called the Special Data Dissemination Standard (SDDS), was established in 1996 to guide countries that have, or might seek, access to international capital markets.[5] The second tier, the General Data Dissemination System (GDDS), was established in 1997 to help countries provide more reliable data. The GDDS focuses on improving statistical systems, while the SDDS focuses on commitments to data dissemination standards in countries that already meet high data quality standards. Both are voluntary, but once a country subscribes to the SDDS, observance of the standard is mandatory. Countries must also agree to post information about their data dissemination practices on the IMF's external website on the Dissemination Standards Bulletin Board (DSBB) and establish an Internet site containing the actual data, called a National Summary Data Page (NSDP), to which the DSBB is linked. The IMF notes that approximately 81 percent of its membership participates in the new data initiatives.

On the other hand, information disclosure of HLIs – including hedge funds – has not been strengthened. The majority view is that HLIs are supposed to serve specific small groups of individual investors and often operate in offshore markets, but that steps are needed to ensure some degree of disclosure by commercial banks which lend to the HLIs. As a result of the recent US subprime loan problem, views are spreading that more information disclosure may be needed by HLIs.

Financial system soundness

Problems in the financial system can reduce the effectiveness of monetary policy, create large fiscal costs related to bailing out troubled financial institutions, trigger capital flight and deepen economic recessions. Financial weaknesses in one country can also trigger contagion effects in others. A sound financial system – comprising banks, securities exchanges, pension funds, insurers, the central bank and national supervisors/regulators – is thus essential for supporting sustainable economic growth and development.

The IMF's main channels for promoting financial system soundness are through its ongoing bilateral and multilateral surveillance, the Financial Sector Assessment Program (FSAP) and the provision of technical assistance. Bilateral surveillance is the process of regular dialogue and policy advice provided to each member country and covers macroeconomic and financial developments and policies. Under the new Mid-term Strategy endorsed in September 2005, the IMF conducts multilateral consultations on common economic and financial issues.[6] Recently, IMF surveillance has also focused more systematically on regional developments, including through increased dialogue with regional institutions and think tanks. Technical assistance refers to measures to strengthen financial infrastructure which may include training and advice on improving monetary and fiscal management, foreign exchange and capital market development, development of the legal framework for banking, and prudential regulations, among other things.

The FSAP was launched jointly by the IMF and the World Bank in 1999. It provides member countries with a comprehensive evaluation of their financial systems, with a view to alerting national authorities on vulnerabilities in their financial sectors and assisting them in designing measures to reduce weaknesses. The FSAP also determines the development needs of the financial sector. Sectoral developments, risks and vulnerabilities are analyzed using a range of financial soundness indicators and macro-financial stress tests. Other areas of financial stability are also analyzed, including systemic liquidity arrangements, institutional frameworks for crisis management and loan recovery, transparency, accountability and governance. FSAP reports are designed to assess the stability of the financial system as a whole rather than individual institutions. As of March 2008, FSAP reports had been prepared on 110 countries.

Crisis management and resolution

New financing instruments and credit lines

In order to play its role in safeguarding the international financial stability, the IMF has introduced new lending facilities. The Supplemental Reserve Facility (SRF) was established in December 1997 and was used in Korea, Brazil, Argentina and Turkey. It provides large financial assistance, without access limit, to members facing exceptional balance of payments difficulties resulting from a sudden and disruptive loss of market confidence. Besides the General Arrangements to Borrow (GAB), a New Arrangements to Borrow (NAB) came into force in November 1998 – doubling the resources of the IMF.

The Contingent Credit Line (CCL) was introduced in 1999 as part of the IMF's efforts to strengthen member countries' defenses against financial crises.

The CCL was intended to be a precautionary line of defense to help protect countries pursuing strong policies in the event of a liquidity need arising from the spread of financial crises. For various reasons, however, the facility was never used and, in November 2003, the CCL was allowed to expire. The new Mid-term Strategy proposes to continue the discussions on high access precautionary arrangements as successor to the CCL. One of the most important issues is how to resolve the trade off between automaticity in drawings and the conditionality to be attached to such drawings.

IMF conditionality

The IMF came in for harsh criticism for prescribing too contractionary macroeconomic policies and too many structural reforms. For example, fiscal policy prescribed in the early phase of the crisis in Thailand and Korea was contractionary despite the fact that the economies were severely affected by the sudden withdrawal of foreign capital. The Indonesian program had over 100 conditions including the dismantling of the clove monopoly.

The IMF now appears ready to avoid a "one-size-fits-all" approach to stabilization without always relying on contractionary macroeconomic policy in the face of crises originating in the capital account. The IMF has also decided to streamline its programs to limit structural conditionality to a core set of essential features that are macro-relevant and in the IMF's core area of responsibility,[7] with a broader approach requiring justification based upon the specific country situation. Hence, IMF conditionality now covers only macro-critical structural reforms. This is an improvement given the lessons learned from the crisis, but it remains to be seen how this will be implemented.

Private sector involvement

The international community has been exploring possible mechanisms for official "standstill" provisions, or private sector involvement (PSI). It has focused on the debt restructuring of international sovereign bonds with the recognition that, at the time of a liquidity crisis, holders of sovereign bonds, along with other creditors, would need to contribute to the resolution of such crises. Two methods have been recommended: a contractual approach and a statutory approach. A contractual approach considers collective action clauses (CACs) in sovereign bond contracts as a device for orderly resolution of crises; their explicit inclusion in bond documentation would provide a degree of predictability to the restructuring process. A statutory approach, such as the Sovereign Debt Restructuring Mechanism (SDRM; Krueger 2002), attempts to create the legal basis – through universal treaty rather than through a set of national laws in a limited number of jurisdictions – for establishing adequate incentives for debtors and creditors to agree upon a prompt, orderly and predictable restructuring of unsustainable debt. The CACs approach has been adopted while a more comprehensive statutory approach has been put on hold.

IMF governance reforms

IMF governance reforms refer to changes in quotas and voting rights, executive board representation and the IMF management selection process. The current distribution of quotas and the relative voice of members within the IMF are raising questions about its legitimacy among its shareholders and other stake-holders. IMF governance reforms are considered as necessary to restore legiti-macy, so that the IMF will acquire the authority and credibility to carry out its missions.

Reform of IMF quotas and voting rights is the most important step to recognize better the new reality of the evolving world economy and finance, i.e. the rising weight of emerging markets including those in Asia. Currently, the industrial coun-tries as a group hold 60.3 percent of the votes, the emerging markets only 20.4 percent, and the rest of the world only 19.3 percent. These ratios have not changed significantly over time. Reforms have begun to take place in several phases. In the first phase, at the 2006 Singapore meeting of the IMF and the World Bank, a decision was made to make ad hoc increases in the quotas of China, Mexico, Korea and Turkey by a small amount. The second and third phases of the reform exercise are to agree on a new quota formula and to further rebalance quotas. Currently, an attempt to increase the quota of emerging markets by 2.7 percent is underway. But clearly more needs to be done by increasing substantially basic votes and reducing substantially the aggregate European Union quotas (Boorman 2008).

Another aspect of the voice and vote issue is the composition of the IMF executive board. Currently the European countries occupy eight of the 24 chairs and are represented in another constituency at the IMF board. A consensus view is that European countries are over-represented at the IMF and that they should agree to reduce their representation in the executive board. It is even more compelling to argue that, with the establishment of a monetary union, Europe should occupy much fewer seats.

Finally, as Mahbubani (2008) has pointed out, the rule that the head of the IMF should be a Western European automatically disqualifies 88 percent of the world's population from leadership of this global economic institution. The choice of the IMF managing director should be based on merit and qualifications and not on nationality.

Summing up, while encouraging progress has been made on crisis prevention efforts, and some progress has been achieved on crisis management and resolution efforts, progress in reforming IMF governance has been very limited. To restore its legitimacy in its operation, the IMF needs significant governance reform. It also needs to address its precarious financial situation as few countries are borrowing from it partly due to the absence of financial crises in emerging market economies.

Reforms of national policies and institutions

Since the Asian financial crisis, the East Asian financial landscape has improved significantly. The current account that had been in deficit in the pre-crisis period has turned into surplus in all crisis-affected countries as a result of a decline in investment. Portfolio investment inflows into the region have resumed, equity prices have been up, and the capitalization of equity markets has expanded. As a result, foreign exchange reserves have kept rising in most countries. Many debtors to foreign creditors have repaid or restructured their short-term external debt so that the ratios of short-term external debt to foreign exchange reserves have declined to levels well below 100 percent (Figure 9.1). All countries that were under the IMF programs have been able to finish repaying their IMF loans.

Reforms of macroeconomic policy framework

Many economies in East Asia have improved the frameworks for macroeconomic policymaking – including monetary, fiscal, exchange rate policies and debt management. They began to introduce independent central banks that tend to pursue inflation targeting. Even without independent central banks or formal inflation targeting, pursuit of non-inflation monetary policy has become the norm. As a result, there has been no significant inflationary pressure, until recently. Fiscal policy has been prudent in the sense of containing large fiscal deficits in most economies. Debt management has also improved – through the establishment of a debt management office in some countries like Thailand – due to the reduction of public debt which was accumulated during the banking sector restructuring and reform.

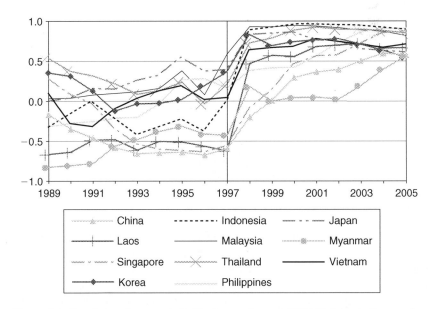

Figure 9.1 Correlations between individual countries and ASEAN+3 (excluding own).

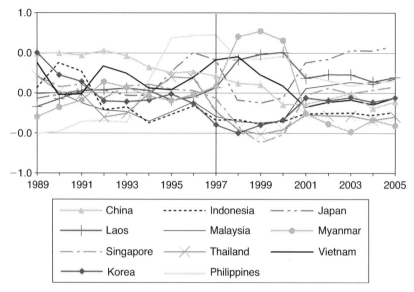

Figure 9.2 Correlations between individual ASEAN+3 members and US.

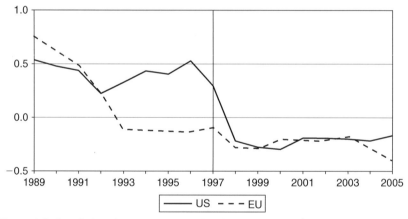

Figure 9.3 Correlations between ASEAN+3 and the US and EU.[1]

Note
1 EU = represented by France, Germany and Italy. ASEAN+3 = 10 ASEAN member countries plus China, Japan and Korea

However, in several countries – particularly China and Vietnam – the monetary policy framework needs to improve substantially by developing and deepening money markets. In these countries, interest rate-based monetary policy has not been working because of the absence of deep and liquid money markets. They tend to rely on quantity control as well as moral suasion. Given the rising level of inflation, recently, there has been a need to fully develop the central bank's capacity to control inflation. In addition, in some cases coordination between monetary and fiscal policies is not adequate. A coherent national framework to manage macroeconomic conditions needs to be established.

Following the initial forced devaluation and the subsequent depreciation of currencies, there has been a general shift toward greater exchange rate flexibility, although there are variations across countries. Indonesia maintains an exchange rate regime close to a free float, despite frequent currency market interventions by Bank Indonesia to smooth the rupiah–dollar rate. Korea and Thailand adopted managed floating with a currency basket as a reference currency (Kawai 2008). Malaysia, which pegged the currency to the US dollar in September 1998 (when it introduced capital outflow controls), officially abandoned their dollar pegs in July 2005 (when China adopted a similar measure) and began to allow currency appreciation within a managed float regime.

Bank and corporate sector reforms

Facing financial and corporate sector distress of systemic proportions, the crisis-affected countries began to resolve financial and corporate sector crises. As a result of these efforts, banking sector indicators have improved steadily (Table 9.2). NPL ratios have kept falling, rates of return on assets and bank equity have been sustained at highly competitive rates, provisioning ratios have increased and risk-weighted capital adequacy ratios among banks remain well above the international 8 percent norm. Overall banking sector profitability has also improved across the region as reflected in banks' rates of return on assets and on equity. With the strong profitability and, in some cases, recapitalization (such as in China), risk-weighted capital adequacy ratios (CARs) are also quite high.

Crisis-affected countries began to embark on bank and corporate sector restructuring and reforms during the crisis period. As a result, financial indicators of commercial banks have improved significantly, the number of commercial banks has been reduced, many banks are better capitalized and have become economically solvent and insolvency procedures and foreclosure laws have been strengthened. With the closure of insolvent banks and/or merger of non-viable banks with stronger, healthier ones, the number of banks has declined, resulting in concentration of banking systems. This has contributed to greater efficiency and profitability of national banking systems as the scale of operation of relatively small and inefficient banks has been reduced.

Crisis-affected economies have also made substantial efforts to strengthen financial sector supervision and regulation. Prudential regulation has been upgraded through better financial and other reporting requirements, independent audits of bank statements and much stricter requirements for establishing new banks. Most banks in the region are now required to maintain minimum CARs above 8 percent of their risk-weighted assets in line with the Basel I accords, with some economies requiring higher minimum CARs.

Many economies have shifted their modality of supervision toward more forward-looking, risk-based bank supervision with greater use of on-site

Table 9.2 Selected financial indicators

9.2a Non-performing loans (% of commercial bank loans)[1,2,3]

	2001	2002	2003	2004	2005	2006[5]
China	–	21.6	17.8	13.2	8.6	7.1
Hong Kong	6.5	5.0	3.9	2.3	1.4	1.1
Indonesia[6]	12.1	8.1	8.2	5.7	8.3	7.0
Japan	7.6	8.8	8.2	5.6	3.8	3.1
Korea	2.9	1.9	2.2	1.7	1.1	0.8
Malaysia[4]	10.5	9.3	8.3	6.8	5.6	4.8
Philippines[4]	17.3	15.0	14.1	12.7	8.2	6.0
Singapore	–	–	5.4	4.0	3.0	2.4
Taipei, China	7.5	6.1	4.3	2.8	2.2	2.1
Thailand	10.5	15.7	12.8	10.9	8.3	4.2
Compromised asset ratios (Indonesia) and distressed asset ratios (Philippines)						
Indonesia	31.9	24.0	19.4	14.2	15.6	16.0
Philippines	27.7	26.5	26.1	24.7	19.7	18.6

Notes
1 – means not available.
2 The table excludes NPLs transferred from bank balance sheets to asset management companies.
3 The measurement of NPLs follows official definitions and differs across economies depending on loan classification (for example, whether a three-month or six-month rule is used), the treatment of accrued interest and whether specific provisioning is deducted from the NPL measure.
4 For Malaysia and the Philippines, reported NPLs are net of specific provisioning.
5 Data for 2006 are for March (Japan), June (distressed assets for the Philippines) and for September (Singapore and compromised assets for Indonesia).
6 Compromised assets in Indonesia include reported NPLs, restructured loans and foreclosed assets for the 16 largest banks; distressed assets in the Philippines refer to reported NPLs, restructured loans and real and other properties owned and acquired (ROPOA).

9.2b Rate of return on commercial bank assets (% per annum)

	2003	2004	2005	2006
Indonesia	2.6	3.5	2.6	2.6
Hong Kong	1.4	1.5	1.6	1.5
Japan	–	0.5	0.8	–
Korea	0.2	0.9	1.3	1.1
Malaysia	1.3	1.4	1.3	1.3
Philippines	1.2	1.0	1.1	1.3
Singapore	1.1	1.3	1.2	1.3
Taipei, China	0.5	0.6	0.3	−0.4
Thailand	0.7	1.3	1.4	0.8

Note
– = not available.

9.2c Rate of return on commercial bank equity (% per annum)[1]

	2003	2004	2005	2006[3]
China	19.0	16.2	17.3	–
Indonesia[2]	19.2	25.4	17.5	28.0
Hong Kong	16.9	18.7	18.4	18.9
Japan	–	8.0	14.0	–
Korea	3.4	15.2	18.4	14.6
Malaysia	15.3	16.0	16.5	16.1
Philippines	9.3	7.6	9.5	11.5
Singapore	10.3	11.8	11.1	12.4
Taipei, China	6.5	8.8	4.4	–7.3
Thailand	15.7	15.7	14.2	8.5

Notes
1 – means not available.
2 Data for Indonesia are calculated by dividing profit/loss by capital from Bank Indonesia banking statistics.
3 Data for 2006 are for September (Singapore) and November (Indonesia).

9.2d Risk-weighted capital adequacy ratios (% of risk-weighted assets)[1]

	2003	2004	2005	2006[2]
Indonesia	19.4	19.4	19.5	20.5
Hong Kong	15.3	15.4	14.8	14.9
Japan	10.9	11.4	11.7	12.2
Korea	11.2	12.1	13.0	12.7
Malaysia	14.0	14.3	13.6	13.1
Philippines	17.4	18.7	17.7	18.5
Singapore	16.0	16.2	15.8	15.4
Taipei, China	10.1	10.7	10.3	10.1
Thailand	14.0	13.0	14.2	14.5

Source: Adopted from ADB, *Asia Economic Monitor*, December 2006.

Notes
1 Figures are based on officially reported risk-adjusted capital adequacy ratios under Basel I and applied to commercial banks (except Korea, where data includes nationwide commercial banks, regional banks and specialized banks). Data for the Philippines is on a consolidated, not solo, basis. Data for Japan is for major commercial banks only.
2 Data for 2006 are for March (Japan) and September (Singapore).

inspections and evaluation of banks' risk management systems in line with Basel II. As the adoption of Basel II Framework begins gradually in 2008, the region's banking systems face a continuing challenge of upgrading of governance and disclosure standards.

In addition, many governments started to make serious efforts at capital market development and opening, together with better regulatory systems, aiming to strengthen accounting and disclosure standards, protect private property rights and improve corporate governance. It is expected that these efforts will further accelerate the development and deepening of capital markets, particularly local-currency bond markets. We are beginning to observe greater diversification of sources of domestic financing, with the relative share of bond financing increasing and that of banks declining (Figure 9.2).

Despite such progress, more efforts are needed. The extent of banking sector consolidation in East Asia may not be sufficient in comparison to international norms (Turner 2007). In many markets, state-owned banks remain dominant and require overhauling and privatization. Regulatory processes need more work, especially in preparation for the adoption of Basel II standards. Systems to manage securities trading, payments and settlement need to be expanded and made more efficient. Securities regulation needs to be upgraded to make markets safer, deeper and more innovative. To support these developments, efforts to improve corporate governance need to continue to make better information available for the private monitoring of markets.

Regional financial cooperation

In the aftermath of the Asian financial crisis, East Asian countries have sought to promote closer monetary and financial cooperation (see Kawai 2005; Rana 2007a, 2007b). There is an ascending order of intensity of these efforts in the sense that they involve progressively increasing constraints on the amount of discretion that individual countries can exercise in the design of macroeconomic policies. By level of intensity, these efforts have ranged from economic review and policy dialogue to establishing regional financing arrangements and deepening of local-currency bond markets, and have eventually moved toward coordinating exchange rate policies.

Regional economic surveillance

In the area of economic review and policy dialogue, there are three major ongoing initiatives (see Table 9.3). First, the ASEAN Surveillance Process was established in October 1998 to strengthen the policymaking capacity within the group. Based on the principles of peer review and mutual interest, this process reviews global, regional and individual country developments and monitors exchange rate and macroeconomic aggregates, as well as sectoral and social policies. Under this process, the ASEAN finance ministers meet annually and the ministries of finance and central bank deputies meet biannually to discuss issues of common interest.

Second, with the formation of the ASEAN+3 Finance Ministers' Process in November 1999, the ASEAN+3 Economic Review and Policy Dialogue (ERPD) process was introduced in May 2000. Under the ERPD, ASEAN+3 finance ministers meet annually and their deputies meet biannually. Initially, deputies would meet for a couple of hours but now their meetings last for two days and discussions focus on:

Table 9.3 Regional forums for policy dialogues[a]

	Finance ministries and/or central banks					Central banks		
Time established	ASEAN (10)	ASEAN+3 (13)	MFG[b] (14)	APEC (21)	ASEM[c] (40)	SEANZA (20)	SEACEN (11)	EMEAP (11)
	August 1967	April 1999	November 1997	March 1994	September 1997	1956	February 1966	February 1991
Japan		○	○	○	○	○		○
China		○	○	○	○	○		○
Korea		○	○	○	○	○	○	○
Hong Kong			○	○		○		○
Taipei, China				○			○	
Singapore	○	○	○	○	○	○	○	○
Brunei Darussalam	○	○	○	○	○			
Cambodia	○	○			○			
Indonesia	○	○	○	○	○	○	○	○
Lao PDR	○	○			○			
Malaysia	○	○	○	○	○	○	○	○
Myanmar	○	○			○		○	
Philippines	○	○	○	○	○	○	○	○
Thailand	○	○	○	○	○	○	○	○
Vietnam	○	○		○	○			
Mongolia						○	○	
Macao						○		
Papua New Guinea				○		○		
Australia, New Zealand			○	○		○		○
Nepal, Sri Lanka						○	○	
Bangladesh, India, Iran, Pakistan						○		
USA, Canada			○	○				
Chile, Mexico, Peru				○				
Russia				○				
EU-27					○			

Source: Adopted from Kawai and Houser (2007).

Notes

a APEC = Asia-Pacific Economic Cooperation; ASEAN = Association of Southeast Asian Nations; EMEAP = Executives Meeting of East Asia-Pacific Central Banks; MFG = Manila Framework Group; SEACEN = South East Asian Central Banks; SEANZA = South East Asia, New Zealand, Australia.

b MFG includes the International Monetary Fund, the World Bank, the Asian Development Bank and the Bank for International Settlements. It was, however, terminated in December 2004.

c ASEM includes the European Commission.

1   assessing global, regional and national conditions and risks;
2   reviewing financial sector (including bond market) developments and vulnerabilities; and
3   other topics of interest.

The value added by regional surveillance is that countries tend to be more frank with each other in a regional forum as they focus on issues of common interest (such as high oil prices, avian flu, global payments imbalances and capital inflows). However, so far, the ERPD is in transition from the simple "information sharing" stage to "peer reviews" among the member countries. Since the ADB, and more recently the IMF, has provided assessments of regional economic and financial conditions and risks, individual countries also provide self-assessments of their respective economic situations. With a move toward "peer reviews" the participating members are expected to conduct more active discussions of other countries' policymaking.

Steps have been taken to monitor short-term capital flows and to develop early-warning systems of currency and banking crises. National Surveillance Units have been established in many ASEAN+3 countries for economic and financial monitoring and operating the early-warning system with ADB support. A Technical Working Group on Economic and Financial Monitoring. A Group of Experts has also been appointed. But the ASEAN+3 does not have a technical secretariat which prepares a comprehensive assessment of member countries' economic and financial outlook and risks.

Third, central bank governors in the region have also developed their own forums for regional economic information exchange, analysis and policy dialogues, including the Executives Meeting of Asia-Pacific Central Banks (EMEAP), South East Asian Central Banks (SEACEN) and South East Asia, New Zealand and Australia (SEANZA). EMEAP is the most prominent group and was organized in February 1991 with the leadership of the Bank of Japan and the Reserve Bank of Australia. Its major objectives include enhanced regional surveillance, exchanges of information and views and the promotion of financial market development. Its activities include annual meetings of EMEAP central bank governors, biannual meetings of the deputy governors and three working groups concerned with bank supervision, financial markets and payments and settlement systems. Like the ASEAN+3 finance ministers' process, EMEAP has no secretariat.

Until its dissolution in December 2005, the Manila Framework Group was another forum that brought together deputies from a wider range of countries for policy dialogue. There are trans-regional forums such as the Asia-Pacific Economic Cooperation (APEC) finance ministers and the Asia-Europe Meeting (ASEM) finance ministers for trans-regional processes.

Regional reserve pooling

Progress has also been made in establishing regional financing arrangements. They are designed to address short-term liquidity needs in the event of a crisis or contagion, and to supplement the existing international financial arrangements. At their May 2000 meeting in Chiang Mai, the ASEAN+3 finance ministers agreed on the Chiang Mai Initiative (CMI) to expand the ASEAN Swap Arrangement (ASA) to all ASEAN members, and to set up a network of bilateral swap arrangements (BSAs) among ASEAN+3 countries. The ASA expansion was done in November 2000, and its size increased from US$200 million to US$1 billion. In April 2005, the ASA size was again increased to US$2 billion. A network of BSAs has been signed among the plus-3 countries (China, Japan and Korea) and between a plus-3 country and a selected ASEAN country. To date, eight ASEAN+3 members have signed 16 BSAs amounting to US$84 billion (see Table 9.4).

One of the important features of CMI BSAs is that members requesting liquidity support can immediately obtain short-term financial assistance for the first 20 percent (originally 10 percent) of the committed amount. The remaining 80 percent is provided to the requesting member under an IMF program. Linking the CMI liquidity facility to an IMF program – and hence its conditionality – is designed to address the concern that the liquidity shortage of a requesting country may be due to fundamental problems, rather than mere panic and herd behavior by investors, and that the potential moral hazard problem could be non-negligible in the absence of tough IMF conditionality. The general view is that, with the region's current limited capacity to produce and enforce effective adjustment programs in times of crisis, linking CMI to IMF programs is prudent, at least for the time being.

Continuous progress has been made to strengthen CMI since its launch, particularly toward its multilateralization. Some of the major developments over the last few years include:

- integration and enhancement of ASEAN+3 ERPD into the CMI framework (May 2005);
- increasing the ceiling for withdrawal without an IMF program in place from 10 percent to 20 percent of the total (May 2005);[8]
- adoption of the collective decision-making procedure for CMI swap activation, as a step toward multilateralizing the CMI (May 2006);[9] and
- agreement in principle on a self-managed reserve pooling arrangement governed by a single contractual agreement as an appropriate form of CMI multilateralization (May 2007).[10]

At their May 2007 meeting in Kyoto, the ASEAN+3 finance ministers "unanimously agreed in principle that a self-managed reserve pooling arrangement ... is an appropriate form of mutlilateralization." They instructed the deputies to carry out further studies on the key elements of CMI multilateralization (self-managed reserve pooling), including surveillance, reserve eligibility, size of commitment, borrowing quota and activation mechanism. At their May 2008 meeting in Madrid, the ministers "agreed that the total size of the multilateralized CMI would be at least US$80 billion." They also "agreed on the key concepts of borrowing accessibility, the activation mechanism, and other elements."

Table 9.4 Progress on BSAs under the Chiang Mai Initiative (as of January 2008)

BSAs	Currencies	Effective/expiration dates	Size
Japan-Korea	USD/Won or USD/Yen Yen/Won or Won/Yen	4 July 2001/27 May 2005; 24 Feb 2006/23 Feb 2009 27 May 2005/3 July 2007	US$10.0 billion (Jap-Kor) US$5.0 billion (Kor-Jap) US$3.0 billion[a] (2-way)
Japan-Thailand	USD/Baht or USD/Yen	30 July 2001/7 March 2005/ 6 March 2007/10 July 2007	US$6.0 billion (Jap-Tha) US$3.0 billion (Tha-Jap)
Japan-Philippines	USD/Peso or USD/Yen	27 Aug 2001/4 May 2006/ 3 May 2009	US$6.0 billion (Jap-Phil) US$0.5 billion (Phil-Jap)
Japan-Malaysia	USD/Ringgit	5 Oct 2001/4 Oct 2007	US$1.0 billion[b] (Jap-Mal)
China-Thailand	USD/Baht	6 Dec 2001/5 Dec 2004	US$2.0 billion (Chi-Tha)
Japan-China	Yen/Renminbi or Renminbi/Yen	28 Mar 2002/27 Mar 2006	US$3.0 billion[a] (2-way)
China-Korea	Renminbi/Won or Won/Renminbi	24 June 2002/27 May 2005/23 June 2007	US$4.0 billion[a] (2-way)
Korea-Thailand	USD/Baht or USD/Won	25 June 2002/12 Dec 2005/11 Dec 2007	US$1.0 billion (2-way)
Korea-Malaysia	USD/Ringgit or USD/Won	26 July 2002/14 Oct 2005/13 Oct 2008	US$1.5 billion (2-way)
Korea-Philippines	USD/Peso or USD/Won	9 Aug 2002/17 Oct 2005/16 Oct 2007	US$2.0 billion (2-way)
China-Malaysia	USD/Ringgit	9 Oct 2002/8 Oct 2008	US$1.5 billion (Chi-Mal)
Japan-Indonesia	USD/Rupiah	17 Feb 2003/31 Aug 2005/30 Aug 2008	US$6.0 billion (Jap-Ind)
China-Philippines	Renminbi/Peso	29 Aug 2003/30 Aug 2007/29 Aug 2010	US$2.0 billion (Chi-Phi)
Japan-Singapore	USD/Singapore Dollar USD/Yen	10 Nov 2003/8 Nov 2005/ 7 Nov 2008	US$3.0 billion (Jap-Sing) US$1.0 billion (Sing-Jap)
Korea-Indonesia	USD/Rupiah or USD/Won	24 Dec 2003/27 Dec 2006/26 Dec 2009	US$2.0 billion (2-way)
China-Indonesia	USD/Rupiah	30 Dec 2003/17 Oct 2005; 17 Oct 2006/16 Oct 2009	US$4.0 billion (Chi-Ind)

Source: Update of Kawai (2007).

Notes

a The amounts are US dollar equivalents.

b The amount excludes US$2.5 billion committed (on August 18, 1999) under the New Miyazawa Initiative.

Asian bond market development

East Asia has come up with a number of initiatives to develop and deepen regional bond markets. Asian bond markets are expected to reduce the "double mismatch" problem, which was at the heart of the crisis, and overcome the so-called "original sin" problem.[11] The basic idea is to mobilize the region's vast pool of savings to be intermediated directly to the region's long-term investment, without going through financial intermediaries outside of the region. Regional financial intermediation through bond markets would diversify the modes of financing in the region and reduce the double mismatch. The initiatives include the APEC Bond Initiative, the EMEAP Asian Bond Fund (ABF) Initiative and the ASEAN+3 Asian Bond Markets Initiative (ABMI).

EMEAP introduced the ABF in June 2003. The idea was to help expand the bond market through demand-side stimulus from purchases by central banks of sovereign and quasi-sovereign bonds issued by eight EMEAP emerging members (including China, Hong Kong, Indonesia, Korea, Malaysia, Philippines, Singapore and Thailand) using all 11 members' foreign exchange reserves. The initial attempt was to purchase US$1 billion of US dollar-denominated bonds (ABF-1). Given the recognition that local-currency denominated bonds need to be promoted in order to address the "double mismatch" problem, the central bankers introduced ABF-2 in December 2004, involving purchases of US$2 billion equivalent of sovereign and quasi-sovereign local currency-denominated bonds.

ABF-2 consists of two components, a Pan-Asian Bond Index Fund (PAIF) and a Fund of Bond Funds (FoBF). The PAIF is a single bond fund index investing in local currency bonds, issued in eight economies. The FoBF has a two-tiered structure with a parent fund investing in eight sub-funds, each of which invests in local currency sovereign and quasi-sovereign bonds issued in their respective markets. PAIF and the eight sub-funds are passively managed by private fund managers against a Pan-Asian bond index and predetermined benchmark indexes in local markets. ABF-2 is designed to facilitate investment by public and private sector entities, through the listing of local currency exchange-traded bond funds – already listed in Hong Kong, Malaysia and Singapore.

The ASEAN+3 finance ministers' process launched ABMI in August 2003. The ABMI aims to focus on facilitating market access to a diverse issuer and investor base and on enhancing a market infrastructure for bond market development, thereby creating robust primary and secondary bond markets in the region. The ABMI initially created six working groups and later reorganized these into four working groups and two support teams (Ad hoc Support Group and Technical Assistance Coordination Group). Currently the four working groups are focusing on:

1   issuance of new securitized debt instruments;
2   establishment of a regional credit guarantee agency to help mitigate risks through credit enhancement;

3   exploration of possible establishment of a regional clearance and settlement system to facilitate cross-border bond transactions without facing the Herstatt risk (i.e. the risk of being in a different time zone); and
4   strengthening of regional rating agencies and harmonization of rating standards.

ADB launched the AsianBondsOnline website in May 2005,[12] which has become a popular one-stop clearinghouse of information on sovereign and corporate bonds issued in ASEAN+3 countries.

Exchange rate issues

Despite close and rising interdependence of East Asian economies through trade, investment and finance, there has been no exchange rate policy coordination in place in East Asia. Moreover, the region's exchange rate regimes are in serious disarray. In contrast to the pre-crisis period when many emerging market economies in East Asia maintained *de jure* or de facto US dollar pegged regimes, the post-crisis period exhibits a greater diversity in exchange rate regimes. The two giant economies in the region, Japan and China, have adopted different exchange rate regimes – Japan a free float and China a heavily managed regime targeted at the US dollar.

Only some research has been conducted, under various forums such as the ASEAN Currency and Exchange Rate Mechanism Task Force, the ASEM Kobe Research Project and the ASEAN+3 Research Group. This will, however, undoubtedly change as the integration process moves forward, business cycles become more synchronized and macroeconomic policy interdependence becomes even stronger. In fact, at the May 2006 meeting, the ASEAN+3 finance ministers endorsed a study on "regional monetary units," or Asian currency units.

New economic and financial risks in East Asia

New financial sector vulnerabilities

As highlighted earlier, the region has achieved a greater level of crisis resilience than in the pre-crisis period. An array of external and domestic indicators suggests that East Asian financial market conditions have improved greatly since the Asian financial crisis. Short-term external debt as a ratio of reserves is much less. NPL ratios have continued to fall. Risk-weighted CARs have improved. Exchange rates have become more flexible. The Bretton Woods institutions have begun to undertake reforms to adapt to the new environment. New standards and codes and data dissemination systems provide more reliable and timely information on economic and financial data which are necessary for well-functioning markets, risk management and market discipline. IMF surveillance systems have also been strengthened to cover financial sector and governance issues and other systemically important issues multilaterally. Several new financing mechanisms have been established. The creation of the Group of Twenty (G-20) and the Financial Stability Forum are also decisive and welcome steps. Regional efforts have also made encouraging progress.

The region also has shown a certain amount of resilience to global and regional turbulence. First, the region did not experience a contagion when the Argentine crisis occurred in 2001 as the country edged closer to the largest sovereign debt default in history.

Second, Indonesia's financial markets and its currency came under pressure in August 2005. The rupiah, which had gradually depreciated against the US dollar through much of the year, fell by 3.6 percent on August 29, its single largest decline since April 2001. The stock market index slid by 18 percent during the month from its April 3, 2005 peak. Worsening investor sentiment also contributed to a sharp reversal of portfolio flows that year. But the contagion was not felt in the other countries of the region. Indonesian markets stabilized after the government announced a major cutback in fuel subsidies, which led to a 126 percent increase in fuel prices. It also raised policy interest rates.

Third, in December 2006, amid concerns of hot money inflow and sharp currency appreciation, Thai officials imposed controls on capital inflows. A 30 percent reserve requirement on short-term inflows unrelated to trade, FDI or portfolio equity was imposed on December 18–19 and modified on January 29 to exempt hedged residential foreign currency borrowing. Subsequently, although the onshore baht has stabilized, the offshore rate has appreciated. This also did not have contagion effects in neighboring countries.

Finally, the US subprime loan crisis and the global financial turmoil have not directly affected Asia's financial institutions due to the relative absence of their exposure to subprime-related products, stronger regulatory and supervisory frameworks and better risk management. Although the full consequence of the subprime and global credit crisis has yet to be revealed, the Asian financial system appears to have escaped from the crisis.

However, vulnerabilities remain in East Asia. Despite improvements in financial indicators, the banking sector's ability to respond to volatile financial conditions may still be limited. Although NPLs continue to fall, problems with restructured loans (Thailand), new NPLs (China), compromised assets (Indonesia) and distressed assets (Philippines) leave banks vulnerable to the emergence of new instability. In many economies, the asset base has been reduced because of significant portions of zero-risk-weighted sovereign securities, but detailed information is not fully available on bank exposure to market risk through holdings of official securities (and private securities and derivatives). As a result, Moody's Investor Services rates large parts of banking systems in East Asia in the low D and E range with the exceptions of Hong Kong and Singapore (Turner 2007). The reasons for these low ratings include relatively strong market views on the need to strengthen risk management and questions about the effectiveness of supervision and regulation.

Currently, East Asia's banking sectors are much less exposed to foreign currency liquidity risks than in the pre-crisis period. But, having moved into new business activities (securities holdings), lending to the property sector and household lending, they have also assumed new risks. Also, economic overheating in several economies can make their financial institutions vulnerable to the bursting of the economic boom.

Challenges for macroeconomic management

In terms of macroeconomic management, the region faces three key risks, and appropriate macroeconomic policy responses are vital. The first is the negative impact of the US economic slowdown (or recession) on the growth prospect of the regional economies. The US housing market collapse, part of the background of the recent subprime loan crisis, will continue to spill over into the construction sector, housing investment and overall economic activity. Tightening credit markets and deteriorating employment prospects in the US could stall household consumption that has been resilient for many years. The stagflationary mix of slowing growth and rising inflation is thus a major risk to the US economy. Its negative international spillovers could dampen growth prospects in many industrialized countries – in Europe and Japan – with cascading impacts on emerging East Asian economies. This risk could be exacerbated by increases in spreads of emerging economy bonds, including those of Asian bonds and severe downward adjustments in many Asian stock prices, which can have dampening effects on firm investment and household consumption in emerging Asia. In addition, banks and investors in the US – which has been exposed to subprime-related securities – have become cautious in managing their portfolios by hoarding cash and reducing loans and investment in order to protect their capital bases. This could indirectly undermine growth prospects in East Asia amid global re-pricing of financial risks.

The second risk is a continued rise in oil and food prices. With precarious supply conditions and inventory rundowns, oil prices continue to rise and further increases remain a possibility. The recent spike in the price of rice, the main staple food of the region, also heightened anxiety across East Asia, highlighting the urgent need to address long-term food security. There is no denying that speculative activities in oil, food and other commodity markets play some important role, and that a large part of the price increase reflects fundamental changes in the global economy – persistent and rising demand for oil, food and other commodities and resources by large, rapidly growing emerging economies, like China and India, which have joined the global market in recent years. With oil, food and other commodity prices at record highs, any further increases in costs could trigger persistent price inflation that can generate a wage–price spiral. Inflation has already reached alarming levels in Vietnam, China and many other economies. Clearly, the inflationary pressures driven by rising energy and commodity prices pose a significant threat to macroeconomic stability throughout East Asia.

The third risk is a possible surge in short-term capital inflows and the consequent upward pressure on the value of regional currencies. Several countries like Thailand and Vietnam had been experiencing excessive capital inflows until the

US subprime crisis broke out. Encountering the subprime problem, many US financial institutions began to secure liquidity and reduce lending and investment abroad. As the US financial system restores its stability and the credit crunch eases, there is a real possibility that capital inflows to East Asia will resume and in a massive way. With the overall confidence in the US dollar eroded, these inflows may generate significant further upward appreciation of East Asian currencies. If not managed properly, they can be another source of macroeconomic and financial-sector instability, by creating overinvestment, over-extension of loans and asset price bubbles in recipient countries. Allowing currency appreciation is advisable in order to stem domestic inflationary pressure and asset price bubbles, but it can also damage a country's international price competitiveness.

An important challenge is to pursue a proper macroeconomic policy mix in the face of these key risks in order to maintain a sound balance between low inflation and sustainable economic growth.

Global payments imbalances and surges in capital inflows

Adjusting to global payments imbalances will be a big challenge for the global and East Asian economy. The international consensus is that these payments imbalances are not sustainable, at least in the long run, and if left unaddressed, their continuation could result in an abrupt and disorderly adjustment of the US dollar. A strong domestic demand increase in East Asia, a savings increase in the US, an orderly depreciation of the real effective exchange rate of the US dollar and an equally orderly appreciation of the East Asian currencies will be needed to reduce the US current account deficit and the East Asian surplus. Nevertheless, risk remains that a disorderly unwinding of imbalances may take place – and indeed it may be already taking place – resulting in economic and financial disruptions and turbulence on both sides of the Pacific.

A general consensus is that, should the current global imbalances continue to grow or international investor tolerance (or expectations) for them change abruptly, significant financial market turmoil could ensue. Both the May 2006 and Feb–March 2007 episodes of increased financial volatility offer glimpses of possible consequences. While in both instances, the turmoil was short-lived and currency adjustments were largely limited, a future shock could be more severe with longer-term consequences. Any such development would clearly require that some or all East Asian currencies not only join, but even lead, the appreciation against the dollar as exchange rate changes could facilitate global adjustment in conjunction with other needed policy steps.

The global payments imbalance problem has been compounded by the US and global credit crisis. As has been argued earlier, massive capital inflows, which are expected at any time in the future, can be a source of macroeconomic and financial-sector vulnerabilities as they put downward pressure on the US dollar and upward pressure on East Asian currencies. In this circumstance, currency appreciation is a good option to contain domestic inflation and incipient asset price bubbles as the authority can gain greater autonomy in setting monetary policy. Given its negative impact on international price competitiveness, however, each economy may find it difficult to allow currency appreciation alone taking into account the neighbors' exchange rate regime. One of the most reasonable strategies would be to address the problem collectively. Lack of collective action can be a source of vulnerabilities.

The policy taken by China is key, as China has been experiencing a massive buildup of foreign exchange reserves due to current and capital account surpluses – with its undervalued exchange rate. Limited sterilization has meant a continuous injection of base money (liquidity) into the economy, excessive monetary and credit growth, posing the risk of accumulating potential NPLs in the bank balance sheets, economic overheating, overinvestment in certain sectors, price inflation, and asset price bubbles in stock markets and housing markets in large cities. This situation is the result of excessive reliance on net exports thereby exposing the country to the vagaries of global demand (Roubini 2007). For China, with a leaky capital account, prudent macroeconomic and financial-sector management requires greater flexibility of RMB. RMB revaluation in July 2005 and its shift to a managed float suggest the beginning of a better arrangement. Further RMB appreciation would make it easier for both China and many other emerging East Asian economies to cope with the forthcoming – and to some extent ongoing – rapid US dollar depreciation.

Next steps for East Asian economic integration

Potential for further economic integration

It is now well understood that business cycles in East Asia are becoming more synchronized, suggesting a good potential for enhancing regional exchange rate and monetary policy coordination (see Rana 2007a, 2007b, and also Kawai and Motonishi 2005 for an earlier study). Using annual GDP growth rates for 11 of the ASEAN+3 countries for which data are available (except Brunei and Cambodia), simple ten-year moving correlations between GDP growth of individual ASEAN+3 members and the group (excluding the reference member) were calculated from 1989 to 2005. Figure 9.3 shows that correlations have been increasing, especially after the financial crisis, suggesting greater synchronization of business cycles among ASEAN+3. On the other hand, correlations between business cycles of individual ASEAN+3 countries and the US appear to be more mixed – increasing in the cases of Korea, Japan, Singapore and Thailand but declining in the case of other countries (Figure 9.4). The ASEAN+3 region's growth correlation with the EU (proxied by France, Germany and Italy), however, appears to be falling (Figure 9.5).

One possible reason for the synchronization of business cycles is the rising trade intensity among East Asian countries. According to the theoretical literature, however, the impact of trade integration on business cycle is ambiguous.[13] If demand shocks dominate, we expect trade integration to increase business

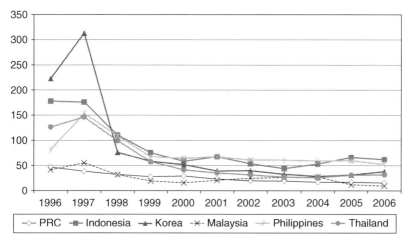

Figure 9.4 Short-term external debt (% of gross international reserves) (source: Institute of International Finance online).

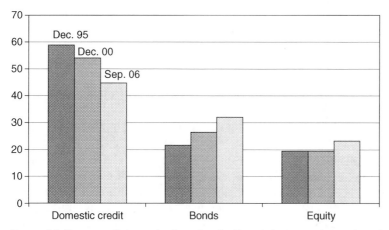

Figure 9.5 Sources of domestic financing in East Asia (as a share of total domestic financing, in %) (source: ADB, Asian Bonds Online website).

Note
1 Countries included are PRC, Hong Kong China, Indonesia, Japan, Korea, Malaysia, Philippines, Singapore and Thailand.

cycle correlation. If general supply shocks dominate, we also expect trade integration to increase cycle correlation as a positive (negative) output shock in a country raises (reduces) its demand for foreign goods produced by neighbors and thus creates positive cycle correlation. On the other hand, if industry-specific supply shocks dominate, the impact of trade integration on business cycle correlation is ambiguous. In countries where trade integration stimulates inter-industry trade (à la Heckscher-Ohlin or Ricardo), it tends to create negative (or low) cycle correlation as countries tend to specialize in different sectors which are subject to different shocks. Where trade integration stimulates intra-industry trade (either of a horizontal nature as in the case of Europe or of a vertical nature as in the case of East Asia),[14] it can create positive correlation as the pattern of specialization occurs mainly within the same industries, each of which is subject to specific shocks.

Further to the seminal paper by Frankel and Rose (1998) and subsequent work by others, Rana (2008) has estimated the following business cycle correlation equation for East Asian countries. To avoid simultaneity problems, the equation uses instruments for the bilateral trade intensity variable based on the gravity model and for pooled data from 1993 to 2004. The estimated equation is as follows:

$$corr\ IPI_{ij} = 0.002 + 0.001 TI_{ij} + 0.532 IIT_{ij} + 0.052 FPC_{ij} + 0.146 MPC_{ij}$$
$$(0.07)\quad (0.05)\qquad (6.11)^{**}\qquad (2.69)^{**}\qquad (4.37)^{**}$$
$$No.\ of\ observations = 332 \qquad R^2 = 0.22$$

where *corr IPI*$_{ij}$ refers to the correlation coefficient of industrial production index between countries i and j; TI_{ij} is the trade intensity index; IIT_{ij} is the intra-industry trade intensity index at two-digit SITC level; FPC_{ij} is fiscal policy coordination; and MPC_{ij} is monetary policy coordination.

This estimated equation suggests that intra-industry trade (together with macroeconomic coordination variables when the crisis dummy is not included) is a major factor explaining business cycle co-movements in East Asia. Interestingly, this means that increasing trade itself does not lead to synchronization of business cycles. In particular, if a trade increase occurs mainly across different industries, it does not foster co-movements of production with trading partners. What counts is the increase in intra-industry trade across countries.

The above findings have important policy implications for the potential for enhancing regional economic integration in East Asia. Bayoumi and Mauro (1999) have calculated an Optimal Currency Area (OCA) index for East Asia based on historical data of debt patterns and nature of disturbances and concluded that "on economic criteria, ASEAN appears less suited for a regional currency arrangement than Europe before the Maastricht Treaty was signed, although the difference was not large." Our finding that an increase in intra-industry trade has led to greater synchronization of business cycles in East Asia, together with the findings of Frankel and Rose (1998) that the level of trade integration can rise significantly after the formation of a currency union, suggest that East Asia, while being a conceivable candidate for a currency union ex ante, could be an even stronger candidate ex post (based on endogenous factors). The latter factors are important because trade expansion due to the formation of a currency union could lead to greater synchronization of business cycles, which would in turn reduce the cost of a union by lowering the incidence of asymmetric shocks. Proponents of a deeper monetary cooperation in East Asia including those making a case for greater exchange rate coordination and a single currency in the region – starting with the introduction of the Asian Currency Unit (ACU) – may have a point. Exchange rate stability in turn should promote further trade integration.

What could be a roadmap for enhancing regional economic integration in East Asia? According to Balassa (1961), the degree of economic integration increases in a linear manner: from FTA, customs union and common market, to economic and monetary union. Although no region in the world has adopted this textbook model in practice, it is worth considering how trade and FDI cooperation may evolve in the future and whether a multi-track approach – a trade track, a financial track and an exchange rate track – is reasonable for East Asia.

Trade and FDI initiatives: consolidation of overlapping FTAs into a single FTA

Proliferation of FTAs

On the trade track, East Asia basically used to adopt multilateralism in designing its trade policy, with the exception of the ASEAN Free Trade Area (AFTA) initiated in 1992. However, the region's approach seems to have changed since the turn of the century. Currently, the region is experiencing a proliferation of FTAs. Within East Asia, 13 FTAs have been in effect or signed for implementation. An additional 31 FTAs have been in effect or signed vis-à-vis non-East Asian economies. The number of East Asian FTAs vis-à-vis South Asia that have been in effect or proposed increased from zero in 2000 to eight in 2006 (Table 9.5). The India–Singapore Comprehensive Economic Cooperation Agreement, which was signed in 2005, covers not only trade in goods but also services, investments and cooperation in technology, education, air services and human resources.

There are positive and negative implications of the spread of FTAs in East Asia. On the positive side, FTAs, if designed properly, can help countries to pursue their dynamic comparative advantage and allocate resources efficiently. Against a backdrop of slow progress in global trade negotiations, good-practice FTAs can promote continuing liberalization, induce domestic and structural reforms in the countries concerned, and widen market access across the region. Trade arrangements with dynamic, competitive partners can also encourage the spread of efficient production practices. On the negative side, FTAs can be trade-diverting and the demands of negotiating many trade agreements place increasing strains on scarce trade negotiation resources of many countries, especially given the expanding scope, content and increasing complexity of recently negotiated FTAs in the region. Multiple rules of origin arising from overlapping FTAs also increase the administrative and business costs especially for small and medium-sized enterprises, giving rise to the infamous Asian "noodle bowl" effect. There is, therefore, a need to consolidate and streamline bilateral/plurilateral FTAs by widening and deepening them into a single, large FTA.

Consolidation into an ASEAN+3 or an ASEAN+6 FTA?

Given the proliferation of FTAs in the region, policymakers should explore ways to reduce negative impacts of having too many overlapping FTAs. First,

Table 9.5 FTAs in Asia, 2000 and 2007[1]

	2000			2007		
	Total	WTO notified	Not notified	Total	WTO notified	Not notified
All agreements	**32**	15	17	**151**	45	106
Bilateral FTAs	**25**	8	17	**115**	35	80
Within Asian sub-regions	**13**	5	8	**37**	17	20
East Asia[3]	**1**	1	0	**13**	5	8
South Asia[4]	**0**	0	0	**5**	1	4
Central and West Asia[2]	**10**	2	8	**17**	9	8
The Pacific[5]	**2**	2	0	**2**	2	0
Across Asian sub-regions	**0**	0	0	**18**	4	14
East Asia[3] + South Asia[4]	**0**	0	0	**8**	0	8
East Asia[3] + Central and West Asia[2]	**0**	0	0	**0**	0	0
East Asia[3] + The Pacific[5]	**0**	0	0	**10**	4	6
South Asia[4] + Central and West Asia[2]	**0**	0	0	**0**	0	2
South Asia[4] + The Pacific[5]	**0**	0	0	**0**	0	0
Central and West Asia[2] + The Pacific	**0**	0	0	**0**	0	0
With non-Asian countries	**12**	3	9	**60**	14	46
East Asia[3] + Non-Asia	**1**	0	1	**31**	5	26
South Asia[4] + Non-Asia	**0**	0	0	**8**	0	8
Central and West Asia[2] + Non-Asia	**10**	3	7	**16**	8	8
The Pacific[5] + Non-Asia	**1**	0	1	**5**	1	4
Plurilateral FTAs[6]	**7**	7	0	**36**	10	26
Among Asian countries	**4**	4	0	**12**	5	7
ASEAN	**1**	1	0	**1**	1	0
ASEAN + Asia	**0**	0	0	**5**	1	4
Others	**3**	3	0	**6**	3	3
With non-Asian countries	**3**	3	0	**24**	5	19
ASEAN + Asia	**0**	0	0	**1**	0	1
Others	**3**	3	0	**23**	5	18

Source: ADB ARIC FTA Database.

Notes
1   Includes FTAs concluded, and under negotiation.
2   Central Asia includes: Armenia; Azerbaijan; Kazakhstan; Kyrgyz Republic; Tajikistan; Turkmenistan; Uzbekistan.
3   East Asia includes: China; Hong Kong, Japan; Korea, Republic of Mongolia; Taipei, China; Brunei Darussalam; Cambodia; Indonesia; Laos; Malaysia; Myanmar; Philippines; Singapore; Thailand; Vietnam.
4   South Asia includes: Afghanistan; Pakistan; Bangladesh; Bhutan; India; Maldives; Nepal; Sri Lanka.
5   The Pacific includes: Australia; Cook Islands; Fiji Islands; Kiribati; Marshall Islands; Micronesia, Federated States of; Nauru; New Zealand; Palau; Papua New Guinea; Samoa; Solomon Islands; Timor-Leste; Tonga; Tuvalu; Vanuatu.
6   Plurilateral FTAs refer to FTAs involving at least three countries of which at least one is an Asian country.

FTAs should be carefully designed to ensure consistency with WTO (GATT Article 24 and GATS Article 5). Second, FTAs should be made compatible with others in the region. A review system to harmonize the tariff structures of FTAs and to impose a common set of rules of origin and insisting on cumulation throughout the region such as the Pan-European Cumulation System may be needed (Baldwin 2007). Third, FTA membership could be expanded and coverage deepened beyond tariffs to eventually establish a single, large East Asian FTA. Fourth, to enhance trade integration, physical connectivity across countries is vital through cross-border infrastructure development and trade facilitation.

A practical approach to East Asian FTA consolidation would be to position ASEAN as the natural "hub" in the region, use ASEAN+1 FTAs as building blocks,[15] and then merge these overlapping FTAs into an ASEAN+3 FTA (EAFTA: East Asian FTA, China's proposal) or ASEAN+6 FTA (CEPEA: Comprehensive Economic Partnership in East Asia, Japan's proposal).[16] This ASEAN-centered approach requires deeper integration of AFTA towards the ASEAN Economic Community, particularly fuller inclusion of CLMV countries (Cambodia, Laos, Myanmar and Vietnam). ASEAN is expected to become a tariff-free economic zone by 2015, when the ASEAN Economic Community will be established. As all ASEAN+1 FTAs are expected to be completed by 2017, it is reasonable to assume that a single East Asian FTA could emerge before 2020.

Kawai and Wignaraja (2008) report computable general equilibrium (CGE) results that demonstrate a large gain from an ASEAN+3 FTA and an even larger gain from an ASEAN+6 (East Asia Summit) FTA. Hence, East Asia needs to aim for ASEAN+6 as the region's goal. If the sufficient depth of integration cannot be achieved among the ASEAN+6 countries due to the diverse interests among the group – particularly between ASEAN+3 countries and India – however, then a realistic approach would be to take a sequential move by starting with an ASEAN+3 FTA and then expanding it to an ASEAN+6 FTA. With such a sequenced approach, there is a need to manage the risk of "noodle bowls" during the transition process. Essentially, any FTA must be designed with a view toward consolidation.

The CGE computation also indicates a negative impact of an East Asian FTA – whether EAFTA or CEPEA – and on the US and Europe which, though small, needs to be addressed by maintaining openness. After the completion of a single East Asian FTA, East Asia may be ready to connect itself with North America and Europe.

Advancing financial cooperation

On the finance track, the recent decisions by ASEAN+3 finance ministers to integrate CMI and ERPD, collectivize the decision-making process of CMI, and create a self-managed reserve pooling arrangement (or a Multilateral Swap Arrangement: MSA) are significant. The next steps are to determine the size of the MSA, define the legal nature of CMI multilateralization, and reduce the linkage to IMF conditionality. Over the medium term, even a centrally administered reserve pool could be developed. As part of this process, a professional secretariat should also be established to support the CMI/ERPD process.

To make the CMI/ERPD effective, concerted efforts should be made to move beyond the simple "information sharing" stage to a more rigorous review stage, possibly in the form of a formal "peer review" and "peer pressure" mechanism of the OECD. Given the important operational role of central banks in extending liquidity support at times of crisis and their potential role in conducting quality surveillance, their governors should be fully involved in the ASEAN+3 process. Once the finance ministers (and their deputies) start focusing more intensively on exchange rate issues – by using an ACU index and divergence indicators – analytical expertise and operational knowledge of central banks are critical to the process.

If the CMI eventually is to become a centralized reserve pooling arrangement that is independent of IMF, a "due diligence" mechanism must be established (Kawai and Houser 2007). The reason is that with such a financing arrangement, the ASEAN+3 group must avoid lending too generously with too little conditionality thereby creating moral hazard for the government at the receiving end. In this regard, a professional secretariat can play a critical role. First, it can produce high-quality country reports, ensuring that all involved with lending decisions have a thorough familiarity with the basic economic conditions of potential borrowers. Second, the secretariat as a neutral agency can recommend a set of lending conditionalities – one that is more focused and more relevant than IMF conditionality in the past – associated with liquidity provision, independently of the specific interests of particular potential lending countries.

Asian bond markets need to be further developed. Regional institutions to deepen local-currency bond markets – such as a regional credit guarantee institution and a regional settlement agency – need to be established. With the progress of market infrastructure reforms at the national levels, a regional regulatory agency that promotes coordination of capital market rules and regulation may be developed in the future.

To summarize, regional financial cooperation may be advanced in the following direction:

- ASEAN+3 finance ministers and central bank governors need to strengthen their policy dialogue, by focusing more intensively on exchange rate issues using an ACU index and divergence indicators;
- CMI needs to be fully multilateralized, its size further expanded and its linkage to IMF conditionality further reduced;
- An independent professional secretariat will have to be created to support the CMI/ERPD process; and
- Various regional entities need to be established to support the development of local-currency bond markets, including for regional credit guarantees and enhancements, regional settlements and clearance.

Exchange rate policy coordination

Collective appreciation of Asian currencies

Given global payments imbalances and possible surges in capital inflows, East Asia faces the risk of an abrupt and sharp adjustment of the currency values vis-à-vis the US dollar. If this happens, many East Asian authorities – even those with currency flexibility – may be tempted to resist market forces in order to maintain international price competitiveness against their regional neighbors, particularly China, should the yuan continue to be heavily managed against the dollar.

To the extent that other policy options like monetary policy easing are inappropriate due to, say, inflationary pressure and incipient asset market bubbles, it is advisable for East Asian economies to allow currency appreciation. If the upward pressure on currencies is region-wide, these economies should adjust exchange rates collectively as this would spread the adjustment cost across East Asia thus minimizing individual economy costs. Simple calculation would indicate that a 20 percent collective appreciation of East Asian currencies vis-à-vis the US dollar implies only a 9 percent effective (or trade-weighted) appreciation against trading partners – given the intraregional trade share being 55 percent. If all other currencies also appreciate vis-à-vis the dollar, the degree of effective appreciation of the East Asian currencies would be more limited (Kawai 2007a).

Joint currency appreciation requires a convergence of exchange rate regimes in East Asia. It is essential for China to further increase its RMB flexibility and pace of appreciation, thereby easing the other neighboring countries' aversion to currency appreciation. This is beneficial to both China's domestic macroeconomic and financial-sector management and East Asia's overall economic management. For this to happen, the existing policy dialogue processes among the region's finance ministers (such as ASEAN+3) and central bank governors (such as EMEAP) can play a critical role.

Exchange rate coordination

The deepening regional economic integration and rising business cycle synchronization within East Asia suggest that East Asia would be better off by maintaining intraregional exchange rate stability. But, currently, there exists no coordination of exchange rate or monetary policies across East Asia as each country wishes to pursue its own domestic objectives. To pursue policy coordination, a gradual, step-by-step approach is appropriate.

The first step is to coordinate informally on exchange rate regimes by moving toward greater exchange rate flexibility, while achieving some exchange rate stability within East Asia. This can be done by those economies under US dollar pegs to increase exchange rate flexibility and by all emerging East Asian economies to adopt managed floating targeted at a basket of G3 currencies (the US dollar, the euro and the yen) or G3-plus currencies (adding emerging East Asian currencies) as a loose reference. The currency weights in the basket and the tightness of exchange rate targeting could vary across countries, at least initially. At this stage, an ACU index can be introduced as a tool for measuring the degree of joint movements of East Asian currencies and the degree of divergence of each currency movement from the regional average set by the ACU. Once China moves to a more flexible exchange rate regime, ACU index movements and divergences of component currency movements can provide more meaningful information.

The second step is to initiate more formal exchange rate policy coordination to ensure some intraregional rate stability without rigid coordination of monetary policy. This may involve stabilizing intraregional exchange rates using a common basket of G3-plus currencies (i.e. the US dollar, the euro and the ACU) as a reference. The basket stabilization policy will be clearly defined with rules on exchange rate parity against the common G3-plus basket, a relatively wide exchange rate band (like ±10 percent) around parity and adjustment of both the parity and the band (along the line of Williamson 2005). The ACU index should continue to serve as an important indicator in measuring joint movements and divergences of East Asian currencies.

"European" vs. "parallel currency" approach

Beyond the second stage, two approaches are possible – the "European" approach and the "parallel currency" approach (Eichengreen 2006). Under the "European" approach, over the medium to longer term, a common basket peg similar to the European Monetary System could be established. Then rigid Maastricht-type convergence criteria could be introduced and eventually, as a final step, a single currency could be adopted. The European approach requires a high level of political commitment in East Asia. In the absence of strong political will, a "parallel currency" approach could be considered. This would involve issuance of an ACU as a parallel legal tender together with national currencies, issuance of ACU-denominated bonds and the establishment of a clearing and settlement system for ACU transactions. In the longer term, as the volume of ACU transactions increases, the ACU could develop into the sole legal tender within the region. The centralized reserve pool could then be converted into an Asian Central Bank.

The appeal of the "parallel currency" approach is dictated more by economic forces (i.e. market forces) than by politics. This is consistent with the greater emphasis placed by East Asian countries on market-led rather than policy-led integration. It also accommodates the fact that the East Asian political context is very different compared with Europe. An underlying commitment to political solidarity drove the transition to a monetary union in Europe. Europe also considered the parallel currency approach, but it was abandoned in favor of the Maastricht process because of the strong political commitment that existed at the time.

Conclusion: the way forward

Having recovered from the 1997–1998 crisis, East Asia is again the most dynamic growth center of the world economy. Crisis-affected East Asia is more resilient to financial shocks as a result of improved external financial conditions (reductions in short-term external debt and accumulation of foreign exchange reserves), restoration of financial health of commercial banks (lower NPL ratios and higher CARs), introduction of a better macroeconomic management framework (including greater exchange rate flexibility) and financial and corporate sector reforms. However, progress has been uneven and significant challenges remain to improve macroeconomic management, financial sector regulation and supervision, and real sector competitiveness not only in crisis-affected countries but in East Asia at large (including ASEAN, China, India and others).

In this chapter, we have argued that the East Asian economies have achieved strong economic interdependence through market-driven integration with the global and regional economies. Expansion of trade, FDI and finance and the consequent business cycle synchronization has created a naturally integrated economic zone in East Asia – though the degree of regional financial integration is still limited. Reflecting rising economic interdependence and in response to the trauma caused by the financial crisis of 1997–1998, East Asia has embarked on various initiatives for regional economic integration, including bilateral and plurilateral FTAs, regional surveillance mechanisms, a regional reserve pooling arrangement (CMI) and Asian bond market development. These efforts are designed to complement the global frameworks governed by the WTO and the IMF.

We have claimed that East Asia can further strengthen its economic resilience by intensifying regional economic and financial cooperation. First, regional trade authorities need to consolidate multiple, overlapping free trade agreements into a single East Asian agreement – particularly among ASEAN+6 countries – so that negative "noodle bowl" effects are minimized and deep integration can be achieved. This will be a basis for greater coherence of rules, standards and procedures across countries in the region, further integration and interdependence with North America and Europe and consistency with the WTO framework.

Second, the regional financial authorities must make greater efforts to strengthen the reserve pooling arrangement (CMI), regional economic surveillance (ERPD) and Asian bond market initiatives. Once the region achieves substantial enhancement of the CMI through further enlargement, full multilateralization, and substantial reduction in its IMF linkages, and once the region strengthens its capacity to formulate independent adjustment policy in the event of liquidity crises, East Asia will have effectively established its own monetary fund that can contribute to regional, as well as global, financial stability without creating fears of moral hazard.

Third, the regional financial and monetary authorities need to strengthen coordination of exchange rate policy – starting with the joint monitoring of regional exchange rates based on an ACU index and the exploration of ways to engineer collective appreciation of the regional currencies vis-à-vis the US dollar at the time of steep dollar depreciation. They need to pursue more systematically mechanisms by which East Asian currencies can be kept relatively stable within the region. Greater political support for economic integration will be needed to further advance significant exchange rate policy coordination. A "parallel currency" approach is worth consideration to move ahead on a market basis.

Finally, the region will have to take steps to overcome the impediments to closer economic integration by encouraging low-income ASEAN members to pursue economic reforms and connect themselves with the regional and global markets and by developing a long-term vision for an East Asian economic community which can be shared by all in the region.

Aside from being multi-track, East Asian integration could be multi-speed as well. On each track membership of countries and sub-regions could be expanded as appropriate. This is what Senior Minister Goh Chok Tong (2006) once referred to as the "variable geometry, flexible borders" approach. Not only could the process be multi-track and multi-speed, it should also be pragmatic, step-by-step, and utilize a bottom-up approach, rather than focus on conceiving and implementing a comprehensive pan-Asian vision or a grand plan, as was done in Europe. Reaching a broad political and social consensus to develop a far-reaching vision of pan-Asian integration does not appear feasible at this stage.

Acknowledgments

This is a combined and substantially revised version of two papers separately prepared by the authors for the Conference on "The Asian Financial Crisis 10 Years Later: What Have We Learned?" organized by S. Rajaratnam School of International Studies of Nanyang Technological University , Singapore on June 25–26, 2007. The authors are grateful to conference participants for valuable comments. The views expressed in this chapter are those of the authors alone and do not necessarily reflect the views and policies of Nanyang Technological University, the Asian Development Bank, its Institute, its Board of Executive Directors or the governments they represent.

Notes

1 Reforms under the auspices of other international bodies such as the BIS and IOSCO are not discussed in this chapter. We mainly focus on the Bretton Woods institutions, particularly the IMF.
2 In this chapter, we do not discuss the social sector implications.
3 In addition, the government must establish effective legal and judiciary systems to enforce property rights and contracts and other supporting institutions that govern private sector economic activity and improve market efficiency. This is essentially a process of institution building.
4 The Korean government, representing the interest of the country's commercial banks, agreed with international bank creditors on a standstill, during which period they negotiated to restructure external debt that was due shortly. The Korean government provided guarantees for debt payment, and the governments of major industrialized countries convinced their banks that the restructuring arrangements would be in their best interest. The restructuring agreement restored the confidence not only in the currency market but also in the financial system, providing a basis for the subsequent recovery.
5 Cady (2004) shows that spreads on new bond issues by developing countries declined by about 75 basis points following SDDS subscription.
6 The first such multilateral surveillance focused on global payments imbalances, involving several systemically important members – US, China, the Euro area, Japan and Saudi Arabia.

7 The IMF's core areas of responsibility include macroeconomic stabilization; monetary, fiscal and exchange rate policy, including the underlying institutional arrangements and closely related structural measures; and financial sector issues including the functioning of both domestic and international financial markets.

8 Joint Ministerial Statement of the 8th ASEAN+3 Finance Ministers' Meeting, May 4, 2005, Istanbul, Turkey.

9 Joint Ministerial Statement of the 9th ASEAN+3 Finance Ministers' Meeting, May 4, 2006, Hyderabad, India.

10 Joint Ministerial Statement of the 10th ASEAN+3 Finance Ministers' Meeting, May 5, 2007, Kyoto, Japan.

11 "Original sin," as hypothesized by Eichengreen and Hausmann (1999), is a situation where emerging economy residents cannot borrow abroad in domestic currency nor borrow long term, even domestically. Hence, domestic banks and corporations tend to face a currency or maturity mismatch or both, thus facing balance sheet vulnerabilities to sharp changes in exchange rates and/or interest rates.

12 This website tracks developments in East Asia's local currency bond markets and provides detailed progress reports on the various ABMI initiatives, among others.

13 According to Calderon *et al.* (2003), the total effect of trade intensity on cycle correlation is theoretically ambiguous and poses a question that could only be solved empirically.

14 One can say that intra-industry trade within Europe is largely a horizontal nature while that within East Asia is largely a vertical nature based on production networks and supply chains.

15 ASEAN+1 FTAs include ASEAN+China FTA, ASEAN+Korea FTA, ASEAN+Japan CEP, ASEAN+India FTA and ASEAN+CER FTA.

16 The Japanese government proposed to establish the Economic Research Institute for ASEAN and East Asia (ERIA) in an ASEAN country to carry out research and analysis on both ASEAN and ASEAN+6 economic integration. This proposal was endorsed at the East Asia Summit meeting in Cebu in January 2007.

References

Allen, M., Rosenberg, C., Keller, C., Stetser, B. and Roubini, N. (2002) "A Balance Sheet Approach to Financial Crisis," IMF, WP/02/210.

Asian Development Bank (2006) *Asia Economic Monitor* (December), Manila.

Balassa, B. (1961) *The Theory of Economic Integration*, Homewood, Illinois: Irwin.

Baldwin, R.E. (2007) "Managing the Noodle Bowl: The Fragility of East Asian Regionalism," Working Paper series on Regional Economic Integration No. 7, Asian Development Bank, Manila.

Bayoumi, T. and Mauro, P. (1999) "The Suitability of ASEAN for a Regional Currency Arrangement," IMF Working Paper No. 99/162, International Monetary Fund, Washington, DC.

Boorman, J. (2008) "An Agenda for Reform of the International Monetary Fund (IMF)," Occasional Papers No. 38 (January), Dialogue on Globalization, Friedrich Ebert Stiftung.

Cady, J. (2004) "Does SDDS Subscription Reduce Borrowing Costs for Emerging Market Economies?" IMF Working Paper No. WP/04/58 (April), International Monetary Fund, Washington, DC.

Calderon, C., Chong, A. and Stein, E. (2003) "Trade Intensity and Business Cycle Synchronization: Are Development Countries Any Different?" Working Paper No. 478, Inter-American Development Bank.

Eichengreen, B. (2006) "The Parallel Currency Approach to Asian Monetary Integration," mimeo (March), Office of Regional Economic Integration, Asian Development Bank, Manila.

Eichengreen, B. and Hausmann, R. (1999) "Exchange Rates and Financial Fragility," NBER Working Paper 7418, National Bureau of Economic Research, Inc.

Frankel, J.A. and Rose, K.R. (1998) "The Endogeneity of the Optimum Currency Area Criterion," *Economic Journal*, 108:449 (July), pp. 1009–1025.

Ghosh, A. (2006) "Capital Account Crisis: Lessons for Crisis Prevention," IMF. Online, available at: www.imf.org/external/np/seminars/eng/2006/cpem/pdf/overvi.pdf.

Goh, C.T. (2006) "Towards an East Asian Renaissance," address at the opening session of the fourth Asia-Pacific Roundtable organized by the Global Foundation, the World Bank, and the Institute of Southeast Asian Studies, Singapore.

IMF Independent Evaluation Office (2003) *The IMF and Recent Capital Account Crises: Indonesia, Korea, Brazil* (July). International Monetary Fund, Washington, DC.

Kawai, M. (2005) "East Asian Economic Regionalism: Progress and Challenges," *Journal of Asian Economics*, 16 (February), pp. 29–55.

Kawai, M. (2007a) "Ten Years after the Crisis: Is Asia Prepared for Future Financial Shocks?" A paper presented to the conference "Ten Years After: Learning from the Asian Financial Crisis – Are Prevention Mechanisms Sufficient to Avoid another Financial Crisis?" (June 29), organized by the Research Institute of Economy, Trade and Industry and the Asian Development Bank Institute, Tokyo.

Kawai, M. (2007b) "Toward a Regional Exchange Rate Regime in East Asia," ADBI, Discussion Paper No. 68, Asian Development Bank Institute, Tokyo.

Kawai, M. (2008) "Toward a Regional Exchange Rate Regime in East Asia," *Pacific Economic Review* 13:1 (February), pp. 83–103.

Kawai, M. and Houser, C. (2007) "Evolving ASEAN+3 ERPD: Towards Peer Reviews or Due Diligence?" ADBI Discussion Paper No. 79, Asian Development Bank Institute, Tokyo.

Kawai, M. and Motonishi, T. (2005) "Macroeconomic Interdependence in East Asia: Empirical Evidence and Issues," Asian Development Bank, *Asian Economic Cooperation and Integration: Progress, Prospects, and Challenges.* Manila: ADB, pp. 213–268.

Kawai, M. and Wignaraja, G. (2008) "Regionalism as an Engine of Multilateralism: A Case for a Single East Asian FTA," Working Paper series on Regional Economic Integration No. 14 (February), Office of Regional Economic Integration, Asian Development Bank, Manila.

Krueger, A. (2002) "New Approaches to Sovereign Debt Restructuring: An Update on Our Thinking," paper presented to a conference on "Sovereign Debt Workouts: Hopes and Hazards" (April 1, 2002), Institute for International Economics, Washington, DC.

Mahbubani, K. (2008) *The New Asian Hemisphere: The Irresistible Rise of Global Power to the East.* Public Affairs.

Rana, P.B. (2007a) "Economic Integration in East Asia: Trends, Prospects, and a Possible Roadmap," Economic Growth Centre Working Paper series No. 2007/01, Nanyang Technological University.

Rana, P.B. (2007b) "Economic Integration and Synchronization of Business Cycles in East Asia," *Journal of Asian Economics*, 18 (October), pp. 711–725.

Rana, P.B. (2008) "Trade Intensity and Business Cycle Synchronization: The Case of East Asian Countries," *Singapore Economic Review*, 55 (August), pp. 279–292.

Roubini, N. (2007) "Asia is Learning the Wrong Lessons from its 1997–1998 Financial Crisis: The Rising Risks of a New and Different Type of Financial Crisis in Asia," manuscript. Online, available at: www.rgemonitor.com.

Turner, P. (2007) "Are Banking Systems in East Asia Stronger?" *Asian Economic Policy Review*, 2:1 (June), pp. 75–95.

Williamson, J. (2005) "A Currency Basket for East Asia, Not Just China," *Policy Briefs in International Economics*, No. PB05–1 (August), Institute for International Economics, Washington, DC.

10 Ten years after the Asian crisis
Is the IMF ready for "next time"?

Stephen Grenville

Ten years after the Asian crisis unfolded, much has changed in Asia. With the present conjuncture, there seems little likelihood of a repeat of the capital reversals of 1997–1998. But this conjuncture is neither sustainable nor sensible: leaving China to one side as a special case, these countries should be investing much more, importing capital, running current account deficits and allowing their exchange rates to appreciate. When this happens, they will grow faster, which they need to do to make up for the "lost years" after the crisis. With the return to normalcy, the core vulnerabilities of the crisis period will re-emerge: volatile international capital flows and fragile financial markets.

There is a variety of opinion of how the Fund performed in 1997–1998, but there is little doubt that it was more successful in some places (e.g. South Korea) than in others (Indonesia). It is not the objective here to rehearse the old arguments, but rather to be more forward-looking: to see whether the Fund's current approach (as influenced by the experience in Asia and elsewhere) seems suited to the sorts of problems which might be encountered.

First we will try to identify potential vulnerabilities. Then we examine the Fund's current policy position in regard to these vulnerabilities. In the third section we will see whether these vulnerabilities are present now, or are likely to return. In the fourth (concluding) section we offer some judgments on how ready the Fund might be for a return to a world of volatile capital flows.

Vulnerabilities

Does the decade-old crisis offer insights on current vulnerabilities? There has been no shortage of explanations offered for the crisis, including crony capitalism, corruption, lack of free-market orthodoxy (having an exchange rate which was neither a firm fix nor a completely free float), absence of democracy, governance deficiencies, moral hazard and lack of transparency. Most of these explanations seem unsatisfying, if only because these circumstances had existed during three decades of extraordinary growth. Defenders of the efficient-markets faith have been inventive in explaining why, if the problems were long-standing and intrinsic, they remained quiescent for so long and emerged so suddenly. Others, perhaps with more sense of the long history of manias and panics (see, for example, Kindleberger (1996)) are readier to accept that market participants, having only an imperfect view of the future, experience episodes of euphoria and pessimism. These changes of view are correlated and so have a big effect on financial markets, especially when these markets lack breadth, depth and resilience.

Even big shifts in sentiment usually have some substantive issue at their base. The key economic problems in 1997 might be identified as:

- Excessive foreign capital inflows in the five years or so before the crisis (either ignorant of or ignoring the problems which later were held to be serious flaws), which fed a local investment and asset boom and created the potential for volatile outflows.
- This was combined with weak and fragile banking systems and unbalanced corporate balance sheets, with serious currency mismatches.[1]

Volatile foreign capital flows

In economics, it is often assumed that the current account is the driver of the balance of payments. But in the case of East Asia in the five years leading up to the crisis, the driver was the capital account. Asia had become the "flavor of the month" in international financial circles, and every portfolio manager wanted to have some exposure to this "economic miracle." This was not irrational or poor judgment. These countries had uniformly recorded quite steady growth of 6–8 percent annually (twice the growth of developed countries), and were offering high rates of return on capital. Equity markets may have been embryonic and with untested governance, but they offered an entrée to this action. Domestically, borrowers in these emerging countries faced interest rates of 20 percent (a typical borrowing rate in Indonesia before the crisis), so were ready to offer lenders an attractive rate. This was exacerbated by the abnormally low interest rates in Japan, which encouraged the "yen carry trade" – borrowing in yen to invest in other currencies such as baht or rupiah. While the financial institutions were often untested and inexperienced, some of them (notably the Bangkok International Finance Facility) were specifically tailored to encourage these flows.[2] All these factors combined to produce a "weight of money" to invest in these countries. The outcome, for Thailand, was five years in which capital inflow averaged 10 percent of GDP annually, and peaked at nearly 13 percent just before the crisis.

The central analytical issue here is the intrinsic vulnerability of capital flows and their sensitivity to exchange rate movements. Capital-flight sensitivity depends on market confidence that the exchange rate is somewhere near its equilibrium value, and that if it is displaced by a shock, it will have a strong tendency to return – so-called mean reversion. This seems a valid, if rough, rule of thumb for the mature economies. For the emerging countries, however (in 1997 and today), the anchoring seems much less secure and well defined. These economies are not in equilibrium, in any sense that an economist can model: relationships are uncertain and coefficients are changing over time. The countries of East Asia are transforming their productive structures to fit the globalized world, undergoing rapid and substantial structural change, which will change the equilibrium exchange rate over time vis-à-vis the mature economies. This might be seen in terms of the Balassa/Samuelson Hypothesis (that fast economic growth is accompanied by an appreciation of the real exchange rate because of differential productivity growth between the tradable and the non-tradable sectors (see Ito *et al.* (1997)). In addition to the Balassa/Samuelson issues (which are about changing relative prices), there are more complex aspects of structural change. These were demonstrated in Japan in the 1960s when the exchange rate could be held at 360 yen per dollar for many years in the face of Japan's productivity revolution, but when floating came in 1971, the currency appreciated by 40 percent in the next five years. Most of the countries of East Asia are currently operating well inside the technological frontier, with capital/labor ratios a tiny fraction of those in mature economies. As capital is gradually built up and technology is transferred, they move toward the frontier, and during this extended process there are high returns to capital. For foreigners, these potential large profits are a magnet in their search for yield. But they are surrounded by uncertainty and a changing environment. Little wonder that there are waves of euphoria and pessimism, which are translated into big fluctuations in what the market regards as a "correct" exchange rate. With this environment in mind, investors will be flighty: when the exchange rate starts to move, they will look to close off their exposure, because their forecasts of the exchange rate are based on extrapolation of the most recent movements rather than mean reversion.

Take, for example, the current case of China. Its exchange rate is no longer absolutely fixed, but is very tightly managed so that it appreciates only slowly. If it was freely floated now, there is little doubt that it would appreciate significantly: Goldstein (2005) puts the equilibrium exchange rate 20–30 percent above the current level. But how should this equilibrium rate be calculated? There is no historical experience in China of a floating exchange rate which might supply some relevant data. In addition, China is receiving substantial capital inflow in response to the perceived profit opportunities there, which will persist for some decades. This implies that it should be well above the appreciation envisaged by Goldstein, to help in the "transfer problem."[3] As well, with the economy running hot, interest rates should be much higher than they are at present, for short-term cyclical reasons, and this would put further upward pressure on the exchange rate. On top of this, there are capital controls (on both inflows and outflows) which will be progressively removed over time, which might affect the exchange rate in either direction.

In short, it is all so uncertain that perceptions of the appropriate current exchange rate can be easily diverted, and by a long way and for a long time. For foreign investors, their knowledge of these countries was often quite superficial (their motivation was diversification, and this was a relatively small investment for them), so the arrival of new information (perhaps just a rumor) might be enough to trigger a fundamental change of view. Capital is flighty because the exchange rate is unanchored, and the exchange rate is unanchored because capital is flighty.

Has any of this changed since the Asian crisis? For the foreseeable future:

- Emerging financial markets will be small relative to international portfolio flows.
- There will be thin information, poorly understood by foreign investors, and the markets will be subject to whims and fashions.
- The "natural rate" of interest (at which domestic markets are in equilibrium) will be higher than in the mature countries because of the intrinsically higher profit opportunities as these countries move to the technological frontier. Balassa–Samuelson effects will reinforce this.
- Yen-carry is still an important motivation for capital flows.
- The resulting capital inflows will put upward pressure on the exchange rate (which some will see as "overvaluation"), making it vulnerable to subsequent downward pressure when sentiment reverses.
- Higher interest rates are an ineffective response to this exchange rate weakness, as the prospect of a depreciation in the near future can only be offset by an unacceptably high interest rate.
- Knowing this, foreign capital will be flighty.

In short, policy should be ready for excessive capital inflow and subsequent sudden reversals.

Influential analysts (e.g. Stan Fischer, IMF First Deputy Managing Director and a key figure during the crisis) have seen the central issue as fixed exchange rates (rather than intrinsic in the nature of international capital flows to emerging markets), with the remedy to be found in free-floating exchange rates.[4] This view is widely shared: in this view, flexible exchange rates, combined with the removal of any government guarantees (with the moral hazard that goes with this) will encourage borrowers to hedge their currency exposure (see Goldstein and Turner (2004)) and, by strong implication, all will be well.

For those who see fixed rates as the chief villain, the key point is that this regime discouraged borrowers from hedging their foreign exchange exposure, as fixed rates gave an exchange rate "guarantee" to borrowers. This not only ignores the reality that many borrowers *did* face shifting exchange rates,[5] but as well, this view misunderstands the macro-level characteristics of hedging. An individual borrower exposed to foreign currency risk can easily arrange with a bank for a hedge. While the risk can be shifted to another resident or to a foreigner, it cannot be removed. If there is a capital inflow, someone (either resident or foreigner) has a currency mismatch. The risk could only extinguish by buying the currency of their exposure, which effectively reverses the capital flow. So if there is capital flow, there is unhedged exposure on the part of a resident or a foreigner and if the cumulated flows have been large, the mismatch will be large.[6,7]

If there is a loss of confidence in the currency and "sudden stop" or reversal of capital, there will be three responses:

- The exchange rate will fall. If foreigners are holding the currency exposure, they will sell the currency to close off their position. If confidence has been lost, it might fall a long way before a buyer is found ready to take on their exposure.
- A fall in the exchange rate administers a balance sheet loss to the party holding the exposure. If hedging has shifted this to foreigners, this will leave domestic borrowers isolated from this element of the 1997–1998 damage.
- At a macro level, the borrowing country has to adjust to the new diminished availability of foreign funding. Part of this adjustment will come with the fall in the exchange rate ("switching"). But given the sudden withdrawal and the need for speedy adjustment (the identities between current and capital account have to hold continuously, in the absence of intervention), the adjustment will probably also require a sharp fall in demand. So the falls in income seen in the early stages of the crisis were the *necessary* response to match the current account with the available funding in the capital account, and would be needed whether the currency exposure is held by a resident or a foreigner.

Thailand in late 2006 exhibited some of the symptoms of this ongoing problem. Even though capital is at present "flowing uphill" from the emerging markets to the mature economies and Thailand's interest rates are significantly lower than the longer-term "natural" rate, Thailand was experiencing a combination of capital inflow and strong trade performance which together put substantial upward pressure on the baht, which appreciated 16 percent in the year prior to the recent capital measures, despite heavy intervention. While this pressure has now been dampened by the unhelpful damage to sentiment through clumsy attempts at restraining capital inflows, the problem remains for India, Vietnam and Korea.

To summarize this section, the intrinsic volatility of capital flows remains, and while floating exchange rates may offer some protection and hedging with foreigners may shift some of the pain, there are still good grounds for "fear of floating," at least as the panacea for volatile capital flows.

Fragile financial sectors

The weaknesses of the financial sector in Indonesia was well-known before the crisis (see Enoch *et al.* (2001) and Montgomery (1997)), but it was accepted that it would take time and major effort (not least on legal, governance and bankruptcy issues) to fix the problems. The Fund's programs of ROSCs[8] and FSAPs[9] has strengthened regulations and encouraged transparency. Today, while there is little doubt that much progress has been made (see Turner (2007)), many of the intrinsic problems remain:[10]

- Shortage of commercial information. Credit bureaus are embryonic and credit ratings still under development.

- As the majority of substantial firms were de facto insolvent during the crisis, unresolved insolvency issues hang over many commercial borrowers.
- Resolution of property rights are poorly defined in the event that the lender needs to seize the collateral security.
- Corporate governance practices and regulation still have a long way to go.
- The operational independence of the regulators is uncertain.
- State-owned enterprises and other powerful borrowers may still be able to apply pressure to obtain loans and may resist proper credit practices.
- State-owned banks, with their inherently flawed governance, are still nearly half of the Indonesian banking sector. Ten years after the crisis, their NPLs are 16 percent.

Much attention has been given since the crisis to financial safety nets. These comprise prudential supervision, lender of last resort (LoLR), depositor insurance and "financial deepening." Let's look at each of these in turn.

Prudential supervision

There is no doubt that this has improved. The issue is not, however, the degree of improvement (after all, it improved in the five years *before* the crisis, from a very low base), but whether it will be sufficient to prevent a systemic or widespread financial crisis. This is not an easy judgment. Much of the improvement has been in terms of liquidity management and reporting: box-ticking and form-filling. The central issue for banks is to ensure that loans are repaid, and this requires good credit management, no connected lending, no special relationships between state banks and state enterprises, quick recognition of problem loans, strong legal systems and well-functioning bankruptcy procedures to gain good title to collateral. None of these elements seems strong in Indonesia and perhaps not in Thailand either.

Lender of last resort

The LoLR (BLBI) in Indonesia was, by common agreement, a disaster. But its deficiencies have not been properly analyzed, to see in detail how to handle the next time. The reaction has been to put in a comprehensive layering of checks-and-balances surrounding use of the LoLR, in particular requiring that it be approved by a group of officials representing the central banks, the Ministry of Finance and the deposit insurance agency. The latter has carriage of bank resolution (although the central bank has all the data and prudential experience). The precedent of imposing long jail sentences on the three BI officials who signed off on the initial BLBI seems almost certain to result in a great reluctance for any future LoLR sign-offs. The Bagehot dictum ("lend freely") simply isn't feasible in Indonesia now. The response to the inadequacies of LoLR in the crisis has been to effectively eliminate LoLR from the armory of policy instruments (or, at best, introduce fatally-extended delays in application).

Deposit insurance

Much hope has been put in the creation of deposit insurance agencies. These are seen in terms of adding to the stability of the banking system, but it is hard to see how they can serve this role, as all cases implemented or under contemplation in East Asia have, as a central characteristic, limits on coverage – only relatively small deposits are covered. Configured this way, deposit insurance can serve two useful functions. First, to assist in the smooth resolution of *individual* bank failures, especially small banks. Second, it may help to limit the degree of government support, by defining the extent of assistance (insurance) beforehand. But it cannot address the problem of *systemic* runs on banks. Non-insured depositors are small in number but large in amount: these depositors are better informed, so will "run" more quickly (especially as they know they are not insured) and their deposits comprise the majority of bank funds, so their "run" will ensure systemic bank illiquidity.

Financial deepening

What about the non-bank financial sector? Former Fed Chairman Greenspan urged its development as a "spare tyre," with the implication that it might provide finance in the event of the banking system getting into trouble, in the same way that the bond market stepped in to provide finance after the Continental Bank illiquidity. While the case for developing the bond and equity markets seems powerful (and this was already underway before the crisis), it has to be accepted that this is a very long-term task, which not only requires market and legal infrastructure, but commercial information which is not available at present nor in the immediate future.[11]

When the bond and equity markets are each substantially bigger than the bank credit market (as is the case in the US), it makes sense to see them as alternatives to the banks as providers of funding for business. But in Indonesia the corporate bond market is minuscule and there have been few new equity issues since the crisis. What seems lacking in the discussion of financial deepening is a sharper sense of priorities, magnitudes and sequencing. All the crisis countries came out of the crisis with large volumes of government bonds, which could have provided the basis for a market with breadth, depth and resilience, providing a well-defined yield curve, getting institutions and the public accustomed to dealing in and holding bonds, and forming the basis for vigorous derivative markets such as repos, which could form the basis of central bank open market operations. This has not happened so far.

While the glamor may be in the sophisticated instruments in financial markets, the heavy lifting will be done by the banks, and the most pressing issue is to get them into the hands of private owners, preferably foreign ones.

The Fund's current position

In the Fund's own analysis of the crisis, there is not much recognition of any deficiencies in its own part, and a tendency to "blame the victim." Michel

Camdessus, returning to Jakarta in 2006 for the first time since the famous crossed-arms signing with then-president Soeharto in January 1998, is reported to have said that, as Indonesia was now going well, this showed that the Fund's prescription had been right all along. More recently, Anne Krueger (2006), Deputy Managing Director, noted:

The Fund was heavily involved in the resolution of these crises. Financial support was often needed more urgently, and on a larger scale, than had been the case in earlier episodes where Fund support was needed. Yet in spite of the difficulties, it is clear that with hindsight the adjustment programs put in place with Fund support were far more successful than most observers believed possible at the time.

For some of us, the sequence was precisely the opposite: we started with the belief that the Fund would succeed and over time came to the realization that it did not.

Clearly there were serious policy and implementation deficiencies both before and during the crisis on the part of the crisis countries themselves. Moreover, as sovereign countries, they were and are responsible for their policies. Much of this territory has been traversed before, so here the aim is to focus, not on what the Fund did and said in 1997–1998, but on what it might do and say today if something analogous arose again. Past performance is not a guide to the future, but it is often all we have. This process is, inevitably, hypothetical, and Fund officials have a variety of views (and their views are often accompanied by a disclaimer that they don't represent the Fund's position).

Recently, some Fund staff *do* seem to accept that volatile capital flows plus fragile financial systems were at the heart of the crisis. In appraising the crisis after ten years, Burton and Zanello (2007) say:

Its hallmark was the sudden reversal of investor sentiment and abrupt withdrawal of international capital. Doubts about the soundness of financial institutions and corporates spread quickly across national borders, creating a vicious circle of capital outflows, plummeting exchange rates, and crippling balance-sheet effects in the crisis-struck countries.

Ghosh's position (2006), too, has a fair overlap with the discussion here: "These countries remain susceptible to shifts in market sentiment.... Most capital account crises appear to have been caused by foreign currency and maturity mismatches on private or public sector balance sheets coupled with a specific trigger – domestic or external."

Lipschitz (2006) analyses the forces driving capital inflows in the same way as we have here:

EMEs are characterized by lower capital:labor ratios than advanced countries and improving total factor productivity. Sizable capital inflows are likely to be an essential part of the income convergence process. The marginal product of capital is a positive function of total factor productivity and a negative function of the capital:labor ratio.

Given relatively low capital:labor ratios, there are likely to be high returns and thus large inflows as total factor productivity levels converge with better institutions and economic governance. [This vulnerability can be avoided] where:

- Unhedged domestic corporations are financed only through domestic-currency bonds and equity.
- Only robust, naturally hedged corporations (i.e. exporters) borrow in forex.
- Consumers borrow in domestic currency paper with large own-equity requirements.
- The government borrows very little and only in domestic currency.
- And banks do maturity transformation with prudent asset-liability management; all forex loans are to hedged corporations.

This would leave no balance-sheet vulnerabilities. But in the real world some countries cannot borrow in domestic currency or long term; therefore use of foreign capital necessarily entails some forex exposure and maturity mismatch.

But very little of these sorts of concerns are found in Fischer's Robbins Lectures (Fischer 2003), his major analysis of the crises.[12] Nor is this found in the more recent analysis of Fund Deputy Managing Director Anne Krueger (2006):

> At first it was assumed in some quarters that these crises reflected capricious shifts in investor sentiment; that national economies were now subject to the whims of speculators
>
>   …
>
> But it became clear that painful though these crises were, they had their origins in underlying weaknesses in the economies affected – weaknesses to which investors had reacted. In some cases, governments had accumulated debts that were unsustainable. In others, rapid private sector credit growth had led to a sharp deterioration in the quality of lending with a rise in the number of bad loans with adverse implications for potential economic growth.

If vulnerabilities re-emerge, despite more flexible exchange rates, what policies are available?

- Market-based measures to restrain excessive inflows, along the lines of the Chilean deposit requirement on short-term inflows.
- Readiness to raise interest rates dramatically.
- Readiness to "lend freely" (by analogy with a bank run).
- Related to this, for the government to take over the currency exposure.

- In the event of a serious reversal, to restrict capital outflows through "stand-still" arrangements for bank-to-bank loans, and enforced "bail-in" of private sector creditors.

How do the Fund's current policies and attitudes match this list?

Short-term inflow controls

The Fund has come to a begrudging acceptance that some controls on inflows may, in some circumstances, be justified. There remains, however, a rather disparaging tone. Just as "real men don't eat quiche," real countries don't resort to capital controls, even market-based limits on inflows. Note the tone in Stan Fischer's (2006) endorsement:

> Evidence from the Chilean experience suggests that controls were for some time successful in allowing some monetary policy independence, and also in shifting the composition of capital inflows towards the long end. Empirical evidence suggests that the Chilean controls lost their effectiveness after 1998. They have recently been removed.

If such short-term capital controls *are* a legitimate instrument of policy, we need the IMF to provide a more fulsome endorsement than this: an unambiguous statement that these measures are not only acceptable, but desirable policymaking in some specific circumstances. That, in itself, would make the measures more effective because the market would spend less time in the sort of counterproductive criticism seen in Thailand late last year.

Higher interest rates

There was always an analytical ambiguity about the Fund's advocacy of an interest rate defense. If the analytical framework was that of portfolio balance, then the interest rates had to be high enough to balance the expectation of *short-term* depreciation. If there was a 50:50 chance of a 2 percent depreciation over the next day (which was not unusual in Indonesia during the crisis), then the annualized rate of interest needed to balance this was more than 1,000 percent. This level was not, in fact, contemplated during the crisis (although in Sweden in 1992, 500 percent was used in the initial defense). So what *was* the analytical framework? How high was "high enough"? Other than urging that interest rates needed to be higher whenever the exchange rate was weak, this is not clear. What we know is that this type of defense has not worked often in the past and is very unlikely to work if there are concurrent problems in the financial sector (see Goldfarjn and Gupta (1999)).

"Lend freely"

The requirements here are that there are sufficient funds (enough to convince the market that there is no need for capital to flee), and that they are made available quickly. The model is Mexico in 1994: $50 billion was made available quickly from the Fund and other sources. Because it was seen by the market as clearly ample to do the job, much less was actually needed ($20 billion). In the Fund commentary during the Asian crisis four years later, parallels with Mexico were *not* drawn and the amounts available for Thailand and Indonesia were much smaller. It's hard to know whether the Fund would have been more successful in these two countries if more money had been available. It could be that the Fund made the right diagnosis in Asia in 1997, but that there were simply not enough funds available to "lend freely."[13]

For the East Asian countries, there are three reasons for concern about the Fund's LoLR role. The first is whether there would be adequate funds to convince foreign capital to stand fast: the required sum might be very large, given that there might well be regionwide contagion. The capital account reversals in Indonesia and Thailand were in the order of 15 percent of GDP, so funding just these two countries would take $60 billion. A 10 percent reversal in China would amount to more than $200 billion. Since 1998, the Fund has shown the capacity to provide greatly increased funding, e.g. in Turkey. Brazil was offered $30 billion of IMF money in 2002, but even these sums seem insufficient for the general problem. These inter-country comparisons raise a second issue. Both Turkey and Brazil have "champions" to push their cases. Asia's champions (Japan? China?) have no track record of being able to deliver: would Asia once again be "short-changed"? What about supplementary bilateral funds on an ad hoc basis, as occurred success-fully with Thailand but unsuccessfully with Indonesian and Korea? The one unani-mous lesson drawn from the Asian crisis is that second-line defenses don't work.[14] The third issue is the speed of disbursement. In 1997 the available funds were not only inadequate: as well, they were "tranched" – i.e. made available over time. The rationale here is a throw-back to the 1980s Latin American crises, where the Fund wanted to make sure that the corrective policies (in those case, macro pol-icies) were being applied. This caution is understandable, but if the problem is analogous to a bank run, then all the money has to be available up front, ready to be disbursed, to convince the market that it isn't needed.

There was frequent mention, in the early days of the crisis, that the Fund lending was "catalytic" and that it would trigger a renewed inflow of private capital (or at least stop the outflow) (see quotes in Hoverguimian (2003), and her Table A showing the predicted outflows and the actuals). She concludes:

> Recent theoretical analysis suggests that this catalytic effect is fragile and will only work in limited circumstances. Empirical evidence bears this out: in most cases the expected turn-around in capital flows has failed to material-ize. There is merit, therefore, in further consideration of alternative responses to capital account crises, including payments stand-stills and roll-overs.

Following the crisis, there was an initiative that would have made available funds with the speed (although not necessarily volume) that is required: the Contingent Credit Line. The CCL would have made "pre-approved" commitments to countries with sound policies. This proposal was met with a universal lack of enthusiasm: potential recipients saw the CCL endorsement as a warning to potential lenders, while others saw technical problems: it would be very difficult to take away the "seal of approval," once given, even if the country became less virtuous. The initiative was not helped by the widespread perception that this was a way of providing ongoing support for certain favored countries, notably Argentina.

Government assumes currency exposure

This provides the potential for discouraging outflows and supporting the exchange rate without the use of actual foreign reserves, but it has a mixed record of success. In Mexico in 1994, as foreigners holding pesos bonds began to worry about their exposure, the government provided exchange rate indexation to encourage foreigners to remain invested (*Cetes* were replaced with *Tesobonos*). This worked only temporarily. In Indonesia in early 1998, there was discussion of exchange rate guarantees for private commercial debt, but the INDRA initiative did not get underway until almost a year after the crisis began, and the initiative soon fizzled out. These two unsuccessful examples contrast with Brazil in 1999 (Bevilaqua and Azevedo 2005), where the government issued its domestic dollar-denominated debt, which then formed the basis of private sector hedging, easing the pressure on the exchange rate (but taking on the currency risk, which in the Brazilian case, turned out to be a good bet). There seems to have been very little analysis of this type of policy and it is not clear what the Fund's attitude is or would be.

Controls on capital outflows: "bailing in" the private sector

If there were not enough funds available to compensate for the fleeing capital and convince it to stand fast, then the only way to avoid a large fall in income was to restrict the capital outflow. When higher interest rates didn't do this, the next step should have been to discourage outflows through some coordinated, organized, probably compulsory, method. This was done successfully for Korean bank-to-bank debt at the end of 1997, and the Fund claims that similar informal arrangements were in place in Thailand,[15] although there is no evidence of this in the balance of payments data, and it was certainly not discussed as part of the multilateral support arrangements.[16] Similarly, the concerted attempts to restructure debt and encourage debt/equity swaps in Indonesia did not get underway until a year into the crisis.

Every country has domestic bankruptcy provisions to handle the *in extremis* case where creditors cannot repay and the only sensible thing to do is to organize a stand-still on repayments and have an orderly resolution. This does require an organized effort and an arbitrator, to ensure fairness and orderliness.[17] This organized process still doesn't seem to be available at the international level.

Where does the Fund stand now on this issue? Some key figures sound quite ambivalent. Fisher (2003), for example, discusses the possibility of "private sector involvement" and adds: "Nonetheless, great care needs to be taken in seeking to coordinate the creditors." Even if some of the Fund staff have moved a long way in the direction of "bailing in" the creditors, they have not been able to sell this view to its member countries. The relatively straightforward issue of sovereign debt restructure was not agreed to by Fund members, despite the Fund staff's strenuous efforts (Krueger 2002). It will be under the same pressure, next time, to keep creditors whole, which makes the cost of rescue hugely greater. Arguments about "lending into arrears" are still unsettled, with the possibility that creditors will use the bargaining weapon of their arrears to hold up a Fund program. Arguments about moral hazard and technical debates about collective action clauses (it seems that collective action would have been possible all along) will once again muddy the waters and muddle the issues, which require quick and decisive resolution. We don't yet have this.[18] In short, the Fund recognizes the need for a different approach, but has not yet been able to persuade its members.

Lessons learned and not learned: "missions accomplished"?

The immediate adjustment of the crisis countries involved a huge redeployment of demand and production, to shift current account deficits into surplus, in order to fund the outward flows on capital account. In Thailand, for example, the current account shifted from 8 percent deficit in 1996 to 13 percent surplus in 1998, a net expenditure movement of over 20 percent of GDP. Having made this painful redeployment, current accounts remained in surplus. In the case of Thailand and Indonesia, this reflects a level of GDP still well below the upward trend line established before the crisis (Type 3 rather than Type 1 in Figure 10.1), and a significantly lower level of investment than in the lead-up to the crisis (or even compared with the period before the pre-crisis boom).

This has left East Asia today in circumstances that are quite different from 1997. Their foreign exchange reserves and current account surpluses have removed their susceptibility to capital reversals.[19] With international capital "flowing uphill" from the emerging economies to the mature economies, capital reversals are not an issue. Foreign debt, both public and private, has been dramatically reduced since the crisis. For the same reason, emerging countries are not accumulating currency mismatches. There is no investment boom: in fact the three IMF-assisted countries recorded investment growth of only 3–4 percent in 2006.[20] Their currencies, if not floating freely, are more flexible. Moreover, the memories of 1997–1998 are still fresh for policymakers, private commercial borrowers, banks and foreign lenders. For its part, with its main potential "customers" for loans (emerging economies) in good shape worldwide, the Fund is flush with funds in the unlikely event that there is any demand for emergency lending.

Thus there seems little risk of a repeat of the Asian crisis any time soon. Does this mean that we should all take quiet satisfaction in a job well done – "mission accomplished"? We will argue here that the responses to the crisis have created problems of a different nature, and today's conjuncture, while not urgently critical, is neither sensible nor sustainable.

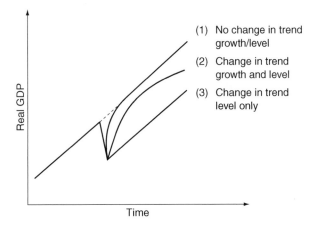

Figure 10.1 Possible post-crisis recoveries.

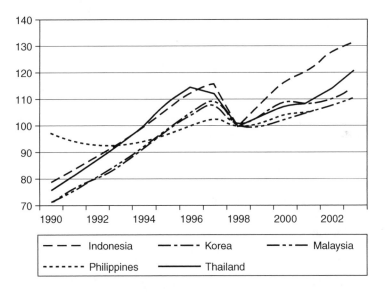

Figure 10.2 Real per-capita GDP, 1990–2003 (1998 = 100) (source: IMF Select Issues Thailand 2006).

Perhaps the sharpest dichotomy between the Fund's prescription and the outcome has occurred with exchange rates. Certainly, all these countries have modified their soft fixes or slowly-moving pegs. Almost everywhere, there is short-term flexibility, and those who want to measure "floating" in terms of short-term volatility (daily bumps in the rate) can find evidence that these countries are floating. But the true substance of floating embodies more than this: the rate should, over time, clear the foreign exchange market when the current and capital accounts are reflecting sustainable positions. This is, of course, not

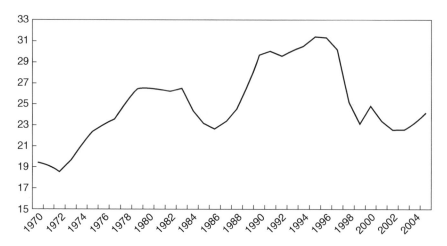

Figure 10.3 Aggregate investment ratio in East Asian emerging markets (gross fixed capital formation as percent of GDP) (source: IMF, World Economic Outlook (WEO) database).

Note

Purchasing Power Parity (PPP) weights: Includes Hong Kong SAR, Indonesia, Korea, Malaysia, Philippines, Singapore, Thailand and Taiwan Province of China.

consistent with the rapidly accelerating reserve build-up in China. Nor is it consistent with the rise in reserves in Korea (see graph), Malaysia (with a current account surplus equal to 15 percent of GDP and reserves equal to 50 percent of GDP) or, on a smaller scale, Thailand with its 30 percent increase in reserves in 2006. Why has there been such a divergence between the central lesson the Fund draws from the crisis and exchange rate behavior in practice since then?

The countries of the region have built up foreign exchange reserves of $2,000 billion, and they are rising at a rate of $450 billion a year (the 2006 increase) or more. This is driven in part by the desire to insure against a repeat on 1997–1998. But it goes further than this. With investment now much slower in all countries except China and Vietnam, one way of promoting growth is to encourage exports – not so much for narrow mercantilist reasons (although these may be present), but to absorb the growing labor force. A loss of international competitiveness vis-à-vis China would not only reduce export share, but would encourage more investment to shift there.

This outcome is far from optimal. Capital flowing uphill, from countries which would seem to have greater need than the mature economies such as the US, seems counter-intuitive.[21] The rising reserves makes money sterilization difficult (China's reserves are equal to 50 percent of GDP, so to sterilize this, bonds of the same magnitude have to be issued (and the interest bill funded)). To reduce the sterilization burden China and Indonesia have resorted to imposing substantially higher reserve requirements on their banks, shifting the

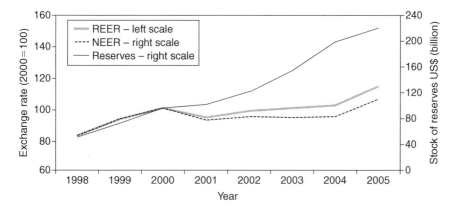

Figure 10.4 Exchange rate and reserves in Korea, 1998–2005[1] (source: IEO 2007).

Note
1 Gross international reserves.

burden through an implicit tax which adds to intermediation margins and hinders the development of a strong financial sector. This excessive liquidity is encouraging banks to fund asset price inflation which is resulting in bubbles in at least two equity markets – China and Vietnam. Interest rates have been kept low for the wrong reasons – to discourage capital inflow, rather than being used as the instrument to contain inflation. The efforts to keep the exchange rate low and stable through intervention are just delaying the inevitable – appreciating real exchange rates are part of this phase of development, and if the nominal rate doesn't appreciate, sooner or later the real rate will, though faster inflation.

Exchange rates lie at the heart of these issues. In the face of strong and unanimous advice that they should adopt "corner solutions" – either immutably fixed or free floating – Asian countries are using slowly-sliding pegs (China) or floating with very substantial intervention (as reflected by continuing increases in reserves in Korea, Thailand in 2006, and Indonesia), or Singapore's version of the "BBC" – basket, band, crawl. Some have seen this as a return to Bretton Woods (Dooley *et al.* 2003), but the architects of Bretton Woods would have seen the need for adjustment in response to the "fundamentals" of a current account surplus running at 10 percent of GDP and growing, as is the case in China. Delays in appreciation increase speculative capital inflows which aims to profit from the eventual appreciation. To the extent that it merely delays the adjustment, the cost of adjustment will be greater. With China's reserves around 50 percent of GDP, a 20 percent appreciation would administer a capital loss to the central bank equal to 10 percent of GDP. Current efforts at diversification of foreign exchange holdings may achieve a better return, but do not remove the funding burden and the exchange rate loss when the rate appreciates. If interest rates are too low and credit growth too fast, this has to end badly, either in inflation or asset price bubbles, as seems to be the case in Chinese equities.

The Fund has, sensibly, not joined in the public international harangue demanding a large appreciation of the yuan, but nor has it been able to play much of a positive role behind the scenes. Part of the problem was that much of the Fund's general analytical message after the crisis was in terms of "corner solutions" – countries either had to have immutable fixes or free floats, and there was no recognition of the "fear of floating" (Calvo and Reinhart 2002). "The lively debates over exchange rate advice have taken place in other fora, in informal discussion, and in individual country cases" (Takagi and Hicklin 2007: 33). Country-by-country, the Fund has accepted the full gamut of regimes (being equally satisfied with BBC in Singapore and a hard fix (often wrongly styled as a currency board) in Hong Kong).[22] But in general, we don't see much support for the BBC policies which Singapore has practiced so effectively.[23]

As a result the Fund has been largely sidelined in a debate where it might have played a useful role. None of the countries of East Asia has been attracted to the idea of a perfectly free float. Much analytical energy has gone into the idea of a regional currency (led by the Asian Development Bank). The idea of a regional currency has at least one attraction – it addresses concerns that individual countries will lose competitiveness vis-à-vis China if they appreciate. But it flies in the face of the economic arguments (encapsulated in the idea of "optimal currency areas") that countries with such diversity of structures, economic maturity and resource endowments as Japan and Indonesia cannot sensibly operate with a common currency. If regional currency does not hold the answer, what does? What should be the Fund's advice? The central elements might be:

• How to anchor the exchange rate against excessive overshoots in either direction.
• How to maintain relative competitiveness, particularly vis-à-vis China.

This might involve acceptance of some BBC-like system plus some regional coordination which involves China moving its rate more than it has done in recent years, with the other non-Japan Asian countries following suit. Could the IMF play this coordinating role? If its success in the wider debate (exemplified by the Multilateral Consultation on Global Imbalances) is any guide, not much can be achieved with the present institutional arrangements. The Fund's regular circus-like meetings are clearly not the place for such coordination, and while the process of small-group discussion is not yet complete, it looks pretty empty so far.

If the sub-optimality of the current conjuncture were to be corrected over time, with some currency appreciation, stronger domestic investment (or consumption in China) replacing exports as a source of growth, current accounts will move into deficit and capital will once again "flow downhill:" the intrinsic attractiveness of these emerging countries, with high profitability as they move towards the technological frontier, will assert itself and the flows will be inward. When this happens, the issues discussed in this chapter will once again be relevant.

Conclusion: the Fund's role

What might the Fund do to hasten this move to a more optimal configuration? When capital inflows return, will the Fund be able to minimize vulnerabilities to capital reversal? What will the Fund be able to do if there is another "sudden stop"?

Perhaps the greatest hurdle for the Fund to overcome is that the last crisis did deep damage to the Fund's reputation in at least four of the countries of the region: Indonesia, Thailand, Korea and Malaysia. This is manifest in the vigor with which the Chiang Mai Initiative has been put in place. The Fund might do better to work with these regional initiatives rather than oppose them, as it did with the Asian Monetary Fund. It showed, too, in the early repayment of Fund loans, with an almost audible sigh of relief as the Fund's close oversight was removed.

The Fund can argue, with considerable justification, that the governments it had to work with (particularly in Indonesia) were divided, un-coordinated and often in disarray. But this is the nature of Indonesia and the nature of crises. So the Fund can't excuse itself by blaming the victim: well-function-ing countries rarely get into trouble, so the Fund has to get used to working with the sort of governments which get into trouble – those which are unable to implement perfect policies, and which make mistakes of analysis and implementation.

If it was hard last time round, it will be that much harder if there is a repeat. Governments in these countries are more democratic (which makes them weaker, less decisive, softer, flakier, perhaps less market-oriented), and so less able to respond with one voice and take hard decisions quickly. Pressures of nationalism and populism seem likely to be considerably greater "next time." Overarching all this, globalization and financial market integration continue their inexorable expansion.

Appendix

Table 10.A1 The credit ratings of banks

	Moody's Bank Financial Strength Ratings[1]			Fitch Individual Ratings[2,3]	
	Mar 1997	*Dec 1998*	*Dec 2005*	*Dec 1998*	*Dec 2005*
Indonesia	D– to D (12)[2]	E (11)	E to E + (9)	E (3)	D to C/D (12)
Korea	D (18)	E+ to D– (19)	D to D (15)	E to D/E (8)	C to B/C (12)
Malaysia	C to C+ (2)	D– (5)	D+ to C– (11)	D/E to D (6)	C/D (12)
Philippines	D to C/D (5)	D to D+ (11)	D– to D (11)	D to C/D (5)	D to C/D (13)
Thailand	D+ (10)	E to E+ (10)	D– to D (10)	E to D/E (12)	C/D (10)
Memorandum:					
United States	C+ to B– (295)	C+ to B (117)	B to B+ (154)	B to A/B (106)	B/C to B (252)
Germany	C+ to B– (29)	C to C+ (35)	C– to C (43)	D to C/D (21)	C/D to C (65)

Sources: Moody's Investors Services and Fitch *Bankscope*; BIS calculations. From Turner, "Banking Systems in East Asia: Ten Years Later," *East Asian Policy Review*, forthcoming.

Notes

1 The Bank Financial Strength Rating Is Moody's assessment of whether a bank is likely to require financial support from shareholders, the government or other Institutions. The ratings range from A (highest) to E (lowest).

2 January 1996.

3 Individual ratings represent Fitch's view on the likelihood that a bank would run into significant difficulties such that it would require support. The ratings have nine different gradations ranging from A (highest) to E (lowest).

Table 10.A2 Moody's Weighted Average Bank Financial Strength Index[1]

	Dec 2002	*Dec 2003*	*Dec 2004*
China	10.0	10.0	10.0
Hong Kong SAR	62.3	62.3	62.3
India	27.5	27.5	24.2
Indonesia	3.0	3.0	7.3
Korea	16.7	18.3	18.3
Malaysia	31.7	33.3	35.2
Philippines	20.4	20.4	19.2
Singapore	74.7	74.7	74.7
Thailand	15.8	15.8	15.8

Source: Moody's Investor Service.

Note

1 Constructed according to a numerical scale assigned to Moody's weighted average bank ratings by country. "0" indicates the lowest possible average rating and "100" indicates the highest possible average rating.

Table 10.A3 Size of corporate bond markets and other channels of local currency funding (selected countries, end-2004)

	Corporate bonds[1]		Other channels as % of GDP		
	Amounts outstanding (USD billions)	*As % of GDP*	*Domestic credit*	*Stock market capitalization*	*Government bonds*
Australia	187.5	27.1	185.4	111.5	13.6
China	195.9	10.6	154.4	33.4	18.0
Hong Kong SAR	61.9	35.8	148.9	547.7	5.0
India	24.5	3.3	60.2	56.8	29.9
Indonesia	6.8	2.4	42.6	24.5	15.2
Japan	2,002.0	41.7	146.9	76.9	117.2
Korea	355.6	49.3	104.2	74.7	23.7
Malaysia	49.7	38.8	113.9	140.8	36.1
New Zealand	29.9	27.8	245.5	41.1	19.9
Philippines	0.2	0.2	49.8	37.5	21.6
Singapore	21.7	18.6	70.1	211.4	27.6
Thailand	31.9	18.3	84.9	67.1	16.5
Memo: United States	*15,116.6*	*128.8*	*89.0*	*138.4*	*42.5*

Sources: IMF; World Federation of Exchanges; Dealogic Bondware; national data; BIS.

Note

1 Domestic and international bonds and notes in domestic currency issued by residents and non-residents.

Notes

1 This diagnosis might be contrasted with earlier crisis experience, particularly in Latin America during the first half of the 1980s, where the capital reversals were symptomatic of other serious domestic macro-imbalances. For Asia, good macro policies (balanced budgets, modest current account deficits and tolerably low inflation) were not enough. For a useful account of the crisis (although less critical of the IMF than this author), see IMF Independent Evaluation Office (2003).

2 Although they may not have been intentionally designed to encourage small Thai firms to borrow in dollars, as they did.

3 Keynes wrote about this problem in 1929 in relation to German reparations (Keynes 1929).

4   Had exchange rates been flexible, the six crises we have discussed in these lectures would either not have happened, or would not have taken the form they did. That is why the shift to flexible rates among the emerging market countries is the most important change in the international financial architecture during the past decade. It will not prevent all external crises, for debt sustainability crises will still occur, but it should greatly reduce the frequency of crises.

Fischer (2001b)

Fixing the exchange rate or protecting an exchange rate provides an invitation to the private sector to bet against the authorities if the capital account is open: in short, the impossible trinity. I believe that the move to flexible exchange rates has made more of a difference to the international financial system than any other change. That change takes away a major risk factor.

Fischer (2006)

5 If borrowers saw the fixed rate as a "guarantee" by the government to always sell them foreign exchange at the current price, it would, indeed, have been a big encouragement to borrow at the lower rates available for foreign-currency loans. But it would have also ignored the fact that Indonesia, for example, had devalued vis-à-vis the US dollar three times in the previous 20 years. It also doesn't fit the case where the borrowings were in non-US dollar currencies (half Indonesia's foreign borrowings were in yen – the "yen-carry-trade" – which currency had moved over a range of 79–149/$US during the first half of the 1990s). So any borrower who thought they had a guarantee was ignoring the obvious reality.

6 Some might note the possibility of shifting the exposure onto a resident counterparty who has an opposed exposure through trade: a borrower shifts the exchange risk to an exporter. There may be limited opportunities to do this, but importers also want cover for their exchange exposure, so most of the natural risk-offset capacity has been used up – certainly there is nowhere near enough to provide an offset for large capital inflows. As a rough approximation the trade flows cancel out the opportunity for using exports to cover foreign borrowing.

7 The first reaction to this pressure may (as in Mexico in 1994) be for the host government to offer to take over the currency exposure in order to prevent the capital flight, thus reverting to "original sin." This may be good policymaking (cf. Brazil in 1999).

8 Report on Observation of Standards and Codes.

9 Financial Sector Assessment Program.

10 See Tables 10.A1 and 10.A2 in Appendix.

11 When assessing the exacting requirements of an equity market, it might be worth noting that the largest insolvency coming out of the Indonesian crisis was a company (APP) registered in Singapore, with its advanced financial infrastructure, not Indonesia.

12   To summarize on the origins of the crises: the Mexican, Thai, Russian, and Brazilian crises all looked more or less like conventional old-fashioned crises, in which an unsustainable current account combined with a pegged exchange rate to lead to a crisis. However neither in Mexico nor in Thailand was there a serious fiscal problem. Financial sector weaknesses appeared especially important in Thailand, not least because its financial sector was much larger than that in the three non-Asian crisis countries. The crises in Indonesia and Korea looked different from the beginning, because both the current account and the fiscal deficits were small, and contagion seemed to play the dominant role. But the contagion hit economies with serious financial and corporate sector weaknesses, whose impact was magnified as market pressures increased.

(Fischer 2003)

13 When we tried to pursue this issue in drafting the IEO document (IEO 2003), the message from the Fund was that shortage of funds had NOT been an issue in devising the response. On the other hand, Lane *et al.* (1999: 21) say:

Large as this official financing was, it would have been sufficient to support the programs in Indonesia and Korea only on the assumption that they would elicit a broad positive response in the part of private markets, specially in the initial phase of the programs.

14 There were many reasons why this was the case, but the most binding was that the US contribution was not seen as "real" money. Following Congress' displeasure that they had been by-passed in the Mexican exercise, the US was no longer able to draw on the Exchange Stabilization Fund, so their contribution was surrounded by the overlapping provisos: it would not be available if the situation proved to be serious, and it was not needed if it was not serious.

15 See Lane *et al.* (1999: 23).

16 At the first assistance meeting for Thailand in August 1997, Australia, as a potential provider of assistance, was looking for some assurance that its money would not simply be used to repay foreign creditors who had undertaken risky loans and were now faced with the consequences of that risk: failure to repay. Our view was that the creditors were "consenting adults" who should have to bear the consequences of the risks associated with their investments. Before the meeting, we asked the Chair of the conference, IMF Managing Director Sugisaki, what would be done to "bail in" the private creditors. He said that nothing would be done. Furthermore, if we raised this issue, the conference would fail and he would publicly blame us for the failure. What can explain this extraordinary attitude, other than pressure on the Fund from creditors anxious that the Mexican precedent (where the creditors were "made whole," without any "haircut") would be followed?

17 Before insolvency regulations were fully developed, this sort of thing was done along the lines of J.P. Morgan's handling of the 1907 banking crisis – the parties were locked in his library and told that they would be allowed out when they had reached agreement. This might have been a model in some cases in East Asia.

18 The Institute for International Finance, which lobbied hard on behalf of the foreign creditors during the crisis, has developed "Principles for Stable Capital Flows and Fair Restructuring in Emerging Markets," covering transparent and timely flows of information, debtor/creditor dialogue and cooperation to avoid restructuring, "good faith" actions, sanctity of contracts and fair treatment. These include the following reference to the IMF:

> In cases where program negotiations with the IMF are underway or a program is in place, debtors and creditors rely upon the IMF in its traditional role as guardian of the system to support the debtor's reasonable efforts to avoid default.

19 Although it is worth noting that Calvo and Reinhart (2000) still see vulnerabilities to "sudden stops" in countries with current account surpluses.

20 There is some evidence that China and Vietnam may have attracted away the manufacturing opportunities that drove their growth in the 1980s.

21 For a possible explanation, see Prasad *et al.* (2006).

22 Assessments of countries' exchange rate regimes are a standard feature of Article IV reports, usually taking the form of a statement noting that the regime in place has served the country well. When advice was given over the evaluation period, it tended to be in the direction of more flexible exchange rates.

(IEO 2007: 32)

23 Here are Fischer's (2003) views on BBC:

> In these circumstances, the band is serving as a weak nominal anchor for the exchange rate, but it is not at all clear why such a system is preferable to an inflation targeting framework. Possibly the band could be thought of as a supplement to an inflation targeting framework, but it would need to be demonstrated what if any benefits that brings. Williamson himself believes that specifying a target exchange rate range may prevent markets heading off on an errant exchange rate path. Another possibility is that by committing weakly to some range of exchange rates, the authorities make it more likely that fiscal policy will be brought into play if the real exchange rate moves too far from equilibrium. Although I do not see how to make these intermediate regimes work for emerging market countries, it is clear that floating exchange rates do fluctuate a great deal, and that it would be useful if it were possible to reduce the range of fluctuations. In these circumstances, the band is serving as a weak nominal anchor for the exchange rate, but it is not at all clear why such a system is preferable to an inflation targeting framework. Possibly the band could be thought of as a supplement to an inflation targeting framework,

but it would need to be demonstrated what if any benefits that brings. Williamson himself believes that specifying a target exchange rate range may prevent markets heading off on an errant exchange rate path. Another possibility is that by committing weakly to some range of exchange rates, the authorities make it more likely that fiscal policy will be brought into play if the real exchange rate moves too far from equilibrium. Although I do not see how to make these intermediate regimes work for emerging market countries, it is clear that floating exchange rates do fluctuate a great deal, and that it would be useful if it were possible to reduce the range of fluctuations.

(Robbins Lecture 2, p. 60)

References

Bevilaqua, A. and Azevedo, R. (2005) "Provision of FX Hedge by the Public Sector: the Brazilian Experience," BIS Paper 24.

Burton, D. and Zanello, A. (2007) "Asia Ten Years After," *Finance and Development*, June.

Calvo, G., and Reinhart, C. (2000) "When Capital Flows Come to a Sudden Stop: Consequences and Policy," in P.B. Kenen and A.K. Swoboda (eds.) *Reforming the International Monetary and Financial System*, Washington, DC: International Monetary Fund.

Calvo, G. and Reinhart, C. (2002) "Fear of Floating," *Quarterly Journal of Economics* 117(2): 379–408.

Dooley, M., Folkerts-Landau, D. and Garber, P. (2003) "An Essay on the Revived Bretton Woods System," NBER Working Paper no. 9971.

Enoch, C., Baldwin, B., Frecaut, O. and Kovanen, A. (2001) "Indonesia: Anatomy of a Banking Crisis," IMF Working Paper 01/52.

Fischer, S. (2001a) "Exchange Rate Regimes: is the Bipolar View Correct?" *Journal of Economic Literature* 15(2) 2001: 3–24.

Fischer, S. (2001b) "The International Financial System: Crises and Reform," The Robbins Lectures, London School of Economics, October.

Fischer, S. (2003) "Globalisation and its Challenges," *American Economic Review* 93: 1–29.

Fischer, S. (2006) "Financial Market Liberalisation," BIS Papers 32, pp. 4–11.

Ghosh, A. (2006) "Capital Account Crises: Lessons for Crisis Prevention," IMF, July. Prepared for the High-Level Seminar on Crisis Prevention in Emerging Market Countries, Singapore.

Goldfajn, I. and Gupta, P. (1999) "Does Monetary Policy Stabilize the Exchange Rate Following a Currency Crisis?" IMF Working Paper 99/42.

Goldstein, M. (2005) "Renminbi Controversies," paper prepared for the Conference on Monetary Institutions and Economic Development, Cato Institute, November.

Goldstein, M. and Turner, P. (2004) *Controlling Currency Mismatches in Emerging Economies*, Washington, DC: Institute for International Economics.

Hovarguimian, C. (2003) "The Catalytic Effect of IMF Lending: a Critical Review," Bank of England Financial Stability Review, December.

International Monetary Fund (2006) "Financial Crises and Growth: in Article IV Consultations," Thailand, Selected Issues.

IMF Independent Evaluation Office (2005) *The IMF's Approach to Capital Account Liberalization*, Washington, DC: International Monetary Fund.

IMF Independent Evaluation Office (2007) *An IEO Evaluation of IMF Exchange Rate Policy Advice, 1999–2005*, Washington, DC: International Monetary Fund.

Ito, T., Isard, P. and Symansky, S. (1997) "Economic Growth and the Real Exchange

Rate: an Overview of the Balassa/Samuelson Hypothesis for Asia," *NBER Working Paper* 5979.

Keynes, J.M. (1929) "The German Transfer Problem," *Economic Journal* 39: 1–7.

Kindleberger, C. (1996) *Manias, Prices and Crashes: a History of Financial Crises*, New York: John Wiley.

Krueger, A. (2002) "Sovereign Debt Restructuring Mechanism, One Year Later," speech at the European Commission, Brussels, December 10.

Krueger, A. (2006) "The New Economic Century: Experience and Opportunity in the Reform Process," address to the Fraser Institute, Vancouver, May 3.

Lane, T., Ghosh, A., Hamann, J., Phillips, S., Schulze-Ghattas, M. and Tsikata, T. (1999) "IMF-Supported Programs in Indonesia, Korea and Thailand," IMF Occasional Paper 178.

Lipschitz, L. (2006) "Notes on Crisis Prevention in Emerging Market Economies," address at the Singapore IMF meeting, September.

Montgomery, J. (1997) "The Indonesian Financial System: Its Contribution to Economic Performance and Key Policy Issues," IMF Working Paper WP/97/45.

Prasad, E., Rajan, R. and Subramanian, A. (2006) "Patterns of International Capital Flows and their Implications for Economic Development," paper presented at the Federal Reserve Bank of Kansas City Conference, August.

Takagi, S. and Hicklin, J. (2007) IMF Exchange Rate Policy Advice. International Monetary Fund Independent Evaluation Office.

Turner, P. (2007) "Banking Systems in Asia: Ten Years Later," *Asian Economic Policy Review* 2: 75–95.

11 The post-Asia-crisis system of global financial regulation and why developing countries should be worried about it

Robert H. Wade[1]

The international finance system has no enforcement mechanism analogous to the state's authority in national financial systems, even as international financial flows have grown to dwarf international real-economy flows. It lacks institutions and organizations that are normal at the national level, such as a central bank, a financial regulator, a bankruptcy court, deposit insurance, and the like. Yet the financial services industry is built on confidence, and lack of confidence in international transactions can be extremely contagious. Hence the desirability of international institutions to provide the international public good of confidence in the international financial system. That means prudential rules, such that all international banks reach an acceptable standard of prudence, and transparency rules, such that all governments, banks and other financial organizations reach an acceptable standard of transparency in their financial accounts.

After the several financial crises of the 1990s the High Command of world finance (US Treasury, US Federal Reserve, G7/G8, IMF, Bank for International Settlements, World Bank) decided that the system for providing these international public goods urgently needed strengthening. Accordingly it reinvigorated the development of comprehensive and universal standards of best practice in such areas as data dissemination, bank supervision, corporate governance and financial accounting, using organizations like the IMF, the Basel Committee on Banking Supervision, the Financial Stability Forum, the G20 of finance ministers, and a gamut of non-official bodies. Enforcement was to come largely by peer pressure and market reactions to information about compliance, such that countries, banks and firms which comply more with the standards gain better access to finance than those which comply less. I call this the standards-surveillance-compliance (SSC) system.[2]

Earlier, through the 1980s and 1990s, the High Command had agreed on a single broad economic policy recipe for countries in general and developing countries in particular, the recipe known as the Washington Consensus, summarized in the commandment, "liberalize the market." The commandment expressed (a) the economic theory that free markets allocate capital efficiently, coupled with (b) the classical liberal norm that freedom and government are opposites – hence the expansion of freedom consists of reducing government "intervention" in free markets.

After the shock of the Asian and other financial crises of the 1990s the consensus shifted from "liberalize the market" to "standardize the market" on a global scale, meaning standardize market institutions around a particular set of political economy models and thereby create a "level playing field" in order to facilitate "globalization." The shift from "liberalize" to "standardize" is not the small step beyond the Washington Consensus that it seems at first glance. While the consensus continues to accept the theory that markets allocate capital efficiently, it emphasizes more than before the need for markets to be governed through rules set in a political process. This amounts to turning classical liberalism on its head, because it gives normative sanction to a big *increase* in governmental and multilateral "intervention." The change from "liberalize" to "standardize" is sufficiently big as to demarcate a shift from the Washington Consensus to the post-Washington Consensus.

The crafting of the standards and rules has been done by an institutional complex including not only developed country governments and multilateral organizations like the IMF, but also by private international financial firms from developed countries and their industry associations and think tanks. Developing country entities have had almost no representation. The resulting regime reflects the collective preferences of developed country governments and financial firms. On the other hand, the more radical proposals for strengthening the international financial system put forward after the Asian crisis – including an array of new international financial organizations whose operations may have reduced the tendency to crisis – would have seriously curtailed the freedom of private financial participants, and consequently have not left the drawing board.

The SSC system described here is just one part of a larger complex of international regimes, backed by the authority of the leading industrial states (often delegated upwards to multilateral organizations), which have the effect of redistributing income upwards to:

1   the industrial countries;
2   the financial sector;
3   the top percentile of world income distribution.

These international regimes have their complements in upwards-redistributing domestic regimes of the leading industrial states. The role of state authority in this upwards redistribution is obscured by the standard framing of "conservative" and "progressive" worldviews as "pro-market" and "pro-government." This framing obscures the point that conservatives often want government intervention which tends to boost the income of the already wealthy, while opposing intervention which redistributes downwards in the form of social programs covering education, health, pensions, unemployment benefit and the like – there the market should reign. The SSC system is part of this broad thrust of rule-making in favor of upwards distribution (Wade 2007).

The chapter describes the evolution of the SSC system, and examines the arguments used to justify it. The next section contrasts the current "smug belief" – former IMF chief economist Kenneth Rogoff's phrase – that the international financial system is robust enough as it is, with the current tendencies toward financial and geopolitical instability, which would seem to warrant more forceful interventions. Then the chapter goes back to the financial crises of the 1990s and shows how they provided support for the idea that major innovations had to be made in the international financial architecture. But in the event the main change was the more modest SSC system – formulation of standards, surveillance of national economies, and (hopefully) compliance by governments and firms. Having described its construction the chapter assesses its effects so far, including on developing countries' access to finance and on the direction of evolution of developing countries' wider political economies.

At the end it advocates three modest changes:

1   revise IMF surveillance standards to give more emphasis to the world economy and policy spillovers from one country to another, and to recognize the validity of alternative ways of reducing harmful spillovers (e.g. accept government guarantees of banks as an alternative to stipulated levels of core capital); here a useful analogy is the idea of "middleware," a piece of software that connects two or more software applications so that they can exchange data;

2   revise Basel II standards in a process where developing country governments and banks have more voice;

3   change global norms to accept capital controls as a legitimate instrument of developing country economic management.

These changes, though modest, would help bring the global economy into closer correspondence with liberal values which it currently short-changes.

The prevailing "smug belief"

Five years on from the start of record-breaking growth rates in much of the developing world "the policy community has developed a smug belief," says Kenneth Rogoff (2007), "that enhanced macroeconomic stability at the national level combined with continuing financial innovation at the international level have obviated any need to tinker with the [international financial] system."

It is a "smug" belief especially because the world economy and the interstate system currently (2007) display signs of fragility that could easily tip the world into economic depression and geopolitical conflict, yet the current period of relative calm in financial markets is not being used to put preventative measures in place. Here are four of these signs.

First, the extraordinarily high and rising levels of debt to equity in the world financial system and the potential for a "great unwind." The assets invested in hedge funds have more than tripled in the seven years since 2000, to around $1,500 bn. As the CEO of a US hedge fund recently noted:

The current situation ... may be even more alarming [than the one which produced the crash of Long Term Capital Management].... [T]he explosion of hedge fund investments in illiquid assets combined with leverage currently pose a greater risk to the global financial markets than we experienced at the time of the LTCM [Long Term Capital Management] debacle.[3]

Second, the run-up in debt reflects the boom in global liquidity, which itself is propelled by:

1   the surge in commodity prices since 2003 to the highest levels in more than two decades;
2   the surge in the US current account deficit;
3   the incorporation of giant savings pools in China and India into world capital markets.

These trends constitute an economic earthquake of equivalent magnitude as the political shock of 9/11. The link with financial instability comes from the way that the boom in liquidity enables many developing country governments to postpone economic reforms, including improved financial regulation; and enables governments of weaker states to "win" (buy) elections without delivering good government, and enables rebel groups to finance militias once they control a commodity-exporting base.

Third, the precarious state of the US economy. Internationally, the US has in recent years been loosing its position of economic dominance both in trade and in finance, especially to the EU and China (European financial markets now have a higher capitalization than US counterparts for the first time in a century). Domestically, the US middle class is being squeezed by falling house prices, spiraling mortgage foreclosures, falling real wages in manufacturing and lower-skill service jobs, historically very high levels of debt to disposable income, economic growth slowing to near 1 percent, and the highest level of inequality between the income of the top 1 percent of households and the bottom 90 percent since 1928. When the Great Depression began in 1929 the US was in the ascendancy. Being in relative decline today may make the US more likely to react to these trends internationally in an even more unilateralist, more defensive, less cooperative way than in the 1930s. We are currently seeing the dark unspooling of this response as the US substitutes bilateral and multilateral trade agreements (such as CAFTA) for commitment to the WTO process. The "one country one vote" principle of the WTO requires too much sacrifice of US national interests; while the bilateral and regional route allows the US to use its "go-it-alone power" to establish agreements loaded with predatory provisions favorable to the US (such as open access for subsidized US agricultural exports and stringent patent protections for US drugs).

Fourth, the relative decline of the US is one part of a larger shift in the inter-state system. In particular, the previously closed club of dominant "insider" capitalist states is under pressure to admit new, challenger states like Russia,

China and Brazil. The rise of states pressing to enter the club of "insiders" has almost always been accompanied by interstate conflict in the past, and there is no reason to suppose that the current rise will not be accompanied by heightened geopolitical tensions and rivalries (hopefully not the twentieth century's head-to-head wars). In particular, neo-imperialism is again in the air. Not only the US variety, sometimes described as "empire without colonies" or "empire lite" (Wade 2003a); but also the less noticed emerging Russian political system, where a kind of neo-imperial ambition can be seen based on Russia's consensual authoritarian rule and its newfound power in energy and raw materials.

The tensions between these emerging neo-imperialisms, especially over access to energy, push the Western side to redouble its efforts to open markets in the rest of the world and reconfigure domestic political economies to facilitate the operations of Western, especially Anglo-American firms – without much more than lip service to the idea of compromise with the national interests and preferences of developing countries. This is a deep paradox of liberalism: in the name of liberalism, the Western side is seeking to build a comprehensive system of global economic standardization, surveillance and correction around one particular kind of capitalism, and to shrink the scope of "policy space" for national political systems. And it is doing so through interstate organizations with democratic deficits so big they could almost be called democratic absences (see below, pp. 229–231).

The petrifying effect of the Asian crisis

Given the current lack of drive needed to sustain even modest and unambiguously positive reforms, we need to remind ourselves just how petrified was the High Command of world finance only eight to ten years ago that the whole world economy, including the biggest industrial economies, would be dragged down as the crisis ricocheted out of Asia and into Russia, Brazil and elsewhere. Paul Blustein, author of *The Chastening* (2001), gives a tick-tock account of how these crises unfolded, and quotes Alan Greenspan in October 1998 saying to the National Association for Business Economics, "I have been looking at the American economy on a day-by-day basis for almost a half century, but I have never seen anything like this" ["this" meaning the disintegration of market confidence]. Blustein also quotes a bond market analyst telling his forecasting consultant, in mid-October 1998, "I've never called you before, and I wouldn't do it, but I owe it to you to let you know, it's never been like this before out there." Stanley Fischer, deputy managing director of the IMF, told Blustein that when the Brazilian governor of the central bank told him, in January 1999, that Brazil would no longer make an iron-clad defense of its exchange rate, "I thought, this is it. We're going to lose Latin America, and then it will go back to Asia."[4] The High Command's worries about the Asian crisis went far beyond the fact that it affected a sizable portion of the world's population in fast-growing and economically important countries. It seemed likely to discredit the hard-won consensus about the virtues of market liberalization and maximum openness for all developing countries. The Asian crisis-affected countries had been regarded as star pupils of the Washington Consensus – indeed their economic success was routinely attributed to their adherence to it and held up as proof of its general validity. The fact that the star pupils tumbled into crisis at the same time was not a good advertisement for the Washington Consensus.

Moreover, the crisis hit only a few years after the Mexican "peso crisis" of 1994, and Mexico too had been regarded as a star pupil of the Washington Consensus. In the wake of the Mexican crisis academics and official agencies rushed to present proposals for safeguarding the world economy against a repeat, including better financial supervision at the international level, more transparency of financial markets, sensible macroeconomic policies and exchange rate regimes, and better monitoring of macroeconomic performance. But once the crisis was seen to be contained to Mexico and not spreading, "complacency soon reasserted itself" (Claessens *et al.* 2003: 6). So the shock of the Asia crisis was compounded by the realization that nothing much had been done to strengthen the international financial system in the several years since the Mexican crisis.

New international financial architecture

In the wake of these traumatic events, leading policy economists tripped over themselves to offer up plans for a "new international financial architecture" (NIFA) – not merely new interior decoration, or even plumbing, but new architecture to create a much stronger supranational authority in financial markets, a change on the order of magnitude as the one initiated at the Bretton Woods conference of 1944.

The NIFA proposals included ambitious new global organizations such as a much larger IMF, a global financial regulator, a sovereign bankruptcy court, an international deposit insurance corporation, even a global central bank. They included the proposal for the IMF to be given greater authority to support standstills – postponement of foreign debt repayments and even controls on capital outflows, which amount to "bailing in" countries' private creditors – so as to give countries protection from creditor panics, analogous to the kind of protection companies get with bankruptcy laws.

In the event, none of these proposals left the drawing board. The IMF has not been super-sized, as some analysts wanted on grounds that the giant size of global financial markets required a big increase in the Fund's resources and staff so that, when crises erupt, it could provide enough hard currency for financial investors not to panic about a shortage of liquidity. On the other hand, nor has the IMF been abolished, as prominent conservatives like former Secretary of State George Shultz wanted; nor even substantially cut, as wanted by the majority on a congressionally appointed panel led by conservative economist Allan Meltzer.

One of the more radical proposals to originate from the official sector – the Sovereign Debt Restructuring Mechanism (SDRM) proposed by Ann Krueger of the IMF, which contained elements of a global bankruptcy procedure – was defeated by a combination of developed country states and private financial organizations at the IMF meetings of March 2003. The SDRM would have involved full debt restructuring: changes in interest rates, reductions in amounts owed, and influence over private investments and contracts. It would have entailed a big jump in the authority of an international organization over private financial markets.

Nor has there been progress on the apparently more modest but still important proposal for institutionalized (as distinct from ad hoc) standstill procedures. Evidence from the crises themselves suggested that standstills – in this case, ad hoc as distinct from institutionalized ones – could be very powerful in managing crises so as to reduce the damage to countries' well-being. Most of the bail-outs mounted by the IMF in the financial crises of the late 1990s failed. But two succeeded: one was the second rescue of South Korea, on Christmas Eve 1997; the second was the second rescue of Brazil in March 1999. The main difference between the ones that succeeded in stopping the panic and those that did not is that the High Command, in the successful cases, cajoled the Electronic Herd (mutual funds, pension funds, commercial banks, insurance companies and other professional money managers) to bail "in" rather than "out" and defer debt repayment; but not in the more numerous unsuccessful ones.[5]

However, it turned out that to get the authority needed for institutionalized standstills (and still more, the SDRM) the Fund would have to change its Articles of Agreement; but Fund members are extremely reluctant to change the Articles of Agreement, having changed the Articles only three times between the IMF's founding in the 1940s and 1999. Also, major industrial countries would have to pass laws recognizing the Fund's authority so that bondholders would be prevented from asserting claims in court.[6] But such laws recognizing the Fund's authority would encounter storms of opposition, because they involve (a) authority to abrogate contracts – the covenants that govern borrowers' obligation to pay interest and principal on loans and bonds, and also (b) authority to block a country's own citizens, as well as foreigners, from moving their money abroad. The US Congress, in particular, would be sure to oppose tooth and nail.

The proposal for Contingent Credit Lines (CCL) was implemented, in that the IMF did create a facility which enables the Fund, for the first time, to lend pre-emptively to help prevent a crisis. However, countries had to volunteer to join the facility, and the IMF had to certify that the country had strong enough economic policies. In the event, no country signed up and even the IMF was unenthusiastic. From the country side, signing up looked like a confession of fragility. From the IMF side, ejecting a country which acquired a new government not to the Fund's liking would send a bad signal to the markets, possibly precipitating a crisis.[7]

In short, there has been little movement on any of the more radical NIFA proposals. The central reason is the unwillingness of participants in private financial markets to accept more international authority or constraints on the markets. They prefer to operate in a world where authority lies mainly with nation states, which gives them more freedom to do what they want than in a regime with stronger supranational authority.

Such movement toward strengthening the international financial system as there has been over the past ten years has been movement towards strengthening developing countries' ability to sustain high integration into the world financial system – on the implicit assumption that the cause of the crises lay with developing countries' weak institutions and practices and not with the international system.

Accordingly, there has been real movement in the area of global economic standardization: standards for good-quality financial data ("transparency"), standards of best practice (including the Basel II capital requirements for international banks), and surveillance of national financial systems by multinational authorities, aimed especially at developing countries.

The central thrust of this effort has been to further constrain policymaking and institutional arrangements in developing countries in order to ensure they fit the preferences of international investors for full openness, arm's-length relations between firms, banks, financial markets and government, and no government guarantees to banks that might give them an "unfair" competitive advantage.

Construction of the SSC system

In October 1998, as the Asia crisis was still unfolding, the G7 finance ministers and central bank governors declared agreement on "the need for greater transparency" (repeating their declaration after the Mexican crisis) – meaning the provision of "accurate and timely" macroeconomic and financial supervisory data, including the reserve positions of central banks and levels of national public *and* private indebtedness.[8] World Bank economists supported this line of crisis prevention with the argument that the East Asian crisis was due in large measure to "lack of transparency" in financial data. In the words of a World Bank paper published in 2001, "The findings suggest that these [crisis-affected] countries did not follow International Accounting Standards and that this likely triggered the financial crisis. Users of the accounting information were *misled* and were not able to take precautions in a timely fashion" (Vashwanath and Kaufman 2001: 44; emphasis added). The IMF argued in 2003 that the global "adoption of internationally recognized standards of good practices [would help] foster financial market stability and better risk assessment." Compliance with standards – said the IMF – would help a country "mitigate the impact of an external crisis by supporting continued access to external borrowing," and "help *prevent* crises" by reducing the cost of foreign capital and thereby help a government "remain solvent in cases it otherwise might not have remained solvent" (IMF 2003). Notice how the underlying theory of crisis protects the IMF and World Bank from blame. It implies that they did not act in advance to counter the build up of crisis potential in Mexico and then in East Asia because they were *misled* by the Mexicans and East Asians. It eclipses an alternative theory, that they (and central bankers) were asleep at the wheel.

The initial concern to improve "transparency" grew into a broader concern to reorder economic activity around the world. The re-ordering had four main components:

1   standards of good information;
2   standards of best practices, including banking supervision, payments systems, corporate governance and financial accounting;
3   systematic surveillance of economies in order to judge compliance with the standards;
4   mechanisms for encouraging governments and firms to comply with the standards.[9]

The Financial Stability Forum (FSF) – established in April 1999 with the G7 finance ministers and central bankers at its core, plus those from four other industrial countries (or territories, in the case of Hong Kong), together with representatives from international financial organizations like the IMF, World Bank and Bank for International Settlements (BIS), and representatives from private sector associations of financial firms – helped to develop standards in many areas, in the domains of banking supervision, risk management systems of banks, financial accounting and corporate governance. The FSF was chaired by the general manager of the BIS. It included no representatives of developing countries.

The IMF was charged with developing Special Data Dissemination Standards (SDDS), mainly for macroeconomic data. The IMF was also to be the primary enforcer of many of the standards, through formal mechanisms of structural conditionality, contingent credit lines and Article IV consultations.

However, these formal enforcement mechanisms were never developed, for the same reason that the more radical of the New International Financial Architecture proposals were not developed. Instead, the IMF – and the "transparency" thrust more generally – relied on indirect enforcement through the response of "financial markets" (Electronic Herd). The IMF would make public the results of the surveillance, either publishing them itself or having the government publish them (and even if the government restricted the public information, the network of experts who did the surveillance was leaky enough to ensure that anyone who wanted to see the results could see them). Financial markets would respond to the high-quality information appropriately; they would lend more funds at cheaper rates to governments that complied more fully with the standards, and less at higher rates to governments that complied less. Knowing this market-driven reward and punishment system, governments would strive for more compliance, and the international financial system would become more stable.

This was the theory behind what I call the Standards-Surveillance-Compliance (SSC) system. In line with the theory the IMF (supplemented by the World Bank) in 1999 set about producing Reports on the Observance of Standards and Codes (ROSCs), and undertaking a Financial Sector Assessment Program (FSAP). Between 1999 and end 2006 the IMF produced 502 ROSCs and the World Bank 92, making a total of almost 600. One hundred and thirty countries had at least one ROSC.

The ROSCs fed into the larger exercise of the FSAP, which had three main assessment components:

1   compliance with standards (based on the ROSC);
2   stability of the financial system;
3   the financial sector's needed reforms.

Operationally, the FSAP exercise may entail, for a large country, a sizable team of people from the IMF, the World Bank and outside consultants, coming to a country and having sustained dialogue with financial authorities on critical matters such as, for example, payments systems, and feeding back their findings to the authorities.

At much the same time on a separate track, the Basel Committee on Banking Supervision, under the umbrella of the Bank for International Settlements (the club of rich world central banks), was developing a new set of standards for banks' capital and for banking supervision. The impetus came from bank regulators feeling overwhelmed by financial innovations in the 1990s, and from banks' development of new kinds of risk assessment models – coupled with the prevailing norm that "markets (as distinct from regulators) know best." Formulating the new set of standards came to be known as the Basel II process, because the original Basel rules had come to be seen as lagging far behind financial innovation. The initial Basel II proposals from the Basel Committee were published in 1999, the Asian crisis having given the project added urgency.

A whole gamut of unofficial, private sector bodies have also been formulating standards with global reach. They include the International Association of Insurance Supervisors, the International Accounting Standards Board (created in 2001), the International Organization of Securities Commissioners, the International Organization for Standardization, the International Federation of Stock Exchanges, and the Institute for International Finance.

Effects of the SSC system

What have been the effects of the drive for transparency, standards, surveillance and correction? At first glance more transparency and clearer standards are as desirable as motherhood and apple pie. But things are not so simple.

On the plus side, the FSAP exercise has produced useful results, according to insiders on the country end. The IMF's FSAP team typically concentrates on "supervising the (national) supervisors" – on examining how the national financial supervisory system is working and making suggestions for improvement. Often its political role is to strengthen the hand of regulators against the government. The regulators can say to the government, "The IMF says X and Y must be done. If we don't comply, we will be subject to international criticism and market discipline." Indeed, quite a few governments have overhauled their financial regulatory system ahead of an FSAP exercise, especially when the government has undertaken in advance to publish the FSAP's findings. (The UK Financial Services Authority, for example, has often been asked to provide technical help to other governments in advance of an FSAP exercise.)

On the other hand, the list of negatives is long. First, the FSAP and the ROSCs have tended to be compiled in a check-list approach. As one involved World Bank insider put it:

> The problem with the FSAP is that the shareholders, primarily G7, burdened it with doing a huge amount of mindless assessments of compliance with a large number of standards. This prevented and/or distracted staff from looking at first-order issues. For example, in [an Eastern European country] two successive heads of the SEC were assassinated by "defenestration" from their office windows. Yet the FSAP concentrated on their compliance with IOSCO standards, even though with this degree of lawlessness, it is difficult to expect any securities market activity except for trade among insiders. Such silly exercises took resources away from consideration as to why some markets were missing or malfunctioning. The British, the French, Canadians, and Americans were the worst in their relentlessly checklist approach to doing assessments. If the Bank and Fund had been serious about this effort, they would have needed a number of new staff to implement it.[10]

In other words, the country assessments tend to lack focus, and to include much detail on so-called "structural" issues which are not closely related to what should be the focus, external stability. (Structural issues refer to institutional domains, such as social security systems or the energy sector, as distinct from macroeconomic policy issues to do with international reserves, external borrowing and fiscal balances.)

Second, as Rachel Lomax, deputy governor of the Bank of England, said:

> The Fund does not devote enough time and effort to overseeing the system as a whole, through assessing global economic prospects and analyzing international economic linkages and policy spillovers (so-called multilateral surveillance).... The Fund needs to be better focused on the big global issues, including financial issues and on the interactions between different regions and countries.[11]

Moreover, the IMF's Independent Evaluation Office found that the Fund's operational staff tend not even to *read* the global stability reports, let alone integrate findings into their bilateral work. Only 14 percent of senior staff said that the IMF's findings from its "multilateral surveillance" were discussed with national authorities.[12] Conversely, bilateral surveillance reports show little discussion of policy spillovers even from systemically important countries like Germany, Russia and even the US.

Third, it seems that on the whole, financial market participants pay rather little attention to the data provided through "transparency" exercises – even though they would presumably no longer be "misled" by the data (as they supposedly were before the Asian crisis). A recent independent evaluation of the IMF's FSAP concluded that: "While many authorities identified the 'signalling role' to markets as one of their motivations for participating in the FSAP exercise, the impact of FSSAs [Financial Sector Stability Assessments] on the views of financial market participants appears *modest*."[13]

Again,

> Our interviews with a wide range of market participants indicate that most have limited knowledge of the contents of FSSAs, a conclusion reinforced by the results of the recent survey conducted in connection with the internal review of the standards and codes initiative. Use of FSSAs by credit rating agencies appears to be somewhat greater, but they have used them only selectively.[14]

Financial markets pay more attention to "traditional" macroeconomic indicators like inflation than to compliance with standards of good financial practice. Most studies of the link between compliance with standards and cost of foreign capital have found no significant impact of the former on the latter.

Yet as noted, the Fund's approach to enforcement of compliance with standards of best practice relies on indirect enforcement through financial markets rewarding high-compliance countries and punishing low-compliance policies. If financial markets do not pay much attention to the data released from surveillance exercises, the enforcement mechanism is hobbled.

Fourth, to the extent that markets do pay attention to the information made available through transparency exercises the effects may be to make financial markets less stable and more prone to crisis. Why? Because these developments, by homogenizing the data about economies and reducing the diversity of opinion on the near future, may accentuate the tendency to pro-cyclical herding behavior – bankers and investors buying what others are buying, selling what others are selling, owning what others are owning.

In short, the Fund's attempt to alter what the High Command took to be a major cause of the Asian financial crisis – to provide more transparency so that users of accounting information would not again be "misled" – may have helped to strengthen financial supervision (through the FSAP process). On the other hand, it has probably had rather little effect on behavior of financial market participants – because they don't use much of the resulting information. Moreover, to the extent that their behavior has been affected by the provision of more transparency, it may be in a more pro-cyclical and destabilizing direction rather than the opposite.

The discussion has been about the impacts of IMF surveillance. What about the impact of the Basel II standards (starting to be implemented in 2008)? It is quite likely that Basel II standards, too, will generate pro-cyclical tendencies and raise the volatility of borrowers' access to bank finance. Avinash Persaud (2001: 61), former head of research at State Street Bank, argues that Basel II's move towards more quantitative, market-sensitive risk management practices reinforces herding behavior and market volatility in a vicious circle. Two other analysts make the same point in the following terms: "The application of models-based risk management may result in the creation of second-order dangers," which "raises questions about the recent move of financial regulators worldwide toward an integration of mathematical risk assessment tools in the regulatory framework" (Holzer and Milo 2005: 17). One reason is that the Basel II standards encourage the more sophisticated banks – those based in developed countries – to adopt a single type of internal ratings-based (IRB) model, a model which relies on current asset prices, which tend to be pro-cyclical, and which raises the capital requirements at times of downturns when banks are less able to meet the requirements. A second reason is that banks will tend to react similarly to similar signals – because they are using the same type of risk assessment model, which leads them to downgrade or upgrade clients *en masse* (Claessens *et al.* 2003).

So Basle II standards, like IMF standards, may well make market participants behave in ways that increase rather than decrease market volatility. But the impact of standards of best practice and their diffusion through regular surveillance is not limited to the behavior of market participants.

Effects on developing countries' access to finance and competitiveness of developing country banks[15]

Standards of best practice are rarely distributionally neutral: they benefit some participants more than others. The standards coming out from the Basel Committee, the IMF, the FSF and the like, and surveillance in line with the standards, may be having at least two far-reaching impacts, which are disadvantageous for developing countries and advantageous for developed countries, especially the Anglo-American kind.

First, Basel II, as compared to Basel I (or as compared to a "first best" solution), will shift competitive advantage even further toward developed country banks and against developing country banks, by raising the cost of finance to developing countries; and will likely hurt development prospects more broadly by making developing country access to finance more pro-cyclical.

Basel II requires banks with less sophisticated risk management systems – which tend to be based in developing countries – to carry relatively more supervisory capital than banks with more sophisticated systems. Therefore it raises their costs of lending relative to those with more sophisticated risk management systems, which tend to be based in developed countries. The latter are allowed to establish their credit risks and capital adequacy themselves ("self-supervise"), subject to the financial supervisor approving their model. Also, Basel II requires bigger differential risk weighting to lower-rated borrowers than Basel I, who are disproportionately in developing countries. And its standards insufficiently recognize risk diversification benefits of lending to clients in developing countries.

The Basel Committee's own most recent quantitative impact study reveals a large variance in the amount of capital required for banks using the different Basel II-based risk assessment methodologies. For example, some banks using the advanced "internal ratings-based" (IRB) approach – coming predominantly from developed countries – are expected to have large *reductions* of their capital requirements of the order of 30 percent. Banks using the simpler "foundational" approach – predominantly from developing countries – are expected to experience an *increase* in their capital requirements of over 38 percent.[16] The Basel II standards thus give structural advantage to large developed country banks, and a structural disadvantage to developing country banks – and to the regional, national and local economies they are nested within.

The upshot is that developing countries under Basel II could face a higher cost of capital and a lower volume of lending than under Basel I, with more pro-cyclical volatility, and with their banks having less chance of establishing international operations and more likely to be taken over by developed country banks (Claessens *et al.* 2003: 17). No country should let its banking system be taken over by foreign banks, even if, in developing countries, Western banks are likely to be more "efficient" than domestic ones; for at times of crisis banks rely heavily on their home state and are likely to sacrifice operations in developing countries in order to protect their home base.

The pull toward norms of Anglo-American capitalism

The second far-reaching impact is the way that the new standards and surveillance mechanisms tend to frame a global "attractor" point, in the sense of taking the Anglo-American or liberal market economy as the "normal" or "proper" kind of capitalism (Vestergaard 2007a). By the Anglo-American or liberal type is meant short-term and arm's-length relations between banks, non-financial companies and the state; non-discretionary regulation which is delegated to "independent" agencies, like the Financial Services Agency in the UK; and banks oriented to maximizing profits. A contrasting type has been common in East Asia, based on longer-term and more "multiplex" relations between companies, financiers and the state, discretionary regulation, and some banks invested with social purposes beyond profit maximizing (including development banks). I have argued elsewhere that this system was an important factor in the very high rates of investment and diversification in capitalist East Asia over the 1950s to the 1980s, particularly because it enabled big firms to carry very high levels of debt to equity compared to counterparts operating in an Anglo-American type of capitalism. High debt/equity ratios supported high rates of investment (Wade 1998a, 1998b, 2004; Wade and Venoroso 1998; Zysman 1983).

As long as the East Asian system operates on the basis of long-term relationships, patient capital and government guarantees, Anglo-American capital is at a disadvantage in these markets. On the other hand, US and UK financial firms know they can beat all comers in an institutional context of arm's-length relations, stock markets, open capital accounts and new financial instruments. Therefore the Asian system must be changed toward theirs. For example, the US Senate passed a Foreign Operations Appropriation Bill in 1998 saying that no US funds may be available to the IMF until the Treasury Secretary certified that all the G7 governments publicly agreed that they will require the IMF to require of its borrowers,

1   liberalization of trade and investment, and;
2   elimination of "government directed lending on non-commercial terms or provision of market distorting subsidies to favored industries, enterprises, parties or institutions" (e.g. elimination of sectoral industrial policy).

When an East Asian economy adopts the High Command's standards of best practice its banks have to operate under much tighter prudential standards, and cannot support debt/equity ratios anywhere close to those they supported before. This puts pressure for change on the whole chain of savings, credit and investment, and curbs the rate of investment.

The Basel Committee's rules illustrate the mechanism by which the SSC system pulls other economies toward the Anglo-American model. The rules have as their ostensible purpose the enforcement of a uniform level of prudence sufficient to make bank failure, and contagion, unlikely. The High Command – taking as "normal" the Anglo-American system of arm's-length relations between banks, firms and government and banks oriented solely to maximizing profits – has defined the level of prudence in terms of the level of the bank's assets, liabilities and core capital. Hence the Basel Committee's rules of prudence translate into rules about capital adequacy. But in a national economy where banks receive government guarantees they have to mobilize less capital for their operations. This has been the case with Japanese banks, other East Asian banks, the German *lande* banks, and developing country development banks. These are different kinds of banks than those assumed in the Basel rules. They are not devoted solely to maximizing profits for their shareholders. Their government guarantees allow them to support a cross-subsidizing mixture of public and private purposes, and to operate with a trading ethic that does not force them to drop unprofitable borrowers overnight. The High Command, however, considers that such banks have an unfair competitive advantage, and wants them to behave like "normal" banks, without government guarantees – which means giving up their mix of public and private purposes.

In other words, the justifiable rules of prudence become rules for forcing convergence of a key feature of political economies to the Anglo-American model, disguised as making a "level playing field" for all competitors.

Moreover, financial systems are sub-systems within a larger institutional complex. Changes in financial systems spillover into changes in related institutional areas, including corporate governance, product markets, labor markets, and further on into the welfare state and education. By making it more difficult for developing countries to reform their financial systems in the direction of the East Asian type the SSC system also makes it more difficult for developing countries to adopt other features of a "coordinated market economy," as distinct from a "liberal market economy" (Hall and Soskice 2001).

So to the extent to which the High Command is able to get its standards of best practices accepted as "normal," and non-compliance as "deviant," it imparts a "global warming" type of change in the international political economy away from coordinated market economies toward the attractor point, the liberal market economy of the Anglo-American type. Therefore the High Command's efforts at surveillance should not be understood as just a small add-on to previous efforts at market liberalization. The drive for "transparency" involves not so much "removing the veil" as a massive program of standardization and reporting, using standards derived from best practice in the liberal market economy type of capitalism rather than from good practice in more coordinated forms of capitalism. It thereby reinforces and legitimizes the injection of the power of dominant states (G7) and multilateral organizations in order to intensify and stabilize financial liberalization. This is why the change is big enough to warrant the label post-Washington Consensus.[17]

The question is whether this shift in political economy in developing countries towards the liberal or Anglo-American type can be justified in terms of improving their prospects for catch-up growth. The answer is, broadly, no, though defending the answer would take us well beyond the limits of this chapter. Suffice to quote here the conclusion of Dani Rodrik (2002), that the "new focus on institutions" is not warranted by the evidence, because "our ability to disentangle the web of causality between prosperity and institutions is seriously limited. [But it is clear that countries do not need] an extensive set of institutional reforms" to spur economic growth.

So how did this agenda of transparency, standards and surveillance crystallize out? The key point is that representatives of developing countries and their financial organizations had virtually no place in formulating the agenda or the implementation. The G7 finance ministers led the debate. Of the bodies which did the further decision-making and implementation, the Financial Stability Forum, the Basel Committee and the OECD include virtually no developing country members, while the IMF and the World Bank are dominated by the G7 states (including via the fact that seven executive directors from developed countries, like Belgium, the Netherlands, Spain and Italy, represent 64 developing countries between them). The G7 states are highly responsive to the preferences of private financial organizations rooted in their states. The large array of international standard-setting unofficial bodies of the kind mentioned earlier have almost no representation from developing countries.[18]

The big international – developed country – banks have an especially effective spokesperson for the industry in the form of the Institute for International Finance (IIF), based in Washington, DC, which does research and lobbying on their behalf. When the Basel Committee on Banking Supervision came under pressure from the states of its members (all developed countries) to consult with "the industry" about improving the working of Basel I in the mid-1990s, the Basel Committee turned to the IIF as its principal interlocutor. In formulating Basel II the Basel Committee relied even more on the IIF. But the IIF has the reputation of being the voice of the international – mostly developed country – banks, and of taking little notice of the preferences of less international banks, including most developing country banks.[19]

In short, the process of formulating how to strengthen the global financial system after the Asian crisis was shaped by the preferences of the developed country states and developed country private financial actors, and very little by developing country states or their private financial actors.[20]

That being said, it is misleading to say that the spread of Anglo-American norms occurred only because of "supply" push as distinct from demand pull. The mechanism of diffusion seems to involve two steps: first, pressure from the IMF, the Financial Stability Forum, the G20 and the like, especially in the wake of the Asian crisis, for countries to adopt best practice standards. These standards are derived from "Western" practice, and especially Anglo-American, as distinct from, say, Japanese, German or Scandinavian. But they are fairly general, for the most part. At the second step, once governments began formally to adopt the standards, they turned to more specific regulations on the books in Western countries, especially to the regulations of Anglo-American countries.

Pushback and pretend compliance

The story of the SSC system cannot stop here, however. The effects of the system on the ground cannot simply be inferred from the features of the system, because compliance, too, is a variable. Developing country compliance with the standards has unsurprisingly often fallen a long way short. In some countries and with respect to some standards a post-crisis surge of formal compliance was followed by regulatory forebearance and selective enforcement – and hence pretend compliance and behavioral non-compliance. For example, in the four crisis-affected countries of East Asia (Korea, Malaysia, Thailand, Indonesia), compliance as of 2006 varied across standards and across countries. In general, compliance with the Special Data Dissemination Standards, for macroeconomic data, has been highest, for the costs of compliance do not bear on private firms and the degree of compliance is relatively easily monitored. Next highest was banking supervision. Compliance with the standards of corporate governance and financial accounting was lowest, for these ones are most costly to the private sector and the most difficult to monitor. Malaysia had the highest overall compliance, then Korea, Thailand and, at the bottom, Indonesia (Walter 2008).

Conclusion

Since the Asian crisis, the High Command of international finance continues to place the onus on developing countries to prevent crises, without changes at the international level to mitigate the intensity of pressures from global financial liberalization. For example, it has rejected such mechanisms for reducing the severity of crisis as the Sovereign Debt Restructuring Mechanism, and standstills more broadly. It has rejected capital controls for developing countries (with qualifications). The fact that the world economy in the past five years has not experienced financial crises like in the 1980s through to the early 2000s is due less to institutional changes than to generally benign world macroeconomic conditions – though as suggested at the start, we are now [2007] in a period of mounting financial fragility.

The central reason why the High Command puts the onus on developing countries is that the High Command includes only slight representation of developing countries, while it includes strong representation of internationally-active private financial firms based in developed countries. Private financial market participants in the West remain hostile to measures which go beyond standardization on a Western, specifically Anglo-American model of arm's-length, short-term capital markets. No surprise, then, that the international financial architecture continues to operate in a way that "externalizes" serious costs onto developing economies.

Looked at more broadly, the SSC system as it is now operating shows the following drawbacks:

1 It tends to treat each national economy as a unit and gives only slight attention to the world economy as a whole and to policy spillovers from "systemically important" economies onto others.
2 It may raise the propensity of financial market participants to "herd," and thereby increase the volatility and pro-cyclicality of developing country access to finance.
3 It tends to give a structural advantage to developed country banks and other financial organizations and a structural disadvantage to those based in developing countries, especially through the dramatic effect on the cost of their capital adequacy requirements.
4 It tends to further shrink developing country "policy space" beyond even that allowed by the Washington Consensus.
5 It tends to further narrow the notion of the national interest to promoting economic growth and increasing personal economic welfare, and to marginalize important developmentalist objectives such as constructing national unity, deepening national economic integration and protecting national culture.
6 It imparts to national economies a gravitational pull towards an Anglo-American type of capitalism and away from other types of advanced capitalism, such as Scandinavian, continental European or pre-crisis East Asian. This pull is in line with the preference of Western investors for developing countries to adopt a regime of full openness and arm's-length, short-term relations between banks, firms and government – a neoliberal system.

The SSC system is therefore problematic from a liberal perspective. In the name of economic freedom – expanding market participants' freedom to move their finance where they wish – it curbs the liberal value of national choice of policy framework by injecting a single model from above. And by nearly excluding developing countries from the standards-setting fora it curbs the liberal value of democratic participation, such that those who are subject to a decision should have some role in making it or at least in holding those who make it to account.

On the other hand, developing countries have by no means complied with the regulatory push emanating from the High Command. They may formally comply and advertise their formal compliance as though it is behavioral compliance. But domestic politics shapes what happens between formal compliance and behavioral compliance. Inside the regulatory agencies and the regulated banks and firms "a varying combination of regulatory forebearance, administrative blockage and private sector non-compliance [can] flourish. The result [is] mock compliance: a combination of considerable formal compliance with international standards and behavioral departure from their prescriptions."[21]

What should be done?

Given that the current international financial regime seems to be working well for developed countries, for the financial sector, and for the top percentile of the world income distribution – as seen in what Rogoff calls the prevailing "smug belief" that nothing much needs to be changed (beyond better implementation of the SSC system) – only modest changes have any chance of being given a second thought, until the next crisis. Here are three modest proposals.

Do more surveillance of the international economy (as distinct from individual countries), and focus bilateral surveillance on issues closely linked to external stability

Both the Fund and the World Bank are – surprisingly – not *world* organizations, in the sense that they pay only secondary attention to the world economy and primary attention to national economies considered as separate units. In the case of standards and surveillance, the Fund should shift the emphasis toward:

1   multilateral surveillance, and;
2   in its bilateral surveillance, the analysis of policy spillovers.

It should be ruthlessly selective in its bilateral surveillance of "structural" issues, and only deal with those which closely affect external stability and policy spillovers to the rest of the world. Partly just to fortify its credibility as a multilateral organization and not an arm of the G7 or the G1 it should – in Rachel Lomax's words – "explicitly recognize members' undoubted right to choose their own policy frameworks, providing that they are consistent with their commitments under the Articles." Lomax's distinction between IMF member states choosing their own policy framework, in line with the spirit of national sovereignty, and members pressed to adopt a homogeneous institutional framework, in line with the spirit of empire ("we will press you do what we think is best for you and us"), is parallel to the distinction between "national treatment" and "deep integration" in trade policy. Under the national treatment principle, governments are free to set tariffs as they will but cannot discriminate between countries; if they lower tariffs on imports from one country they must lower them for all countries. Under deep integration governments must change institutions deep within borders in line with models ratified in multilateral fora dominated by developed countries.

The distinction is also analogous to the one between an organization where user departments choose their own software systems, bottom-up, with the *facilitation* of a central information department (and within broad limits of intercommunication), and one where a central data processing department makes top-down decisions about software for the whole organization and does the processing itself. The former may rely on "middleware," a piece of software that connects two or more software applications so that they can exchange data.[22] Middleware provides an analogy to the kind of rules that the international financial regime should aim for.

The point of backing off from structural issues, of course, is to make the business of forming standards and monitoring compliance less of a Trojan Horse for the injection of Anglo-American political economy into the rest of the world. Or in Martin Feldstein's words during the Asia crisis, "[The IMF] should strongly resist pressure from the United States, Japan, and other major countries to make their trade and investment agenda part of the IMF funding conditions" (Feldstein 1998: 32).

Revise Basel standards in a process less dominated by developed country states and developed country banks

The Basel II standards are to be implemented around the world. Yet the Basel Committee has indicated that the process of standardizing capital adequacy and supervisory standards must evolve in a way that responds to innovation in international financial markets. This calls for changes in the way the Basel Committee structures its interaction with outside groups. The consultation process with both non-Basel Committee banking supervisory agencies and with the private sector should be more transparent. The Basel Committee has initiated a semi-transparent consultative process, where it posts the openly solicited comments received on design proposals. This is a step in the right direction, but the Basel Committee's way of dealing with these comments is completely opaque. The use of independent external auditors to assess comments received and interactions between the Basel Committee and outside groups would improve the transparency and accountability of the Committee. Such formalization of procedure could also give leverage to developing countries when new proposals are being made.

Currently, developing country banking regulators and banks are experiencing great difficulties in implementing Basel II. In particular, the few developing country regulators and banks trying to implement the more advanced risk assessment methodologies are encountering severe problems.[23] At a minimum there should be better provision of technical assistance to developing countries to implement these standards, while still giving autonomy to developing countries to decide on the extent they implement Basel II standards, given competing national priorities.

Discussions of a Basel III – which are expected to begin over the next few years – should involve developing countries more than in the previous rounds. Here regional organizations have a potentially important role – such as the Association of Supervisors of Banks of the Americas, and the Latin American Bank

Federation. The new standards should give higher weighting to the risk-reducing effects of international diversification of borrowing and lending – including to and among developing countries.[24] And attention should be given to a less uniform "cookie cutter" approach – to standards which are more regionally differentiated, with surveillance by regional organizations; and to the distinction between the capital requirements of internationally active banks and national development banks (as more countries begin to revive their development bank system).

Basel III should also grapple with the fundamental question of whether regulating levels of capital adequacy is the best way to promote greater bank stability; and open up scope for bank stability options outside of more intensive application of the Basel II standards.[25] The options should include a range of legitimate ways to achieve adequate levels of prudence to protect the international financial system against loss of confidence. For example, they should include not only prescribed levels of core capital but also government guarantees. And the options should include ways of providing liquidity during a crisis – because contrary to the thrust of Basel II the problem for banks during a crisis (especially for banks in developing countries) is often liquidity, not capital.

Distinguishing between "functions" (adequate prudence) and alternative institutional arrangements for fulfilling a given function is a first step toward expanding the scope for national autonomy.

Capital controls

Since the dominant developed country states continue to place the onus on developing countries for avoiding crisis (rather than change the operation of the international system to make crisis less likely) developing countries should draw the lesson. They have to protect themselves. Some in Asia have managed to build up large foreign exchange reserves by way of self-insurance. But large reserves have high costs. A partial alternative is to make more use of capital controls to curb capital surges in and out.

At the international level, standards of good practice should permit states to impose restrictions – as well as regulations – on portfolio capital mobility. For as free trade champion Jagdish Bhagwati declared, "In my judgement it is a lot of ideological humbug to say that without free portfolio capital mobility, somehow the world cannot function and growth rates will collapse."[26]

We know from the East Asian experience and much other that capital inflow surges can generate pressure for exchange rate appreciation, a domestic credit boom, loss of export competitiveness, and hence can raise the risk of sudden "bust" triggered by panicky capital withdrawal. Controls on inflows and outflows can dampen these surges. In particular, controls on outflows can help deal with the liquidity problem just mentioned, that during a crisis liquidity rather than capital is often the issue for banks.

Moreover, capital controls on inflows can also be effective as a macroeconomic management tool, to curtail demand at times of boom, when tax increases for the same purpose are too slow or precluded for political reasons. Restrictions on inflows allow domestic interest rates to be raised to curb aggregate demand, in a way not possible in the absence of the controls. Without the controls raising the cost of short-term foreign loans, domestic borrowers would simply switch from domestic to foreign loans, undermining monetary tightening.

Chile's non-interest-bearing reserve requirement on capital inflows, plus a stamp duty type of tax on foreign credits, were effective in the first half of the 1990s in securing both of these kinds of benefits – shifting the term structure of the country's foreign obligations toward the long end and raising the effectiveness of monetary policy for macroeconomic stability.

The US Treasury, of course, strongly opposed Chile's capital controls. During the 1997 US–Chile negotiations for Chilean access to NAFTA the US side demanded the Chileans get rid of them.

But for reasons both of national sovereignty – "members' undoubted right to choose their own policy frameworks," in Lomax's phrase – and of effectiveness in preventing financial crises and maintaining macroeconomic stability, multilateral rules should explicitly recognize countries' right to use capital controls. There should be no revival of the G7 push through the 1990s to revise the Articles of Agreement of the IMF so as to add the goal of promoting free capital mobility to the existing statement of goals, or to give the IMF jurisdiction over the capital account.

These policy suggestions – to focus IMF surveillance more on "multilateral" and less on "structural" features of national economies distant from the economy's external stability, to revise Basel II with more voice for developing countries, to give scope for countries to use capital controls, and more generally to distinguish between the functions that have to be met and alternative institutional forms for meeting those functions, using "middleware" as an analogy – reflect a wider concern to blunt the momentum toward "deep integration" or "standardization " of national economies. Standardization means implicitly the liberal market economy of the Anglo-American world as distinct from more coordinated forms of market economy found elsewhere (Wade 2003b and 2006). There are no good grounds in terms of efficiency, growth or morality for the rest of the world to accept the Anglo-American form as the global model. But to change global norms requires a prior change in global governance, such that Europe's present overrepresentation shrinks and the South's underrepresentation grows. The top table needs to be expanded to include perhaps 20 important states – chosen not by the US and Germany, as was the present G20, but by regional election; and with a cabinet of the G4 – the US, Japan, EU and China, with outreach to Britain on certain financial issues.

Notes

1 In addition to the cited references I have drawn on discussions with Jane D'Arista (Financial Markets Center, www.fmcenter.org), Jakob Vestergaard (visiting fellow, Center for the Analysis of Risk and Regulation, LSE), Kevin Young (PhD candidate, Government Department, LSE), Charles Goodhart (Financial Markets Group, LSE)

and Howard Davies (former head of the UK Financial Services Authority and current director of LSE).

2 A finer distinction might be made between standards which are set by international agreement, as in the executive councils of IMF, World Bank, Basle, WTO, etc., and unilateral action by the US Treasury which in effect sets standards by, for example, making certain banks or certain countries' banks dangerous to deal with.

3 Tavakoli (2007) says,

> Due to the use of structured products and derivatives hedge funds can take on hidden leverage above and beyond that which can be explained by polling prime brokers. Furthermore, illiquid structured products will experience a classic collateral crash when hedge funds try to liquidate these assets to meet margin calls or collateral "cures."

4 Blustein (2001), at 349, 351, 357 respectively.

5 "Electronic Herd" comes from Thomas Friedman via Paul Blustein (2001: 2).

6 Yet when mini-crises arose in Ecuador, Ukraine and Pakistan in late 1999 and early 2000 the Fund and the G7 did make official loan packages dependent on the willingness of those countries' bondholders to permit a restructuring of their claims (Blustein 2001: 386).

7 See IMF Fact Sheet dated July 2, 2000 entitled "Progress in Strengthening the Architecture of the International Financial System" (www.imf.org/external/np/exr/facts/arcguide.htm), which gives a link to 2001 updates of the Fact Sheet. It speaks volumes that there are no later updates (an observation for which I thank Jane D'Arista). See also IMF (2003).

8 G7 (1998).

9 My argument on transparency and surveillance is indebted to Jakob Vestergaard (2007a and 2007b).

10 Anonymous, April 2007.

11 Rachel Lomax, "International Monetary Stability – can the IMF make a Difference?" lecture delivered at Somerset House, London, November 1, 2006, p. 8.

12 Independent Evaluation Office of the IMF (2006), available at: www.imf.org/external/np/ieo/2006/ms/eng/pdf/report.pdf.

13 Independent Evaluation Office (2006: 13), emphasis added.

14 IEO, 2006, report on the evaluation of the FSAP, at 57. See also IMF (2005). The latter reports that the use of ROSCs by market participants is low, and has not increased in recent years (as indicated by responses to the question, "To what extent do you use ROSCs in your work?"). The most used information was about compliance with Basel Core Principles and Data Dissemination; but even these scored only in the low 3's on a scale of 1 (not at all) to 5 (a very great deal).

15 I am indebted to Kevin Young for points made in this section.

16 Basel Committee on Banking Supervision (2006: 2)

17 This is a central point of Vestergaard (2007a).

18 The G20 grouping of developed and developing country finance ministers, formed in 1999 by the Clinton administration, is less a forum of debate than an occasion for a Durkheimian effervescence of faith in free markets and the Washington Consensus. In meetings below ministerial level, representatives of Australia and Canada have aggressively led the cajoling of consensus, while representatives of major developing countries sit mute. See for example Gruen *et al.* (2002).

19 This, notwithstanding that 52 percent of its membership comes from developing countries.

20 This point is central to Claessens *et al.* (2003).

21 Walter (2008), Chapter 7.

22 See http://en.wikipedia.org/wiki/Middleware.

23 This is illustrated in the BIS-housed Financial Stability Institute's own surveys conducted in 2004 and 2006 to test the efficacy of adoption of Basel II standards in countries outside the rich country members of the Basel Committee. The results reveal that the number of non-rich-country banks which plan to implement the advanced internal ratings-based approach to credit risk fell by 60 percent between 2004 and 2006. See Financial Stability Institute (2006: 11). Also Fight (2006). My thanks to Kevin Young for these points.

24 For an overview and discussion of these proposals before the Basel Committee, see Griffith-Jones *et al.* (2004).

25 See, for example, Kregel (2006), available at: www.socialwatch.org/en/informesTematicos/102.html.

26 Bhagwati, interview in *Times of India*, December 31, 1997.

References

Basel Committee on Banking Supervision (2006) *Results of the Fifth Quantitative Impact Study*, Basel: Bank for International Settlements, June 16.

Blustein, P. (2001) *The Chastening: Inside the Crisis that Rocked the Global Financial System and Humbled the IMF*, New York: Public Affairs.

Claessens, S., Underhill, G. and Zhang, X. (2003) "Basel II Capital Requirements and Developing Countries: a Political Economy Perspective," typescript, Center for Global Development, October.

Feldstein, M. (1998) "Refocusing the IMF," *Foreign Affairs*, March/Apr.

Fight, A. (2006) "Emerging Markets Struggle with Basel II," *The Financial Regulator* 11(3): 31–34.

Financial Stability Institute (2006) "Implementation of the New Capital Adequacy Framework in non-Basel Committee Member Countries," Occasional Paper No. 6, September.

G7 (1998) Statement on the World Economy, Declaration of G7 Finance Ministers and Central Bank Governors, London, October 30.

Griffith-Jones, S., Segoviano, M. and Spratt, S. (2004) "CAD3 and Developing Countries: The Potential Impact of Diversification Effects on International Lending Patterns and Pro-Cyclicality," Institute of Development Studies, Sussex University, mimeo, August.

Gruen, D., O'Brien, T. and Lawson, J. (eds.) (2002) *Globalisation, Living Standards and Inequality: Recent Progress and Continuing Challenges*, Reserve Bank of Australia.

Hall, P. and Soskice, D. (2001) *Varieties of Capitalism: The Institutional Foundations of Comparative Advantage*, New York: Oxford University Press.

Holzer, B. and Millo, Y. (2005) "From Risks to Second-order Dangers in Financial Markets: Unintended Consequences of Risk Management Systems," *New Political Economy* 10(2): 223–246.

Independent Evaluation Office (2006) Multilateral Surveillance, Evaluation Report. Independent Evaluation Office of the IMF.

IMF (2000) "Progress in Strengthening the Architecture of the International Financial System," Fact Sheet dated July 2.

IMF (2003) *Review of Contingent Credit Lines*, Washington, DC: The International Monetary Fund.

IMF (2005) "The Standards and Codes Initiative – Is It Effective? And How Can It Be Improved?"

Independent Evaluation Office of the IMF (2006) "An Evaluation of the IMF's Multilateral Surveillance," February.

Kregel, J. (2006) "From Monterrey to Basel: Who Rules the Banks?" *Social Watch*.

Persaud, A. (2001) "The Disturbing Interactions between the Madness of Crowds and the Risk Management of Banks in Developing Countries and the Global Financial System," in Griffith-Jones, S. and Bhattacharaya, A. (eds.) *Developing Countries and the Global Financial System*, Commonwealth Secretariat.

Rodrik, D. (2002) "Getting the Institutions Right," working paper, Kennedy School of Government, Harvard University.

Rogoff, K. (2007) "No Grand Plans, but the Financial System Needs Fixing," *Financial Times*, February 8.

Tavakoli, J. (2007) "Greater Global Risk Now than at Time of LTCM," letter, *Financial Times*, May 7.

Vashwanath, T. and Kaufman, D. (2001) "Towards Transparency: New Approaches and their Application to Financial Markets," *The World Bank Research Observer* 16, 1.

Vestergaard, J. (2007) "Managing Global Financial Risk? The Post-Washington Consensus and the Normalization of Anglo-American Capitalism," typescript, Center for the Analysis of Risk and Regulation, LSE, June.

Vestergaard, J. (2007) *Discipline in the Global Economy: Panopticism and the Post-Washington Consensus*, Copenhagen Business School.

Wade, R. (1998a) "The Asian Debt and Development Crisis of 1997–?: Causes and Consequences," *World Development*, 26, 8.

Wade, R. (1998b) "From 'Miracle' to 'Cronyism': Explaining the Great Asian Slump," *Cambridge J. Economics*, 22, 6.

Wade, R. (2003a) "The Invisible Hand of the American Empire," *Ethics and International Affairs*, 17, 2.

Wade, R. (2003b) "What Strategies are Viable for Developing Countries Today? The World Trade Organization and the Shrinking of 'Development Space'," *Review of International Political Economy*, 10, 4: 621–644.

Wade, R. (2004) *Governing the Market*, Princeton: Princeton University Press.

Wade, R. (2006) "Choking the South," *New Left Review* 38, Mar/Apr: 115–127.

Wade, R. (2007) "Globalization, Growth, Poverty, Inequality, Resentment and Imperialism," in J. Ravenhill (ed.) *Global Political Economy*, London: Oxford University Press.

Wade, R. and Veneroso, F. (1998) "Two Views on Asia: The Resources Lie Within," By Invitation, *The Economist*, November 7–13: 19–21.

Walter, A. (2008) *Governing Finance: East Asia's Adoption of International Standards*, Ithaca: Cornell University Press.

Zysman, J. (1983) *Governments, Markets, and Growth: Financial Systems and the Politics of Industrial Change*, Ithaca: Cornell University Press.

Part IV

Conclusions

12 Conclusions

Hubert Neiss

The wide-ranging discussion during the conference showed broadly similar views over many issues, but also made it clear that there are few black and white issues and that we have to be nuanced and subtle in our assessment. Let me now go through the main topics.

Origin and causes

There was a consensus that the Asian crisis was simultaneously a capital account crisis and a banking crisis, triggered by a change in market sentiment. This change did not come out of the blue, but came in response to emerging weaknesses in the balance of payments and the banking systems of the countries affected. The main causes of these weaknesses were pointed out to be premature capital account liberalization (except in Indonesia which had liberalized long ago) and inadequate banking supervision. In the boom years before the crisis, this had led to excessive short-term foreign borrowing by banks and excessive longer-term lending to corporations (including for doubtful projects), resulting in a currency and maturity mismatch, and a deteriorating loan portfolio. To these weaknesses some speakers added deteriorating macroeconomic developments, in particular a falling return on investment and rising current account deficits, and some speakers quoted the prevalence of "cronyism," poor governance and corruption – issues which got ample publicity during the crisis. These flaws, undesirable as they are, may have been contributing factors, but I never thought they could be made responsible for the crisis. (If this were the case, the crisis should have come much earlier and encompassed many more countries.)

Record of developments

The evolution of the relevant variables has been amply demonstrated by the speakers in tables and graphs, and I don't need to repeat the details. The following features stand out:

- the recession was sharp but short;
- the restoration of a strong external position – after a collapse of the exchange rate and a depletion of foreign exchange reserves – was rapid;

- the recovery of growth was also impressive, but it was pointed out that growth remained below the pre-crisis trend.

Some differentiation between countries was also observed:

- The Philippines and Malaysia had somewhat smaller declines in real GDP and the exchange rate. I think this is due to a stronger starting position: both countries had a lower level of foreign debt and a less vulnerable banking system because they had taken some banking reforms prior to the crisis, in response to earlier banking problems.
- Indonesia suffered the largest decline of real GDP and of the exchange rate. I attribute this to the fact that Indonesia suffered a major political crisis at the same time, with heightened uncertainty and growing public unrest. In addition, Indonesia also had a severe drought causing a serious rice shortage, and there was a fall in oil prices.
- Korea had the strongest recovery. I think this is mainly due to the authorities' greater decisiveness in implementing the crisis program than was the case in the other crisis countries. We did not quite resolve the question whether the lower post-crisis growth trend was due to under-performance or to natural maturation of the economies. The latter is probably true only for Korea, where potential growth is now estimated at 5–6 percent compared with 7–8 percent pre-crisis. In the Southeast Asian countries potential growth may also be lower (although we don't have solid estimates), but the actual growth performance of around 5 percent is very likely to be below potential. In this context, substantially lower rates of investment than before the crisis were of concern to several participants. It was recognized, however, that some of the investment before the crisis was excessive and went into low-return projects. What to do about the present sub-optimal investment performance? Governments cannot decree higher investment, but they can do a lot to improve the investment climate. The measures for achieving this are well known, but action has been slow.

Record of policies

Under the crisis programs supported by the IMF, countries tightened fiscal policy, raised interest rates, rescued and restructured banks, and restructured corporations. In addition, they implemented structural reforms over a broad area, including external liberalization, internal market opening, dismantling of monopolies, strengthening of institutions and improving the legal system. (Malaysia, which dealt with the crisis without an IMF program, took initially a similar approach. Later it was modified: the exchange rate was fixed again and capital controls where imposed, while bank and corporate restructuring was continued.) While the record of policies is fairly clear, the views on their appropriateness started to differ as the crisis deepened. Some policies still remain controversial, and in our discussion on lessons from the crisis, several policy mistakes were mentioned.

Policy mistakes

Not all policies turned out to be wrong, but some mistakes inevitably occurred because the nature of the crisis was initially not fully understood, and action had to be taken in a hurry, without the luxury of much discussion and reflection. The initial program for Korea, for instance, had to be finalized in one week, since usable reserves had run out and the international community was not prepared to provide a quick bridging loan; nor did the Korean government want to declare a default. (When India had a BoP crisis in 1991, the Bank of Japan and the Bank of England provided a bridging loan to avoid default; at the outset of the Korean crisis, I had unsuccessfully suggested that the Japanese and the US central banks provide similar help to Korea.)

Here is the list of the policy mistakes mentioned in our discussion:

- Fiscal tightening – this was clearly wrong and after a while the course was reversed. Fiscal tightening was meant to contribute to market confidence, but instead it contributed to the recession. However, I would point out that the damage was limited. Because of the usual bureaucratic delays in implementing expenditure cuts, they did not fully materialize as the policy was changed in the meantime. The exception was Thailand, where the increase in the value added tax at the start of the program had an immediate impact.
- Increase in interest rates – this measure was highly controversial at the time of the crisis, but was not mentioned prominently in our discussions. My answer to the criticism is: since massive and quick financial support was not available, a default was to be avoided, and a standstill agreement with banks was slow in coming, and there was no other means to stop the precipitate fall in exchange rates than a sharp and short rise in interest rates. (The effectiveness of this had been demonstrated by other countries hit by foreign exchange crises earlier, including Hong Kong in 1998.) However, I think the mistake was that interest rates were increased only hesitantly instead of sharply (particularly in Indonesia and Korea), because of political resistance, and then were kept high for too long, because of fear that a quick reduction would throw the foreign exchange market again into turmoil. This of course contributed to the depth of the recession. (It was indeed a difficult call, and the IMF preferred to err on the side of caution.)
- Structural reforms – during the crisis, they were widely opposed as too intrusive and distracting attention from crisis management proper, and similar misgivings were voiced in our meeting. My answer is this: If governments had at that time not tackled some long-overdue reforms, neither would the required support from official lenders (IMF, IBRD, ADB) have been forthcoming, nor would market confidence have been restored. So, there would have been no choice anyway. But governments themselves recognized the need for reforms and used the crisis as an opportunity to correct some deep-seated structural flaws which may have contributed to the crisis. Nevertheless, the criticism of some speakers of excessive and sometimes irrelevant reform

conditions in the IMF crisis programs is justified, and this was later also recognized by the IMF. But let's not lose sight of the fact that most reforms would have been needed even without a crisis (but would have been more difficult to implement in good times), and that they have proven to be beneficial to the economy. I have not heard any of the earlier critics arguing that they should be reversed (governments could now do that if they wanted, but apparently they don't).

- Delayed and slow corporate restructuring (particularly in Thailand and Indonesia) – this was due to the technical and political difficulties involved in this task as well as to an insufficient understanding, at that time, of the adverse macroeconomic impact of damaged corporate balance sheets.
- Hesitant introduction of a "blanket guarantee" for bank deposits (in particular in Indonesia), because of the much quoted "moral hazard" (i.e. it would lead to indiscriminate depositing as well as to indiscriminate lending) and of the potentially large liabilities of the government – this was clearly a mistake (which was made despite the fact that before the Asian crisis other countries, including Japan, had used a blanket guarantee successfully to avoid a panic of bank depositors). However, it was corrected subsequently.
- A related frequent criticism, made again in our discussions, refers to the closure of 16 banks in Indonesia at the start of the program, when criteria for closing were not transparent, the deposit guarantee was insufficient, and the execution was flawed – I think the significance of this event was and still is exaggerated. The 16 banks were a tiny part of the banking system, and the underlying reason for the growing panic was the lack of trust of the people in the president's willingness and ability to implement the crisis program. Let me also point out that all other bank closures during the crisis, including the subsequent closures of many more and larger banks in Indonesia, were executed successfully. (Critics of the 16 banks' closure never mention this.)
- Inadequate expansion of social protection – this was due to technical difficulties to target the most seriously affected (especially in Indonesia) and to bureaucratic inefficiency. I would also mention that to some extent, such measures were against the prevailing philosophy of governments, and taken only half-heartedly. In addition to these policy failures, other critical issues were mentioned in our discussions:

  - Creditor banks were bailed-in too late. True, but in the absence of an institutional framework for doing so, this was a sensitive issue. There was fear (justified or not) that convening an emergency meeting of banks at the outset of the crisis and before an IMF program was in place could increase market nervousness and accelerate capital outflows. The problem was the lack of an institutionalized mechanism to deal with such emergencies (and we still don't have one).
  - Lending packages (as decided by the IMF, IBRD, ADB and bilateral donors) were too small – this is true especially in the case of Thailand (where it was pointed out that support was less than the forward

exchange obligations of the Bank of Thailand), but also for the other countries since the "second line of defense" from bilateral sources was not really usable. The announcement of these supplementary bilateral resources had initially a favorable psychological effect, but markets soon understood that they were unlikely to be forthcoming.

- Failure to impose capital controls – some among us have argued that with insufficient official support and no immediate bailing-in of foreign creditor banks, controls on capital outflows should have been applied, like in Malaysia. I am not sure whether this would have worked. First, apart from Korea, the other crisis countries did not have the institutional capability to enforce capital controls at a time of a severe confidence crisis (particularly not in Indonesia where even the smuggling of rice out of the country could not be controlled during the rice shortage; in the Philippines, government officials said at that time that capital controls would only increase corruption). Second, the example of Malaysia itself is not conclusive: The controls were only introduced after the peak of the crisis had passed, i.e. when substantial capital flight had already occurred and the exchange rate had already dropped sharply – as had real GDP. Nobody can say whether the controls would have worked and saved Malaysia from suffering a similar crisis as the other SEA countries, if capital controls had been imposed at the outset of the crisis.

To conclude this part, I offer some thoughts about the "mistakes of the IMF," as the policy mistakes were referred to by some participants, without wishing to be apologetic:

- To some extent, the mistakes have to be shared by the governments of the crisis countries who did not reveal the true situation, did not act preemptively, particularly in Thailand, and in the case of Indonesia, failed to implement the first two programs.
- The World Bank and the ADB also have to take some share, as they were involved in the program formulation and decided their contribution to the support package. (I would mention in particular that, from the third Indonesian program onwards, a World Bank and an ADB representative were invited to participate in all program negotiations and to sign off on the draft Letters of Intent, after consultation with their respective headquarters.)
- The larger international community also has to take its share. Program content and amounts to be disbursed were ultimately decided by the IMF member countries represented in the IMF Executive Board (and the support provided by the World Bank and the ADB was decided by their respective Executive Boards). While each large country made its preferences and misgivings on the draft program known to staff and management (bilaterally and in informal Executive Board meetings during the crisis), in the end, they all voted for the programs (there were not even abstentions). Some speakers pointed out that the

US was the driving force in suggesting several program conditions. Yes, but let's bear in mind that the US vote was just some 19 percent of the total vote.

• Finally, while we have to look at policy mistakes in order to draw the proper lessons from the crisis experience, we have to do so from a broader perspective and I would say this: Despite a number of mistakes, the overall strategy, which was aimed to overcome the crisis quickly and to initiate a sustained recovery was right. And it turned out to be highly successful, as we all know in retrospect. In 1998 and even in 1999, many did not believe this, including serious analysts of the crisis. (A copy of *Time Magazine* of June 21, 1999 has the cover "Asian Recovery – Don't Bet on it," by Paul Krugman.)

Lessons

There was agreement that some important lessons were learned, some were only half-learned, and some were gradually forgotten. To generalize a bit, the first category includes government policies, the second regional cooperation, and the third the reshaping of the international financial system. The lessons referring to crisis management itself were quickly learned:

• relax fiscal policy
• declare a blanket guarantee up-front
• close banks in an orderly way, with clear pre-announced criteria
• restructure corporations early on
• initiate overdue structural reforms immediately, but stick to the basics and don't burden programs with measures of secondary importance
• expand the social safety net and protect the groups most severely affected.

Because of these lessons, I am sure things would be done differently the next time around.

The lessons in crisis prevention have also been learned by governments:

• keep exchange rates flexible
• keep a high level of foreign exchange reserves
• maintain macro-stability
• establish procedures for early resolution of banking problems
• establish central bank independence
• maintain strong banking supervision
• strengthen other regulatory institutions (as well as commercial courts)
• monitor short-term capital flows and impose restraints on these flows if necessary.

Regarding flexible exchange rates, in our discussion, the limited flexibility in the former crisis countries and the gradual approach to flexibility taken by China were supported as contributions to market stability. I am not sure. Countries could allow exchange rates to be somewhat more flexible without suffering serious damage, as it has recently been demonstrated by the Euro-area. Regarding foreign exchange reserves, the massive accumulation has often been criticized because of the currency risk involved and because these resources could be put to better use domestically. In our discussions, reserve accumulation has been generally supported as a necessary second-best solution ("self-insurance"), in the absence of an effective lender of last resort. I fully agree with this. The cost of maintaining high reserves is an insurance premium which countries should be willing to pay in order to avoid another capital account crisis. Nevertheless, at some point, I would expect governments to conclude that the costs are high enough compared with the risk. We will then see, apart from further shifts into non-USD currencies, an easing of reserve accumulation through investment in other foreign assets, further exchange rate depreciation, and further import liberalization – all of which is desirable. Also learned were lessons for better regional cooperation, but only by half. In our discussions, we have heard about a multitude of initiatives by ASEAN+3 (concerning swap agreements and bond markets), FTAs (as a second-best solution), and institutionalized policy dialogues (a marked change from pre-crisis tradition when policy makers were shy to comment on each other's actions). This is all very hopeful. But when we look for the substance behind this flurry of activities and multitude of schemes, my impression is that we are still far away from an effective coordination of economic policies and from a pooling of reserves of a sufficient scale to establish an effective lender of last resort. And, as several here mentioned, the speed to get there is slow. (Earlier, the question was asked whether the Asian Monetary Fund (proposed in mid-1997 by Japan), if everybody had agreed to its establishment, would have made a difference to the crisis. The answer was ambivalent, but my answer is clear: Theoretically yes, but at the speed things have been moving, the AMF would not have been ready to operate in time to have an impact on the Asian crisis. And if there was a crisis now, countries would still depend on the IMF for immediate and massive BOP support.) It was also mentioned that welcome changes were made in the IMF: Standards and codes and best practices; data dissemination; streamlined conditionality; improved surveillance; capital market monitoring; financial sector assessments; etc. (The World Bank and the ADB were not mentioned regarding post-crisis performance, although I think that participants agree that these institutions are also in need of reform.) However, there was agreement that the international community failed in three essential areas to make the IMF more effective in the next crisis:.

- the expansion of lender of last resort capability
- the institutionalization of sovereign debt resolution
- the institutionalization of private sector involvement (e.g. stand-stills)
- the adjustment of voting rights to reflect today's economic realities.

In these areas, after some initial rhetoric about a new "financial architecture," the lessons of the crisis have been quickly forgotten. The mentioned improvements in several areas benefiting the international financial system are marginal and cannot outweigh the failure to act on these substantial issues. (This shows again that good times are bad times for reform.)

Conclusion

Before finishing, I would like to draw two more lessons.

First, the crisis took everybody by surprise. (Even in Thailand nobody expected a crisis of that magnitude.) Lesson: Be prepared for the unexpected. We have all agreed that another Asian crisis, while possible, is highly unlikely since countries are in a much stronger position (BoP and reserves, macro situation, banking system, institutions and structural changes). However, unlike old generals fighting the last war, we have to be aware that it is not enough to be prepared for a return of the last crisis, because the next crisis may be different. There was a hint by some speakers that it could be triggered by a disorderly unwinding of global imbalances. It could also be triggered by a sudden and severe oil shortage, or by some political catastrophe.

Second, at the outbreak of the crisis, nobody understood it fully (explanations as well as criticisms of policies came only later), and as a consequence, some wrong policies were applied. Lesson: In the event of new crisis, be quite flexible in the policy response and be prepared to change policies quickly as events unfold and the situation becomes clearer.

In conclusion, let me say that our discussions did not only contribute to the ongoing task of establishing the historical record of the Asian crisis (which is still incomplete), but, by discussing the lessons, I hope it also contributed to a better understanding of preparedness for the next crisis. This in my view is the essence of the exercise, and it could make the world a safer place.

Index

Printed in the United States
by Baker & Taylor Publisher Services